ECCLESIASTES

LIFE WITHOUT CHRIST IS MEANINGLESS

The Proclaim Commentary Series

THE PROCLAIM COMMENTARY SERIES

ECCLESIASTES
LIFE WITHOUT CHRIST IS MEANINGLESS

OLD TESTAMENT
VOLUME 21

MATTHEW STEVEN BLACK

PROCLAIM
PUBLISHERS

WENATCHEE, WASHINGTON

Ecclesiastes: Life without Christ is Meaningless
(The Proclaim Commentary Series)
Copyright © 2022 by Matthew Black
ISBN: 978-1-954858-37-4 (Print Book)
         978-1-954858-38-1 (eBook)

Proclaim Publishers
PO Box 2082, Wenatchee, WA 98807
proclaimpublishers.com

Cover art: *Solomon the Wise*

Notes: (1) Ancient quotations have been at times changed to the ESV as well as some archaic language updated, and additional phrases added for clarification. At times verse references (non-existent until recent times) have been interspersed as well to guide the modern reader. (2) We have done our best to be careful in footnoting. Due to the nature of the sermonic material, various items are quoted freely, and may not have proper footnoting. If any great error is noticed, please contact the publisher, and it will be remedied in whatever way is available to us.

First Printing, January 2023, Manufactured in the United States of America

---

Dedicated to my firstborn son William Black. Your practice of the fear of the Lord has often challenged me to higher ground.

And to my brother-in-law Jason Wenger. Thank you for being a bright example of wisdom and the fear of the LORD. Out of all the people that I know, you have demonstrated to me how to live life in the richest and most meaningful way, in devotion to Christ.

CONTENTS

14

ABBREVIATIONS

Common

cf – Latin "conferatur", compare, or see, or see also
ff – and following (pages or verses)
i.e. – Latin "id est", that is
e.g. – Latin "exempli gratia", for example

Books of the Bible

OLD TESTAMENT

Genesis	Gen	Esther	Est
Exodus	Exo	Job	Job
Leviticus	Lev	Psalms	Psa
Numbers	Num	Proverbs	Pro
Deuteronomy	Deut	Ecclesiastes	Ecc
Joshua	Josh	Song of Solomon	Song
Judges	Jdg	Isaiah	Isa
Ruth	Rth	Jeremiah	Jer
1 Samuel	1 Sam	Lamentations	Lam
2 Samuel	2 Sam	Ezekiel	Eze
1 Kings	1 Kgs	Daniel	Dan
2 Kings	2 Kgs	Hosea	Hos
1 Chronicles	1 Chr	Joel	Joel
2 Chronicles	2 Chr	Amos	Amos
Ezra	Ezr	Obadiah	Oba
Nehemiah	Neh	Jonah	Jonah

Micah	Mic	Zechariah	Zech
Nahum	Nah	Malachi	Mal
Habakkuk	Hab		
Zephaniah	Zeph		
Haggai	Hag		

NEW TESTAMENT

Matthew	Mt	2 Timothy	2 Tim
Mark	Mk	Titus	Titus
Luke	Lk	Philemon	Phm
John	Jn	Hebrews	Heb
Acts	Acts	James	Jas
Romans	Rom	1 Peter	1 Pet
1 Corinthians	1 Cor	2 Peter	2 Pet
2 Corinthians	2 Cor	1 John	1 Jn
Galatians	Gal	2 John	2 Jn
Ephesians	Eph	3 John	3 Jn
Philippians	Phil	Jude	Jud
Colossians	Col	Revelation	Rev
1 Thessalonians	1 Thess		
2 Thessalonians	2 Thess		
1 Timothy	1 Tim		

INTRODUCTION

The end of the matter; all has been heard. Fear God and keep his
commandments, for this is the whole duty of man.
ECCLESIASTES 12:13

In Ecclesiastes, King Solomon, after a life of great wisdom and then great failure, concluded that a mere human being cannot fully understand life or control it. From the human point of view, life looks like a lot of vanity and folly. But if you look at life from God's perspective, it is his gift to us. He wants us to enjoy it and use it for his glory. Real satisfaction and richness in life comes when Jesus Christ is at the center.

Our Jewish friends read Ecclesiastes at the annual Feast of Tabernacles, a joyful autumn festival of harvest. It fits! For Solomon wrote, "There is nothing better for a person than that he should eat and drink and find enjoyment in his toil. This also, I saw, is from the hand of God" (2:24). Even the Apostle Paul (who could hardly be labeled a hedonist) said that God gives to us "richly all things to enjoy" (1 Tim 6:17).

Life without Jesus Christ is indeed "vanity and vexation of spirit" (1:14). But when you know the Lord personally, and live for him faithfully, you experience "fullness of joy and pleasures forevermore" (Psa 16:11).[1]

AUTHOR

Solomon is named as the author in the first verse as the "son of David, king in Jerusalem" (1:1). King Solomon, who, when asked by God what gift he would like, responded that he would like wisdom. God

---

[1] Warren W. Wiersbe, *Be Satisfied*, "Be" Commentary Series (Wheaton, IL: Victor Books, 1996), 9.

was so pleased with his answer that he not only made Solomon the wisest ruler on Earth, but also added wealth and honor (2 Chron 1:7-12). There are many stories about the wisdom of Solomon found in 1 Kings 1-11, and in 2 Chronicles 1-9. However, when we get to Ecclesiastes, we find Solomon reviewing his life as he nears his own death.

The argument for Solomon's authorship is quite clear. Many of the actions that Solomon describes in the book of Ecclesiastes mirror the sort of accomplishments that are recorded of Solomon in 1 Kings and 2 Chronicles. In addition, the Preacher makes many claims to great, vast wealth and unparalleled wisdom, which is recorded in detail in the two books previously mentioned.

DATE

According to Jewish tradition, Solomon wrote Song of Songs in his youth, compiled Proverbs in his middle years, and wrote Ecclesiastes near the end of his life. If that is true, then this book is of near infinite value because it is the final reflections of one of the wisest men to ever live (1 Kgs 4:29). Solomon died in 931 B.C., so he must have written Ecclesiastes shortly before his death.

MESSAGE

If it is true that Solomon wrote Ecclesiastes near the end of his life, then it can be interpreted as Solomon's return to the faith. We are told in 1 Kings that Solomon was led astray from the Lord by the false gods of his wives (1 Kgs 11:4). Thus, Ecclesiastes are likely Solomon's final reflections on life and whatever conclusions he has made.

In some ways, the apostle Paul summed up the entire theme of the book of Ecclesiastes in Philippians 3:8 when he called everything outside of knowing Christ "dung."

Primarily then, Solomon's words are recorded here to show us that wealth, success, and prosperity do not ultimately satisfy. The message of Job is that even when we have nothing, God is everything. But in Ecclesiastes we see the converse. Even if you have everything, if you don't have the Lord at the center, everything is vanity and useless.

Solomon was a man to whom God had given everything. He was the epitome of the American dream. In terms of political power, Solomon was greater than the President of the United States. In terms of religious authority, Solomon had more than the Pope. In terms of intelligence, Solomon had more than Einstein. In terms of wealth, Solomon, in his day, surpassed Bill Gates. In terms of women, Solomon sank as low as Hugh Hefner. We are told that the daily provisions for his personal staff were enough to feed 35,000 people (1 Kgs 4:22-23). That's 35,000 servants that waited on him, hand and foot. Solomon had it all. In addition, God granted Solomon a peaceful reign on the thrown of Israel for forty years (1 Kgs 11:42). That is the longest time of peace that Israel has ever seen! Not only did countries not attack Israel, but also during Solomon's reign, they came from all across the globe just to give him money. One would think that Solomon lived the good life and died the happiest man alive, but then we get Ecclesiastes. His final words to us are that "all is vanity" without the fear and love of God at the center. Without Christ, life is meaningless and vain.

TESTIMONY

I have rarely spoken with anyone about this book who did not find it at least a little depressing. I have even heard people claim that it was their favorite book because it reminds them just how futile life really is. To an extent, these things are true. Ecclesiastes is not the happiest book that one may read, true. It does a great job of describing the futility of life, also true. However, I do not find Ecclesiastes depressing, nor do I believe that it is one gigantic downer. Instead, Ecclesiastes is one of the world's first philosophical works. Many people, including myself, would call it the greatest work of philosophy ever written. In fact, it appears to me that what most people call depressing is actually the presentation of life's difficult questions. No other book calls us to face the reality of our mortality and depravity like Ecclesiastes. It addresses the human condition in such a way that Solomon is attempting to give words to experiences that are beyond words. Ecclesiastes is not an easy book, and it will not be content with simply being a "good read" or an interesting book. This book does not need to be depressing, but if we study it well, Ecclesiastes will cut through any shallowness in our souls, leaving behind a desperate need for God to provide our lives with meaning, satisfaction, and joy.[2]

---

[2] Cole Newton, "Background on Ecclesiastes," *B. C. Newton: Rooted Theology for the Unwithered Church*, Blog. December 15, 2020, https://bcnewton.co/2018/02/03/background-on-ecclesiastes/.

The book of Ecclesiastes shaped the thinking of Paul for sure. He said all is dung and worthless without Christ. I believe it has also shaped my thinking. As a young man, I had so much zeal, but not much wisdom. As a result, I was often impatient in my "righteousness." I aimed for goals but not for God's glory ultimately when I think about it. As I've matured in Christ, I've seen that nothing can actually be enjoyed without Christ at the center. As Paul said, "For me to live is Christ, and to die is gain" (Phil 1:21). Without Christ, life is tedious, tasteless, and vain. But with Christ, all events in life work for our good, God's glory, and our true peace and satisfaction in him who is on the throne. Hallelujah!

Matthew Steven Black
Elgin, Illinois
January 26, 2023

1 | ECCLESIASTES 1:1-8

LIFE WITHOUT CHRIST IS MEANINGLESS

Vanity of vanities, says the Preacher,
vanity of vanities! All is vanity.
ECCLESIASTES 1:2

You've heard the saying: "The grass is always greener on the other side of the fence"? What do we mean by that? When we are unsatisfied with life, we tend to dream of a better place that will take away all our problems. When we feel lonely, desperate, and exhausted we tend to dream of all the possibilities in life that are really not realistic. We dream of a new job that will make everything better. We might even dream of a special person coming into our lives to make everything better. Some might dream about how they might get out of their circumstances. Why? Because life is not satisfying. That is, it is not satisfying unless Christ *is* your life.

In other words, there is no greener grass on this earthly life apart from Christ. There is no fullness of joy apart from his presence. You must find your contentment in Christ. If you want greener grass, then water your own grass with all the water Christ has to offer. Find contentment in Christ alone.

THE MAN WHO WROTE THIS BOOK (1:1, 12)

He calls himself a preacher and a king. He's writing from a point of wisdom, but you get the idea that some of it comes through the weariness and hardness of a life of sin. In all likelihood, Ecclesiastes is Solomon's last writing after he had fallen deeply into idolatry and every kind of sin and come to repentance. He is likely writing from a position of not only wisdom, but also humility, having been humbled by his own failures.

Solomon is a Preacher

Ecclesiastes 1:1 | The words of the Preacher.

The author of Ecclesiastes is a wise sage, one who knows much. Solomon, we know, was the wisest man in all the world outside of Jesus Christ. This great king, you'll remember, was given one wish from God, and he could have anything.

1 Kings 3:5 | At Gibeon the Lord appeared to Solomon in a dream by night, and God said, "Ask what I shall give you."

Since he chose *wisdom* over and above a long life or riches, God gave him all three. With such wisdom, Solomon designates himself as "the Preacher" (Heb. "*Qoheleth*"). *Qoheleth* was a public teacher. Yet "Preacher" may be the best translation of all. The Hebrew root of the word *qoheleth* literally means "to gather, collect, or assemble." Some scholars take this as a reference to the way the author collected various proverbs and other wise sayings together into one book. However, that is not the way this form of the word is used anywhere else in the Bible or other Hebrew literature. Instead, the verb *qoheleth* refers to the gathering or assembly of a community of people, especially for the worship of God. So *Qoheleth* is not so much a teacher in a classroom but more like a pastor in a church. He is preaching wisdom to a gathering of the people of God.[3]

This context is clearly reflected in the title this book is usually given in English. "Ecclesiastes" is a form of the Greek word *ekklesia*, which is the common New Testament word for "church." An *ekklesia* is not a

---

[3] Philip Graham Ryken, *Ecclesiastes: Why Everything Matters*, Preaching the Word (Wheaton, IL: Crossway Books, 2010), 16.

church building but a congregation—a gathering or assembly of people for the worship of God. The word "ecclesiastes" is the Greek translation of the Hebrew word *qoheleth*. Literally, it means "one who speaks in the *ekklesia*"—that is, in the assembly or congregation.[4]

Solomon has learned much about the vanity of life through his wrong choices in following the idolatry of pagan women. Now he is gathering us as a preacher would his congregation, and he is teaching us two things: without the faith life is meaningless, and only through a worldview of faith can everything have meaning.

Solomon is a King

Ecclesiastes 1:1, 12 | The words of the Preacher, the son of David, king in Jerusalem. **12** I the Preacher have been king over Israel in Jerusalem.

He calls himself a king and introduces himself as King David's son—quite obviously this is Solomon—he notes that he once ruled over Israel. His point in bringing up these lofty qualifications is not a spirit of pride, but a desire to show us how he as the king had unlimited resources to investigate the best life had to offer. He's stating his qualifications and saying, I've been all there is to be and done all there is to do, and it's all vain.

By the way, it is ok to state your qualifications, but we are not to boast in doing so. Someone may have earned a degree in a college, or a certificate of learning. It's ok to mention that as long as it is without pride or boasting. We are recognizing a gift from God and the person's responsibility to be a good steward with what God has given him.

Solomon is a Sinner, Saved by Grace

King Solomon began his reign as a humble servant of the Lord, seeking God's wisdom and help (1 Kgs 3:5–15). As he grew older, his heart turned away from Jehovah to the false gods of the many wives he had taken from foreign lands (1 Kgs 11:1ff). So this is an old man, given much time to ponder after wandering terribly away from God. He's done it all. He experienced every idol from fame to sex to power to money. And all of it without God is painful and vain. He writes this from a perspective "preacher" not in the sense of the ordained office,

---

[4] R. N. Whybray, *Ecclesiastes, The New Century Bible Commentary* (Grand Rapids, MI: Eerdmans, 1989), 2.

but as one who has repented and learned from his sins and found God to be gracious. What does this tell us?

We need to be reminded that there is no more gracious, forgiving, merciful and kindhearted being in all the universe than God almighty. The tragedies of sin are unspeakable. But "where sin abounds, grace much more abounds" (Rom 5:20, KJV). Solomon is eminently qualified to tell you that life without your Creator, who we know from the New Testament is Christ—life without Christ is empty!

The theme of the book is repeated throughout and again very distinctly in the last chapter. Solomon says in Ecclesiastes 12:13 (KJV), "Let us hear the conclusion of the whole matter: Fear God and keep his commandments: for this *is* the whole *duty* of man." This is beautiful. Don't look for greener grass. The purpose of man is to serve God where you are with what he's given you. Stop looking for greener grass. Can you think of places in the Bible that tell us that God is our all and our satisfaction? David says these things often in the Psalms.

Psalm 63:3 | Because your steadfast love is better than life, my lips will praise you.

Psalm 16:11 | You make known to me the path of life; in your presence there is fullness of joy; at your right hand are pleasures forevermore

Psalm 42:1-2 | As a deer pants for flowing streams, so pants my soul for you, O God. ² My soul thirsts for God, for the living God. When shall I come and appear before God?

You need also to remember that as great as his mercy is, so are the consequences of ignoring God's offer. God will not force you to go his way. You can go your own way for as long as you want. But it will never get any better. Christ alone can fill us. He can change us. But he wants not only to change us, but to realize valuable truths from it. You can become wiser and stronger despite selfish, sinful choices. God is in the business of turning tragedies into triumphs, tax collectors into teachers, adulterers into his holy servants. Every one of us deal with the deep temptations toward idolatry in our lives. You ask, how do I let go of those idols and lay hold on God as my all in all?

THE MADNESS OF LIFE WITHOUT CHRIST (1:2-7)

The first step to being filled by Christ is by seeing the madness of life (1:2–11, *cf* 1:14–15, 17–18). There is no greener grass without Christ. In fact, a preliminary investigation into this chapter quickly reveals some bitter truths about life without Christ. It's ugly. Life without Christ is a chocolate covered roach. It's sweet on the outside, but ugly on the inside.

The promises of life apart from Christ are deceitful. In every false idol there is both ecstasy and agony. You have pleasure in sin for a season, and it is ecstasy, but then it doesn't fulfill, and it is agony. Apart from Christ, life is a roller coaster of ecstasy and agony. In Christ, life is filled with the steady stream of love, joy, and peace. There is a purpose to all the madness. Without Christ all you have is madness and addiction. The madness of life makes people do all kinds of things.

Life is hard, and men turn to pornography and lust. Women may turn to romance novels. Soon their marriage is on the rocks or destroyed altogether. When life is hard it pushes people to be TV zombies, or overeating, or addictions of all kinds. Some girls turn to anorexia or bulimia. Young people are committing fornication all over the place, and they live on the ecstasy of "secret waters" (Pro 9:17-18).

Without Christ there is no real purpose in life (1:2–7, 14, 17). There's this drive in us to better ourselves. To make something of ourselves. God put within us a conscience to tell us that we ought to reflect him and that we are failing miserably. We were created to be image bearers of God. C.S. Lewis said there were two main pillars to the futility of life without Christ. "First, that human beings all over the earth, have this curious idea that they ought to behave in a certain way, and cannot really get rid of it. Secondly, they do not in fact behave in that way."[5] People try to fight against the futility with anger, anxiety, and despair. They try to break free from it by seeking idols of all sorts including earthly comforts, carnal escapes, and relief of all kinds. Even good things can be turned into idols. The point is without Christ, seeking relief from futility is indeed futile.

---

[5] C. S. Lewis, *Mere Christianity*, C.S. Lewis Signature Classics (San Francisco: HarperOne, 1980), 8.

No Purpose in Everything

Ecclesiastes 1:2 | Vanity of vanities, says the Preacher, vanity of vani-
ties! All is vanity.

Everything is vain, says Solomon. What is he saying? Some trans-
late it "meaningless." But the best way to think of this Hebrew concept
is "superficial." Solomon will soon name everything under the sun like
work, relationships, food, fun, etc., is fine, but it is merely superficial
without the knowledge and fear of God. We might express it even more
clearly as new covenant Christians. Because our purpose is to live for
Christ, and that purpose is in every human being's heart, we look for
something to live for. But everything outside of Christ is vain.

Everything is transitory and therefore superficial with no lasting
value or eternal meaning unless Christ is at the center. Fallen humanity
is caught in the trap of the absurd and pursue empty pleasures. They
build their lives on lies[6]

What is Solomon saying? He's not a bitter old man just being pes-
simistic and grouchy. He's warning here. He's essentially saying that
whatever is done selfishly and simply to enjoy as an end in and of itself
always disappoints. In other words, the promises of money, sex, and
power are all empty outside of God. The Lord told us as much in his
ministry.

Mark 8:36 | For what shall it profit a man, if he shall gain the whole
world, and lose his own soul?"

What's the answer? Gaining the whole world profits nothing. Even
if you could gain the whole world, it would not bring you the happiness
or meaning you deeply desire. It's all vanity apart from knowing Christ.
Paul gets even more graphic and specific concerning the vanity of life
in Philippians.

Philippians 3:8 | I count all things *but* loss for the excellency of the
knowledge of Christ Jesus my Lord: for whom I have suffered the loss
of all things, and do count them *but* dung, that I may win Christ.

According to Paul, life without Christ is not merely vanity, it is
dung—refuse. It's sewage! Single people might think marriage will

---

[6] Duane A. Garrett, *Proverbs, Ecclesiastes, Song of Songs*, vol. 14, The New
American Commentary (Nashville: Broadman & Holman Publishers, 1993), 283.

solve their problems. If your motive is not Christ, it's sewage! Married people might say, "I married the wrong person." You might think, "I know my life will be better when I get that promotion. It'll solve so many problems." Or, "If only I had a better job." Or, "If only I had a better relationship with my parents." If you are thinking, *[fill in the blank]* will solve my problems, and that blank is not filled with Christ, you have entered into idolatry in your heart. Idolatry is a state of heart that is perpetually enslaved to unhappiness because idols cannot fulfill the human heart. Someone said it this way, "Only one life. 'Twill soon be past. Only what's done for Christ will last." Without Christ there is no real purpose or meaningful happiness in life. It's all futility and vanity.

No Purpose in Work Itself

Ecclesiastes 1:3 | What does man gain by all the toil at which he toils under the sun?

In the Old Testament, the phrase *"under the suni"* occurs only in Ecclesiastes (1:3, 9, 14; 2:11, 17, 18, 19, 20, 22; 3:16; 4:1, 3, 7, 15; 5:13, 18; 6:1, 5, 12; 8:9, 15 [twice], 17; 9:3, 6, 9 [twice], 11, 13; 10:5).[7] "Under the sun" is a way of saying, "This is the common experience of man."

Without Christ there is no lasting work in life. Everything on earth is temporary and fading. Your work without Christ is the same as all the others. Whether you are filthy rich or a poor person, your work is meaningless and vain without Christ. What is one king among a thousand? They did all their work, and it was all in vain if they were without Christ. What do you do for a living? There are a thousand others that do the same thing. If you die, someone will take your place. Even if you think you've made a difference, without Christ, your life and your work doesn't matter in the end.

No Purpose in Culture

Ecclesiastes 1:4 | A generation goes, and a generation comes, but the earth remains forever.

---

[7] Michael A. Eaton, *Ecclesiastes: An Introduction and Commentary*, vol. 18, Tyndale Old Testament Commentaries (Downers Grove, IL: InterVarsity Press, 1983), 68.

Without Christ life is meaningless monotony. A purposeless life is not worth living. Nature cycles, but if there is no purpose to it, it's all vain. History moves on. A generation comes and goes. The earth remains. The transitory nature of human generations contrasts with the seeming permanence and apparent immutability of the physical world. Cultures develop in each generation, but no culture has the power to change the course of nature. We live. We die. Like ants on a rock, we leave no trace of having been here. Without experiencing walking with God through a life of faith, the birth of one generation and the passing of another seems like the mere passing of nature's cycles.[8]

No Purpose in Nature Itself

Solomon begins to talk in more detail about how the "earth remains forever." He speaks of the sun rising, the wind blowing, and the rivers running. All beautiful and wonderful things. But if that is all one has to hold onto it is merely the philosophy of fundamental naturalism. A person without the fear of God has no other hope but what he sees. That philosophy divorced from God leads to a dangerous political and philosophical worldview.

Those in the Nazi party in World War II Germany were national socialists. Their worldview was built on the idea of fascism and Marxism. The thrust of the Marxist worldview sounds attractive: put all your energy and effort into a focus on the natural realm. Everything is about leveling the playing field for the oppressed. Sounds appealing. So what was wrong with national socialism in Germany? What's wrong with Marxism today? Marxism and its political child, national socialism, emphasize the natural realm to the utter exclusion of the supernatural. There is no meaningful morality because there is no moral standard outside of self. The religion of Marxism is secular humanism. Humanism in and of itself is good and well. We should help and care for the human race. But the underlying motive cannot be secular but sacred. We have to live as those made in the image of God. Without this purpose, all we have is nature, and that is utterly meaningless. Solomon points us to the vanity of nature, as glorious as it is, without the fear of the Lord (a concept for faith in the Old Testament). Solomon makes

---

[8] Garrett, *Ecclesiastes*, 284–285.

clear that nature, in and of itself, can never provide mankind with any meaningful purpose for living.

The Sun Rises

The sun rises, Solomon says, and yet there is still no meaning in life. All we do without the fear of God is to observe nature.

Ecclesiastes 1:5 | The sun rises, and the sun goes down, and hastens to the place where it rises.

The intricate patterns of the cycle of nature declare the glory of God (Psa 19:1) but mock the atheist. [9] For the unbeliever, the sun, the wind, the running rivers, instead of exalting God, all declare the meaninglessness of his life. On the other hand, the rising sun is a tribute to God for the believer. But for the godless person, the sun is a marker for his countdown to oblivion. The verb translated "hastens" means "to pant."[10] The sun is like a runner endlessly making his way around a racetrack, but sadly for the unbeliever, there is no end to the race. The sun has no purpose but to point to the meaningless of life.

The Wind Blows

Solomon moves from the sun to the wind. Since nature declares the glory of God (Psa 19; cf Rom 1:18ff), you would think that it would inspire the entire world to worship God, but the lost world is blind to the glory of God in the sun and in the wind. They close their eyes to the miraculous ecosystem God has created.

Ecclesiastes 1:6 | The wind blows to the south and goes around to the north; around and around goes the wind, and on its circuits the wind returns.

It is interesting to note how the Preacher uses the sun, wind and rivers as his metaphors of meaninglessness. In other passages of Scripture, they are used to describe the joy and hope to be found in God. (Mal. 4:2; John 8:12; 3:8; 7:38).[11]

Yet as you consider the sun and the wind as a teaching tool, they, like the lost world, are in constant motion but never arrive at any fixed

---

[9] Jim Winter, *Opening up Ecclesiastes*, Opening Up Commentary (Leominster: Day One Publications, 2005), 19.

[10] Garrett, *Ecclesiastes*, 285.

[11] Winter, *Opening up Ecclesiastes*, 19.

goal or lasting rest.[12] There is no rest, no meaningful joy, no tangible meaning to life without our Creator at the center.

The Rivers Run

This next verse is as profound as it is instructive. Solomon speaks of the circuits of the streams and rivers that run to the sea, long before these things were established in modern science.

Ecclesiastes 1:7 | All streams run to the sea, but the sea is not full; to the place where the streams flow, there they flow again.

We see that Solomon is using the sun, wind, and seas as a metaphor for the meaninglessness and futility of life without God. All the activity of nature is monotonous (round and round ... ever returning) and wearisome (*cf* Jer 14:6), without effecting any progress or reaching any fixed goal.[13] This is the central loss for the unbeliever. Life is meaningless without God at the center, and so then eternity is meaningless. A person without Christ is thrown into the lake of fire that burns forever. Nothing productive or joyful is found in an eternity without Christ.

To summarize this portion of Scripture (1:1-7), we might say—you get up and go to work every day. You eat, you sleep, you work, you go on vacation, you do it again and again, and then you die. What's the point? If we have no cosmic purpose, then life is meaningless! That goes for the Christian. Anything attempted in the flesh is wasted. We could lay up treasure in heaven. We could have lasting fruit in eternity. Life is only meaningless and unsatisfying if we leave God out of the picture. Consider that when we see the sun rise and the wind blow on each new day, we can say "Great is your faithfulness" (Lam 3:23).

THE MEANING OF LIFE IS IN CHRIST (1:8)

Solomon tells us that he is wearied trying to explain this to people, because they don't get it! Man cannot see or hear spiritually because the human race is naturally born "dead in trespasses and sins" (*cf* Eph 2:1-3).

---

[12] Donald R. Glenn, "Ecclesiastes," in *The Bible Knowledge Commentary: An Exposition of the Scriptures*, ed. J. F. Walvoord and R. B. Zuck, vol. 1 (Wheaton, IL: Victor Books, 1985), 980.
[13] Ibid.

Ecclesiastes 1:8 | All things are full of weariness; a man cannot utter it; the eye is not satisfied with seeing, nor the ear filled with hearing.

When you try to tell people that life without God is vain, it is wearisome because they are so busing trying to fill their eyes and ears to satisfy them. This is why we have 24-hour news and movies coming out every other day. Man's appetite is never filled or satisfied apart from God. To try to explain this to people is wearisome. Solomon says something similar in his proverbs.

Proverbs 20:27, NLT | Just as Death and Destruction are never satisfied, so human desire is never satisfied.

Where then is true happiness found? In Christ alone. While the fleeting delights of earth are meant for our enjoyment and encouragement, they are not our savior or ultimate end. They are the mere wrapping paper, not the gift. Ultimate satisfaction cannot be found in food or pleasure or even the more sacred things of life like family or ministry. No joy and satisfaction can be tasted in the Lord alone.

Psalm 34:8 | Oh, taste and see that the Lord is good! Blessed is the man who takes refuge in him!

Psalm 16:11 | In your presence is fulness of joy; at you right hand there are pleasures for evermore.

Colossians 2:10 | You are complete in him [Christ], which is the head of all principality and power.

Have you ever been driving, listening to the radio, and the signal gets mixed? Trying to serve God in a day of media is like getting a mixed signal. You hear the word, but it has no power because it's mixed with all kinds of stuff that God is no okay with. We need to clean up our signal. We need to get a stronger signal and cut off all the competing signals. Ask yourself—am I more concerned about the news than the good news? Knowing Christ and walking in obedience to Christ alone will bring spiritual joy—the ecstasy of sin is *dull* compared to our *joy* in Christ.

Conclusion

Are you searching for greener grass? Then you need to water your own lawn. Don't look for a person or a job or anything else in this world for greener grass. That's all covetousness, and it cannot deliver. All the flesh can give us is empty fantasies and promises that will never come true. You must water your own heart with the water of God's presence and the joy of reading his word and hearing his voice.

2 | ECCLESIASTES 1:9-18

KNOWLEDGE WITHOUT CHRIST IS MEANINGLESS

I applied my heart to know wisdom and to know madness and folly. I perceived that this also is but a striving after wind. For in much wisdom is much vexation, and he who increases knowledge increases sorrow.
ECCLESIASTES 1:17-18

We are always looking for something better. The cycle of soul hunger never stops because we are never satisfied unless we are satisfied in Christ. Do you remember the solution to the greener grass syndrome? You don't go looking for greener grass. There is not a "better" situation out there. You've got water your own grass with the water of a spiritual relationship with Jesus Christ.

We have seen that without anchoring our life to Jesus Christ, everything is vanity. The word "vanity" means meaningless. Consider verse 2, "Vanity of vanities, saith the Preacher, vanity of vanities; all *is* vanity." Solomon says, "Everything is meaningless." Everything, Solomon? "Everything." What about marriage? "Meaningless." What about knowledge and wisdom? "Meaningless." What about pleasure?

"Meaningless." What about wealth? "Meaningless." There is nothing that can satisfy us "under the sun" apart from God.

In other words, Solomon tried everything under the sun, and while he found a temporary pleasure in all good things that God has given, there was always a ceiling. There is a certain limit to joy and meaning and purpose to all things in this life apart from God. But we were not created to live as animals for only those things under the sun on this earth. We were created to enjoy the pleasure of God which is beyond the sun. We need to live for the Son of God, not for that which is under the sun on this earth. Life without Christ is meaningless.

One of the first things we are tempted to take the place of Christ in our lives is knowledge. Information. Wisdom. Philosophy. Knowledge of political systems. Sports knowledge. Wikipedia is vain unless it is used to employ your understanding of this world for the glory of God. Knowledge is a superficial goal that cannot satisfy the heart of man. We were not made for mere knowledge or mere relationships or mere work. All of these things are means for an end, and that end of all satisfaction is to know God through Jesus Christ. Mere knowledge is vain? Meaningless? Yes. Our society seems to believe that if we can pour enough money into education, our children will be who they need to be. We need to listen to Solomon.

Ecclesiastes 1:17-18 | I applied my heart to know wisdom and to know madness and folly. I perceived that this also is but a striving after wind. **18** For in much wisdom is much vexation, and he who increases knowledge increases sorrow.

Did you hear Solomon? "I've experienced wisdom and knowledge, but it only vexed my spirit." Knowledge, information, wisdom apart from God will tickle your intellect for a while. But apart from God, it is vain. Sometimes as Christians we think if we need more knowledge, more information, more books, more internet searches, we can find the answer.

T. S. Eliot said, "All our knowledge brings us nearer to our ignorance."[14] That is exactly what Solomon says: "When we increase knowledge, we increase sorrow" (1:18). As far as wisdom was

---

[14] T.S. Eliot. *The Rock*. Directed by E Martin Browne and R. Webb-Odell, 28 May 1934, Sadler's Well's Theatre, London, England.

concerned, the fuller that Solomon got, the emptier that he felt. It had not yielded the satisfaction he was looking for. Remember, Solomon was granted the gift of wisdom and knowledge. Because he was king, he had seemingly unlimited time to explore it. He was such a diplomat that he had connections and resources to any knowledge he desired in the ancient world. But knowledge without meaning and purpose in the Lord is nothing but vexation of spirit.

Consider the sum total of all of our knowledge, which doubles every 2 ½ months. Consider all of the progress we have made technologically, medically, scientifically, economically, and militarily. Has it made life more rich, fulfilling or satisfying? Or are we more enslaved and out of our minds? What good has all this information done us? Without God it information meaningless! The only knowledge that matters is that we know Jesus. In Acts 4, we discover the knowledge that really matters.

> *Acts 4:13*, KJV | Now when they saw the boldness of Peter and John, and perceived that they were unlearned and ignorant men, they marveled; and they took knowledge of them, that they had been with Jesus.

It is said that John Bunyan's entire library consisted of the Bible and Foxe's Book of Martyrs. He had very little learning, but he had learned Christ (Eph 4:21). Yet so many without Christ go after knowledge. Solomon gives us three motives people may have as they pursue knowledge.

THE DISAPPEARANCE OF KNOWLEDGE (1:9-11)

It's fascinating to me what people thought was worthwhile in each generation. People from my day would find video games boring as kids. We would much rather ride our bicycles for ten hours a day than stay cooped up inside. If you grew up in the Middle Ages, a young boy might trap a rabbit or some animal, partially for sport, and mainly to bring it home for a good meal. It's funny how so much of the past is forgotten. Knowledge may be around forever on the internet, but what people really take is has a shelf life. We forget. Knowledge, in a way, disappears at least in regard to what is important or interesting. For those into sports, who won the NBA (basketball) championship last year. It's not important anymore (maybe unless it's your home team." We forget more knowledge than we remember.

Solomon says life apart from Christ is a meaningless rut. Life has little pizzazz outside of Christ, so we try to add a spark of joy to the treadmill of life. Imagine a big sign hanging over this passage that says, "welcome to the treadmill of life." New things are constantly invented, yet there is really nothing new to the "rat race." Solomon wants us to know that apart from meaning in Christ, everyone on earth spanning every generation is in a predictable meaningless rut. People have been working themselves to death for no real purpose since the beginning of time at the fall of man in Genesis 3. Without Christ, we are merely getting on a hamster wheel, or we are swimming around the fishbowl. Choose your metaphor, but without Jesus, life is utterly meaningless because what you do will be replace and forgotten.

The Fact of Knowledge

Ecclesiastes 1:9 | What has been is what will be, and what has been done is what will be done, and there is nothing new under the sun.

Knowledge can be a wonderful thing. It has brought much joy to many generations, but it is not the ultimate goal. The discovery of new things and information can be intoxicating. In every generation we have new inventions that will solve our problems. My father remembers when TV was invented. You may remember 8-track tapes. Wasn't that great? There's a new diet fad every other day. We get new technology or a new celebrity, a new movie or TV show. I remember when they came out with the Kindle and iPad which are supposed to be the future of books. Whatever comes out next, it's really nothing new. It's just another distraction to make you forget that you are on the treadmill of life. Apart from God, your life is in a predictable, meaningless rut. New knowledge can be so helpful in the realm of technology or medicine. It can be fascinating. But without God, it leaves us unsatisfied.

You say, well Solomon knew nothing of the internet, of VCRs or CD players. That's right—what he's referring to is the social and spiritual aspects of who we are. Mankind has not changed. *Time has changed much, but it hasn't changed man himself.* Generation after generation of human beings do the same vain things in relation to God, the world, and one another. We may make new discoveries, but they spin us in the same rut of a purposeless existence if we live life without God.

The Fascination with Knowledge

Ecclesiastes 1:10 | Is there a thing of which it is said, "See, this is new"? It has been already in the ages before us.

We get so excited about new things. Today there is a new fascination with social justice and rioting for the rights of the oppressed. Yet, turn back the clock to 1968 in our country and you see a very similar summer to the summer of 2020. It's a cycle.

Sinners and struggling saints get caught up in the treadmill. We work ourselves to death without realizing that our purpose is to live "for the glory of God." How much meaning is there in all this new stuff? It's all going to be forgotten. Do you remember that before CDs we had vinyl records? Remember when a VCR cost $500? Some of our young people have hardly seen a VCR. The rate at which we obtain stuff and get rid of it is amazing. Count all the garage sales on any given nice weather day. Better yet go to one. Better yet, have one! You'll see all the things you though you could live with out, but you have now forgotten.

Learning new things is so much fun, no doubt. Exploring new ideas is invigorating. God wants us to do this. He told us to dominate the earth in his creation mandate. That means we need to take what God created and be creative. There's a certain legitimate fascination with doing that. But the attainment of knowledge is not an end in and of itself. It is a means to an end. Only God can be the end and goal of everything we do.

The Fading of Knowledge

Ecclesiastes 1:11 | There is no remembrance of former things, nor will there be any remembrance of later things yet to be among those who come after.

Knowledge is exciting, but knowledge fades. Sure, we have our history books and our science books and our biographies. But there is certainly a mindless whirl to all that we have. In days past so much was forgotten. We had no internet, no printing press. So much can be retained today, or so we think. I often go to funerals, and one thing strikes me in a profound way. This person had a whole life to live, but it's all summarized in a few sentences on the back of a little card or funeral program. Most people's lives amount to very little. That is unless we invest in eternity. Once we make God the center of our knowledge, then eternity is affected.

We see this play out in life over and over and over again, that a gadget or a new bit of clothes or a new house or a new boat or a new car, it brings this weird relief and excitement to life. Doesn't it? Have you ever thought about how weird that is, that a *new cell phone*, the cool one, makes you feel better? It has an emotional effect on you. You get it, and you just hold it. When you're around people, you pull it out to check the time. I mean it's this really weird, "This validates the reason I'm here." The Scriptures are saying, "Give me a break." Trinkets are trinkets. What matters is God! "For me to live is Christ!" (Phil 1:21).

We all come to a point as we mature in life where we see things don't satisfy, and so many of us turn to knowledge to dull the pain. It doesn't work. Pursue Christ first, and only then will knowledge have purpose and meaning.

THE DISSATISFACTON OF KNOWLEDGE (1:12-14)

An Unlimited Opportunity

Ecclesiastes 1:12 | I the Preacher have been king over Israel in Jerusalem.

We go after knowledge because we want to experiment with life. *We have a morbid curiosity to know what's out there.* As we go down the treadmill of life, there are many things to take our mind off the treadmill. It's like those fancy schmancy work out gyms that have TVs attached to the treadmills. People want to take their mind off the pain of stretching their body.

Life hurts, and one of the ways we distract ourselves is through what I call "information overload." We live in an age that seeks after wisdom and knowledge and information in place of God. How many channels do we need on a television? The average person with a remote control will change channels 350,000 times in his lifetime. We have 24-hour news cycles. You can turn on the news channels and a thousand other channels on your TV or on the Internet and waste your life gaining meaningless knowledge. Now you say, Solomon didn't have the Internet. No, but he did something far beyond what any of us have ever done as far as experimenting. Solomon's exploration of life. Solomon didn't have Google or the internet, but he did have unlimited resources to seek out information.

An Unsatisfying Opportunity

Ecclesiastes 1:12-13 | I the Preacher have been king over Israel in Jerusalem. [13] And I applied my heart to seek and to search out by wisdom all that is done under heaven. It is an unhappy business that God has given to the children of man to be busy with.

The word "search out" means to investigate, explore, or experiment. So the king—wealthy, wise, powerful Solomon, set out to explore all that is done under heaven. He's got an experiment going. He's going to use the five senses: taste, touch, seeing, hearing and smell. So, he's going to use his five senses with all his wealth, power, and wisdom, and he's going to use those five senses to apply those five senses to the seven favorite things among men. Here are the seven favorite things: wealth, power, religion, friends, work, knowledge, and pleasure. Solomon decides to explore everything. There was no one who was more curious than Solomon. In his day he was the ultimate knowledge surfer. If there was an internet, he'd not only surf it, he would own it. Solomon's dissatisfaction with life.

An Unrealistic Opportunity

Ecclesiastes 1:14 | I have seen everything that is done under the sun, and behold, all is vanity and a striving after wind.

With unlimited resources, Solomon gained all the knowledge he could about everything it left him unsatisfied. It was unrealistic to think knowledge could ever fill the void in the human heart. Knowledge, instead of helping Solomon, it hurt him. It brought him pain. He had that ache that he was wasting his life. Knowledge, if it not attached to Christ just makes us prouder, self-centered, unhappy people. "Knowledge puffs up" (1 Cor 8:1). Knowledge is dangerous if it doesn't lead us to God. You've heard the saying, "curiosity killed the cat." That thirst for knowledge killed the cat. Without God we cannot know the truth, we cannot know ultimate reality. We learn in the New Testament: "You will know the truth, and the truth will set you free" (Jn 8:32). Without Christ, we can only live according to invented realities with "everyone doing that which is right in his own eyes" (Jgs 17:8; Pro 21:2).

Let your mind go back to the Garden of Eden and see how dangerous curiosity without Christ is. It is interesting that at the beginning Satan's temptation of Eve was for knowledge, specifically the "knowledge of good and evil". Like Eve, we all have a sinful desire for the curious. Curiosity not only killed the cat, it killed the entire human race.

Let me give some practical warnings. Internet curiosity kills marriages. If you surf the internet with no goal in mind, but just "out of curiosity" let me tell you, you are a candidate for a terrible fall. You will sin, it's just a matter of time. We cannot test God. If you play with fire you will get burned. Some of you are curious about email. You have to check it every five minutes. That curiosity is really an ache for God. Some of you are curious about Facebook. You can spend hours there. Others can text and use that cell phone God gave you. If you are spending inordinate amounts of time on this stuff, you are looking for satisfaction in a place that cannot fulfill you. Do you spend inordinate amounts of time texting, spending time on the computer, video games, or with your smart phone? Life is about people, not technology. You are probably robbing your family of quality time if you are hooked on curiosity and knowledge.

There is a solution to this problem. Turn your cell phone off at night when you are home. If you are home, people can get a hold of you through the old-fashioned line-based telephone. If you only have a cell phone, then have the spouse with the least called phone keep their phone on. If you have a cell phone biologically attached to your ear, then you need to turn off your phone at night and ask God to help you not to abuse it! This goes for any technology. The TV is the same way. Channel surfing will get you spiritually dirty. I don't know of a time when I just channel surfed with no objective but to be mindlessly entertained, and I got hit with something I didn't want to hear or see. It's like David says:

> Psalm 101:3 | I will set no wicked thing before mine eyes: I hate the work of them that turn aside; it shall not cleave to me."

What do you really get from the news? What is your purpose? Have you considered the dangers of internet use with no fences and no accountability?

THE DAZZLE OF KNOWLEDGE (1:15-18)

Ecclesiastes 1:15-18 | What is crooked cannot be made straight, and what is lacking cannot be counted. [16] I said in my heart, "I have acquired great wisdom, surpassing all who were over Jerusalem before me, and my heart has had great experience of wisdom and knowledge." [17] And I applied my heart to know wisdom and to know madness and folly. I perceived that this also is but a striving after wind. [18] For in much wisdom is much vexation, and he who increases knowledge increases sorrow.

We go after knowledge because of our high expectations for life. We have high expectations to succeed. We want to divide and conquer. We want to do something significant. Perhaps we can't bring world peace, but we often have high idealistic goals. There's a problem though. Many times, our expectations wrongly focused. It seems like knowledge can really change things and really make a difference. But it really depends what kind of knowledge we are talking about. Knowledge alone can help society and push if forward, but it cannot offer an lasting and eternal solution for mankind, unless it is found in God himself.

Knowledge is Not the Ultimate Solution

Ecclesiastes 1:15a | What is crooked cannot be made straight.

The soul of man is crooked, and it cannot be made straight through mere knowledge. We need something more than intellectual stimulation. It is so tempting to trust in knowledge alone. A new mindset, a new class, a new principle. How long does that last? Knowledge is good and right, but it not the goal. Fulfilling our intellectual curiosities can be fun and exciting, but apart from first knowing God, knowledge can leave us unsatisfied and even in great psychological pain.

We often get idealistic expectations that distract and disappoint us. We want to believe that we can really make a difference. My brother is doing something really cool this year. He's biking across the country, from California to North Carolina for a young cancer patient. He wants to raise awareness and funds for a cure for forms of childhood cancer. That's a noble good thing. On May 22nd we are going to have a fundraiser Cystic Fibrosis in Naperville. We love to participate in "Great Strides" every year. These are all great things, but let's not fool ourselves. The greatest problem that our children face is not cancer, and it is not cystic fibrosis. The greatest enemy is *sin*. Whether we find cures for these diseases, our children are going to spend their lives somewhere forever. They will either be judged by their behavior or by their trust in Christ. Unless we are involved in spreading the Gospel, what we do will not last ultimately.

We cannot expect to straighten out that which is crooked (1:15). That's not my job or your job. That's Jesus' job. So many people get involved in politics because they want to straighten everything out. Verse 15, "That which is crooked cannot be made straight"—only Jesus can make the hearts of men straight. Our government will not and cannot be straightened out until Jesus comes again. What is crooked cannot be straightened out, except by Jesus' grace. Our expectations are wrongly focused. Our expectations are also unrealistic.

Knowledge is Not the Ultimate Satisfaction

Ecclesiastes 1:15b | What is lacking cannot be counted.

The word "lacking" is pointing to those things we "long to attain." We have romantic thoughts about the greener grass. Things would be better, if only... The problem is all of the "if onlys" that do not and will never exist in people's minds are so many they cannot be numbered. So we might find out information about so many things in life dreaming about unrealistic things. And it's all a waste. Listen to Solomon's conclusion.

Ecclesiastes 1:16-18 | I said in my heart, "I have acquired great wisdom, surpassing all who were over Jerusalem before me, and my heart has had great experience of wisdom and knowledge." **17** And I applied my heart to know wisdom and to know madness and folly. I perceived that this also is but a striving after wind. **18** For in much wisdom is much vexation, and he who increases knowledge increases sorrow.

Solomon experiences the high life of wisdom and the low life of folly and madness. Knowing all that the high life offers without Christ is vain. What Solomon did was, he marbled everything and encrusted it in gold. He ate caviar; he went to the opera; he went golf clubs and the elite night clubs. He spent his wealth and power. He did all that the rich and famous do, and he found it to be meaningless. And so, after he

THE PROCLAIM COMMENTARY: ECCLESIASTES

had acquired all that stuff and had all those things and did all the things that the rich did, he decided to go the other direction.

Knowing all that the simple life offers without Christ is vain. So, then Solomon looked down and found some country folk and hung out with them to live the simple life. And drank he drank Diet Dr. Pepper and played horseshoes and went to the Sox games and ate macaroni and cheese and hamburger stirred up in a pot. And he even hated on the Cubs a little bit, and after he did all that, he found out that this also was meaningless.

Solomon even went a little stupid here with the low life and showed it was vain. He played with "madness and folly" (1:17). He gave himself to the stupid stuff. He goes into this a little more in chapter 2, but he finds out everything he can about pleasure. He tries everything he can possibly try of this world's pleasure.

He's tried both the high life, and the simple life, and even the low life. He's got all the knowledge; he's done all the experimentation with life that can be done. He's surfed the information superhighway of his day. He's watched Fox and CNN, done 10,000 texts, gotten every car, had every girl, thrown every party. He knows everything there is to know. And what is his conclusion?

Ecclesiastes 1:18 | For in much wisdom is much vexation, and he who increases knowledge increases sorrow.

Knowledge without Christ can bring much vexation and sorrow.

Conclusion

For some people, they think seeking after knowledge is the way to satisfy themselves. Solomon tried to educate his way to satisfaction! He thought if he could learn enough, if he could earn enough degrees that he would experience fulfillment! But the more he learned the less he knew and the less he liked what he learned!

Now, I'm all for education! I believe you ought to get all the education available! But I want to tell you that education without God is just brilliant foolishness. A person who has knowledge in his head but doesn't have God in his heart, is nothing more than a clever devil! Information, knowledge, and learning is all meaningless without Christ.

3 | ECCLESIASTES 2:1-11

PLEASURE WITHOUT CHRIST IS MEANINGLESS

I said in my heart, "Come now, I will test you with pleasure; enjoy yourself." But behold, this also was vanity. I said of laughter, "It is mad," and of pleasure, "What use is it?"

ECCLESIASTES 2:1-2

Solomon, the wisest man in the history of the world outside of our Lord, uncovers a serious scandal and controversy in the world. Can a person be happy by acquiring knowledge? The government campaigns all tell us that education is the answer. Solomon shoots that down and says "No, after getting all the wisdom and knowledge that a human being can have, I still have an emptiness, an ache, a pain, and a vexation in my soul and in my spirit." So instead of knowledge, Solomon turns to pleasure.

Ecclesiastes 2:1-11 | I said in my heart, "Come now, I will test you with pleasure; enjoy yourself." But behold, this also was vanity. ² I said of laughter, "It is mad," and of pleasure, "What use is it?" ³ I searched with my heart how to cheer my body with wine— my heart still guiding me with wisdom—and how to lay hold on folly, till I might see what was good for the children of man to do under heaven during the few days of their life. [4] I made great works. I built houses and planted vineyards for myself. [5] I made myself gardens and parks, and planted in them all kinds of fruit trees. [6] I made myself pools from which to water the forest of growing trees. [7] I bought male and female slaves, and had slaves who were born in my house. I had also great possessions of herds and flocks, more than any who had been before me in Jerusalem. [8] I also gathered for myself silver and gold and the treasure of kings and provinces. I got singers, both men and women, and many concubines, the delight of the sons of man. [9] So I became great and surpassed all who were before me in Jerusalem. Also my wisdom remained with me. [10] And whatever my eyes desired I did not keep from them. I kept my heart from no pleasure, for my heart found pleasure in all my toil, and this was my reward for all my toil. [11] Then I considered all that my hands had done and the toil I had expended in doing it, and behold, all was vanity and a striving after wind, and there was nothing to be gained under the sun.

PLEASURE THROUGH PARTIES (2:1-3)

Solomon fields another experiment. He went after knowledge and was left empty, and now it is time to experiment with pleasure. "What if I could fulfill all the desires of my flesh and have all the pleasure that a human being could possibly enjoy? Then I would be happy!" Solomon actually attempts this experiment. Solomon, who is king of Israel, is going to use his almost unlimited wealth and immense power, which is beyond what any of us can fathom, and he is going to fulfill every imagination his heart can dream up as far as pleasure goes. And his goal is to see if there is any meaning and any lasting value and purpose to what he is doing under the sun. Solomon's first experiment begins with pleasure through parties.

His Motto: If It Feels Good Do It

Ecclesiastes 2:1 | I said in my heart, "Come now, I will test you with pleasure; enjoy yourself." But behold, this also was vanity.

The slogan of our society today can be reduced to six single-syllable words, "If it feels good do it." Solomon lived this 3500 years ago. So here in Ecclesiastes 2, Solomon wants to put pleasure to the test. Solomon is going to put pleasure to the test.

Solomon who has infinite resources and time is going to use all his imagination and creativity to launch an experiment with pleasure and see if there is any fulfilling and satisfying purpose to it, in and of itself apart from God. He's already admitted the meaninglessness of pleasure without Christ by saying: "Behold, this also is vanity" (2:1). At the end of the day, pleasure cannot fulfill us in a meaningful and lasting way. There is no lasting value in earthly comfort. It is a gift from God, and it must be enjoyed with God.

The Mirth of His Banquets

Ecclesiastes 2:2 | I said of laughter, "It is mad," and of pleasure, "What use is it?"

Solomon might have had jesters and comedians. He laughed so hard day after day after day. But at the end it was all of no value to him. There was no fulfillment. Laughter is good medicine of course. Sometimes humor and wit have a wonderful way of communicating truth. Even sarcasm has its place. But it cannot take the place of Christ.

Solomon later says rightly, there is "a time to weep and a time to laugh" (3:4). Laughter is a wonderful gift from God. Solomon tells us in his proverbs that "A joyful heart is good medicine" (Pro 17:22). Christians who are walking with God have much laugh about and be joyful, for but laughing away our problems and sins is not the solution. Some sitcoms and comedians can be fine, but without Christ they only serve to distract people from the coming day when we will meet God. When all is well with your soul and you are walking with God, there is "joy unspeakable and full of glory." There is joy in his presence (Psa 16:11).

The Massiveness of His Banquets

Ecclesiastes 2:3 | I searched with my heart how to cheer my body with wine—my heart still guiding me with wisdom—and how to lay hold on folly, till I might see what was good for the children of man to do under heaven during the few days of their life.

The size of Solomon's banquets would have had was beyond comprehension. Solomon says, "I'm going all out, using all my unlimited resources as king, all my unhindered time, and my fantastic creativity to consume as much pleasure as I possibly can." You cannot imagine the epic banquets Solomon had. Solomon begins to throw the largest parties the world has ever seen. He's going 7 days a week for an extended period of time with his pleasure experiment. No one is really sure how long he continued this way. He had massive amounts of food. In case you wonder if Solomon tried hard enough, consider 1 Kings 4.

> *1 Kings 4:22-23* | Solomon's provision for one day was thirty cors of fine flour and sixty cors of meal, [23] ten fat oxen, and twenty pasture-fed cattle, a hundred sheep, besides deer, gazelles, roebucks, and fattened fowl.

We have to be careful not to compare ourselves with Solomon, thinking our day would be better than his day. Now for every party he has the commentaries say, he would have hosted between 15 and 20 thousand people. Whatever pleasures you could imagine—if you only had the money. He did it. He had an epic series of parties, night after night. There was no time clock for Solomon. He could do whatever he wanted whenever he wanted. If he wanted to sleep till 11 in the morning, he did. If he wanted to stay up all night, he did. Eventually he got tired of all the pleasure and the partying. His conclusion? It's vanity (1:1); it is madness (2:2), it's of no use (2:2), it's folly (2:3). In other words, it leaves you wanting more. It cannot satisfy. People fix their hearts on all kinds of pleasures and enjoyments under the sun, but at the end of the day, without God they are empty and leave an ache of unfulfillment in the soul.

PLEASURE THROUGH PRODUCTIVITY (2:4-6)

So Solomon moves from pleasure through parties to pleasure through productivity. We have all these people who say, if I could get the house I want and the car I want and the little vacation house on the lake, I would be happy. Solomon is out to prove you wrong.

> **Ecclesiastes 2:4-5** | I made great works. I built houses and planted vineyards for myself. [5] I made myself gardens and parks, and planted in them all kinds of fruit trees.

Solomon moves on from narcissistic pleasures to more productive pleasures. He starts building elaborate houses with elaborate gardens and parks. When he says he "built great works" (2:4), he's talking about a palace and other houses for all his wives and concubines. Solomon's palace was massive. The temple took seven years to build. Solomon's house on the other hand took fourteen years to build.

Solomon undertook great projects. There is something that is satisfying about getting your own home. There is also something about working hard all day going after your dream and accomplishing it. Solomon did all that.

You might get some genuine satisfaction out of your flower garden and your nicely kept lawn. You fix it up. You plant the marigolds and petunias. You put in some shrubs. You add a horseshoe pit and your bar-b-que grill. You plant trees and put in the mulch everywhere. You are feeling good, sitting on your porch, and enjoying your yard. Solomon I'm sure would appreciate your garden, but he planted forests and orchards and parks on his back 900 acres! Solomon had massive irrigation pools constructed for his parks and orchards and forests.

Ecclesiastes 2:6 | I made myself pools from which to water the forest of growing trees.

To this day, if you went to Jerusalem, southwest of Jerusalem, you would come to this place where there are all these craters in the earth, and it's called "The Pools of Solomon." This is where Solomon dug these huge, cavernous holes in the earth, filled them with water to water all the gardens and national parks and everything else he built out. So Solomon builds the most amazing place on earth, and at the end he says, "it's all vanity." Solomon admits he had all the money, all the time, all the creative powers, but utopia on earth just didn't satisfy him (2:1).

PLEASURE THROUGH PROSPERITY (2:7-8)

Since parties and productivity didn't work, Solomon tries a third path for pleasure, that of prosperity and ease.

Ecclesiastes 2:7-8 | I bought male and female slaves, and had slaves who were born in my house. I had also great possessions of herds and flocks, more than any who had been before me in Jerusalem. [8] I also gathered for myself silver and gold and the treasure of kings and provinces. I got singers, both men and women, and many concubines, the delight of the sons of man.

The Prosperity of Servants

Ecclesiastes 2:7a | I bought male and female slaves, and had slaves who
were born in my house.

Solomon had servants. Solomon could afford to possess anything
material he chose. This even included fellow human beings! Power over
people has always been a strong driving force within the human psy-
che.[15] Solomon need not do anything for himself. In this experiment
with prosperity, he might have woken up late, and somebody cooked
breakfast for him. He moved on from there to get massage number one.
He got the facial, the pedicure. He did nothing for himself. He sat back
and enjoyed his riches and wealth.

Being able to do what you want when you want to will not bring you
happiness. Have you ever turned on those "success" shows and found
out how you could make money from home doing nothing? Listen, if
you could make money from home doing nothing, we'd all be rich! Yet
people fall for it!

The Prosperity of Ranches

Ecclesiastes 2:7b | I had also great possessions of herds and flocks,
more than any who had been before me in Jerusalem.

Solomon had ranches with horses and cattle and sheep. This included a massive amount of land. King Solomon had so many animals
that every day the chefs in his royal kitchen would prepare "ten fat
oxen, and twenty pasture-fed cattle, a hundred sheep, besides deer, ga-
zelles, roebucks, and fattened fowl" (1 Kgs 4:23).[16] He had the best food
and the best cooks. He could have filet mignon anytime he wanted. He
took advantage of all his wealth and power and spent it on himself. Anything he wanted he enjoyed it. You might want a boat—Solomon could
buy the harbor! Indeed, Solomon had more land and animals than anyone before in Jerusalem before him. Solomon was the ultimate refined
landowner. His own slaves, herds, and flocks (the real measure of
wealth to the average man of his time) were greater than any in local
history (*cf* 1 Kgs 4:20–23).[17]

---

[15] Winter, *Opening up Ecclesiastes*, 37.
[16] Ryken, *Ecclesiastes*, 49.
[17] Garrett, *Ecclesiastes*, 292.

The Prosperity of Riches

Ecclesiastes 2:8a | I also gathered for myself silver and gold and the treasure of kings and provinces.

Exactly how rich was King Solomon? How much gold and silver did he possess? There are four primary ways King Solomon, in a fairly short period of time, became the wealthiest king alive. He was made rich through commerce and trading, gifts he received, tribute money paid to him and heavy taxation.

His commerce and trading endeavors were amazing. His partnership with Hiram brought him, every three years, things like ivory, monkeys, apes, etc. (1 Kgs 10:22-23).

Another way Solomon became so rich was by large and generous gifts from other nations. For example, the Queen of Sheba made a special trip to Jerusalem to hear Solomon's wisdom. She was so impressed that she gave him camels, jewels, five tons of gold ($250 million), and other gifts (2 Chron 9:1, 9). The Bible says that everyone who came to inquire of the king's wisdom brought him a gift: animals, spices, precious metals, and so on (1 Kgs 10:25).

Many nations brought Solomon tribute money. Tribute is money or goods paid by kingdoms or countries in acknowledgment of another country's superiority. Many nations "brought tribute and served Solomon all the days of his life" (1 Kgs 4:24). Not to mention, the people of Israel were taxed heavily by Solomon (1 Kgs 12:4).

Solomon's wealth was incredible! We read that he would receive on average over a billion dollars of gold (666 talents) each year (1 Kgs 10:14-15). The king became so immensely rich that all his cups were made of gold (not one was made of silver (1 Kgs 10:21). His wealth was so vast that precious metals were as common in Jerusalem as stones (2 Chron 1:15; *cf* 1 Kgs 10:27).

And yet all these unimaginable amounts of money did not satisfy Solomon. Like so many in the billionaire's club, he said, even with all the money that can be had by a human being, life is still vain, meaningless, useless, without purpose. Money cannot fill the great void we have in our hearts. Our hearts were made to be satisfied by the infinite God alone.

The Prosperity of Music

Ecclesiastes 2:8b | I got singers, both men and women.

Solomon had his own orchestras. Solomon didn't have an iPod. He didn't download music. He had enough money to buy the band! Any music he wanted he brought in to play for him. Music was a rare pleasure in those days, but Solomon could afford to bring it into his own home, engaging entire orchestras to play and choirs to sing for his pleasure.[18]

Today people cannot live without their music. Some of you are listening to your streaming music in church, outside of church. You can barely put it down to eat dinner. Music is a wonderful gift of God, but if you are using it to escape the pain of this life, make sure you have Jesus at the center of it. Worship music can lift your burdens, but music by itself is an insufficient savior.

The Prosperity of Carnality

Ecclesiastes 2:8c | And many concubines, the delight of the sons of man.

Sex is a more common pleasure, but few people have ever experienced it on quite the scale as King Solomon. Here he speaks of many concubines, but 1 Kings 11:3 gives us the raw statistics—seven hundred wives and princesses, with three hundred concubines—more sexual partners than anyone could imagine. The erotic luxury of this vast harem was the royal icing on his cake of pleasure.[19] Solomon lived out the intimate sensual fantasies in his mind and indulged in sexual pleasure.

What about pornography? Pornography is a scary word that we want to say is other people's problem. David Powlison says, "The first part of the word pornography, "porné," means immorality and the second part, "graph" means to write, draw, or portray."[20] Pornography is about picturing, imagining, and fantasizing about immorality. You may not be aware of it, but soft-core pornography is everywhere you look. It

---

[18] Josephus. *Antiquities of the Jews*, Book 8, Chapter 7.
[19] Ryken, *Ecclesiastes*, 49.
[20] David Powlison. *Breaking Pornography Addiction*. Available on the web at: http://ccef.org/breaking-pornography-addiction-part-1

is on about every other commercial on television. It's all over the billboards. And it's not just in the media. In our world, both men and women dress to attract attention and to elicit romantic or erotic feelings in others. We are all bombarded with pornography every day—it's the atmosphere we live in.

What is the answer to pornography? We must understand that God has a place for fulfilling sexual desire. "Marriage is honourable in all, and the bed undefiled: but whoremongers and adulterers God will judge" (Heb 13:4, KJV). Married men need to be loving and treating their wives in the right way. Married ladies need to be there for the needs of thier husband. We are prone to criticize Solomon for his excursions with 700 wives and 300 concubines, but in the world today, men are having those kinds of fantasies in their minds with the internet and other gateways to porn. Now marriage is not the solution. Marital intimacy is a beautiful picture of Christ and the church (Eph 5:22ff), but it is only a picture. It cannot bring satisfaction without Christ at the center. The ultimate solution whether you are single or married concerning sensual imaginations is self-control, satisfaction in Christ, and living in the real world where we value people around us as made in the image of God. Escapism will end for the Spirit-filled Christian. Sin will not have dominion over the Christian who is growing in grace and walking in the word.

PLEASURE WITHOUT CHRIST CANNOT SATISFY (2:9-11)

Now let's look at Solomon's conclusions. He basically says all the pleasure in the world is completely empty without knowing the Lord.

Ecclesiastes 2:9-10 | So I became great and surpassed all who were before me in Jerusalem. Also my wisdom remained with me. [10] And whatever my eyes desired I did not keep from them. I kept my heart from no pleasure, for my heart found pleasure in all my toil, and this was my reward for all my toil.

Solomon never forgot what his goal was. His "wisdom remained" with him. He never lost sight of the goal, which was to see if there was any value in pleasure for pleasure's sake.

Solomon took in his pleasure. Party after party. Night after night. After so many months, it got old. There is a ceiling to pleasure. Then he moved to productivity. He took in the beauty of his palace and houses and forests and orchards and parks. That got old after a while too. There had to be something more. So he took in pleasure. He did nothing for himself. He spoiled himself with music and ranching, and pleasure with his wives and concubines. Solomon went from the party scene, to the productivity scene, to the prosperity and pleasure scene, and he says that all he had was momentary and fleeting fun. What did he get out of all of it? Pleasure—momentary, fleeting pleasure that is here for a moment and then it is gone!

Ecclesiastes 2:11 | Then I considered all that my hands had done and the toil I had expended in doing it, and behold, all was vanity and a striving after wind, and there was nothing to be gained under the sun.

A rich life of pleasure without God is empty. Here's the conclusion. Sex and pleasure and food and joy are all God's idea. God creates the world and puts two unclothed people in the Garden and says, "Be fruitful and multiply." Pleasure in Christ is beautiful. But you take it outside of Christ and it gets messed up. It's vanity. Fleeting. It brings you no meaningful or lasting return outside of that fleeting moment.

Conclusion

Now you may be feeling a bit messed up in this world. Perhaps you are struggling with addictions to this world's pleasure. You can't stop watching TV. You are addicted to your music. You might be addicted to pornography. You might be addicted to food. Calvin famously said, "The heart is an idol making factory."[21] Any time you worship idols, the pleasure lasts for a moment, but the anxiety, anger, and despair cling to our souls. Pleasure outside of God cannot satisfy but leaves us violated by sin.

God is not a spoilsport. He is not trying to take pleasure away from us but to give it to us. Once we learn how to find our satisfaction in God himself, then all of his other gifts become the best and truest pleasures. Happily, we do not have to be as rich as Solomon to experience meaningful hedonism. We simply have to see what is in the world around us and know that it comes to us as a gift from God.[22]

---

[21] John Calvin, *Institutes of the Christian Religion*, Ch XI, Para 8.
[22] Ryken, *Ecclesiastes*, 54.

It's ok to want pleasure. But you must find your ultimate pleasure fulfilled through your walk with God. Pleasure must be gained God's way, in God's presence, living life the way God designed it. Remember there is a ceiling to earthly joy. If all you have is earthly joy, you will find your spirit all messed up inside, vexed with anxiety and frustration and despair. Real, lasting, meaningful joy is found in Jesus alone. All the other pleasures he gives us are like wrapping paper. Don't delight in the wrapping paper. Delight in our true joy and delight, our Lord Jesus Christ. He is the greatest and most satisfying gift. "You make known to me the path of life; in your presence there is fullness of joy; at your right hand are pleasures forevermore" (Psa 16:11).

4 | ECCLESIASTES 2:11-26

WORK WITHOUT CHRIST IS MEANINGLESS

*There is nothing better for a person than that he should eat
and drink and find enjoyment in his toil. This also, I saw,
is from the hand of God, for apart from him who can eat or
who can have enjoyment?*

ECCLESIASTES 2:24-25

Thus far we have seen that you can have all the knowledge and human wisdom this world can offer and it won't satisfy you. Satisfying all your curiosities will not satisfy you. What if I had all my
curiosities satisfied—nope. Tomorrow you'll have another one. You'll
always be hungry.

What about pleasure? What if I had a wife that would satisfy me in
the bedroom? What if I had all the best food and never went hungry?
What if I could actually life all my dreams, build whatever I wanted,
vacation wherever I wanted. Nope that won't satisfy. Solomon partied
and banqueted more than any one on earth and it didn't satisfy him.

Now we are going to try another experiment. What about work?
Can I be happy if I make the goal of my life work? Will work make me
happy? Will job security and a dream job make me happy? You can
guess what the answer is. No way.

I remember living in Spain, and I would ask my neighbor: "How was work?" "What?" he asked in unbelief. Work is work." I understood. He had a great job, but he put up with it. He lived for vacation. He lived for the weekend. God has given us a completely different mindset with the Christian work ethic. Our nation is founded on the work ethic. What is the secret? Christians turn their work into worship for God. It becomes pleasurable even in the worst working conditions.

We read of the great King Solomon. At one time in his life, his job was his life. He neglected everything so that he could be a success at his calling. But he wasn't happy. He had to give up that idol of work for lasting eternal pleasure. He had to make the Lord his joy, and the man became completely satisfied. It's Solomon's story. We are going to find according to Solomon work alone can never satisfy a person. Work instead is to be turned into worship in service to our great God.

WORK ITSELF IS NOT THE ANSWER (2:11-15)

Here we have Solomon's summary statement of the rest of the chapter: he was the king—everything he imagined he built. He put his heart and soul into working and imagining and not just having one business, but a hundred. And at the end of the day, he got no deep satisfaction or meaning from all his work.

Work Doesn't Profit

Ecclesiastes 2:11 | Then I considered all that my hands had done and the toil I had expended in doing it, and behold, all was vanity and a striving after wind, and there was nothing to be gained under the sun.

Solomon's work was fleeting, like a striving after the wind. Where is the temple Solomon built? What about his palace? All turned to dust. We can work and work, but what are we doing it for? Wisdom? Wealth? Pleasure? Why do you work? At the end of the day, any reason for working outside of God's glory that is found "under the sun" is worthless. It's going to leave you empty and aching. The New Testament says it this way, "For what is a man profited, if he shall gain the whole world, and lose his own soul? or what shall a man give in exchange for his soul?" (Mt 16:26). Solomon's proposition here is that work cannot satisfy the heart of man. He had all the power and money to prove this proposition. You can't outdo Solomon.

Work Doesn't Satisfy

Solomon now tells us that work is limited in what it can do for you. It cannot bring you lasting satisfaction (2:12). It also cannot solve the problem of death and dying (2:13-15).

Ecclesiastes 2:12 | So I turned to consider wisdom and madness and folly. For what can the man do who comes after the king? Only what has already been done.

Solomon had all the wisdom a man could have. He also experimented by going against wisdom with madness. And then he tried folly and foolishness. None of it was satisfying. All the toil of his hands could not satisfy. Why? Because work is limited. Whatever area of life we choose to work in, work cannot not get you what you want. That's found in Christ alone. Solomon has all the wisdom to prove that work cannot satisfy you. What is anyone going to do that comes after King Solomon? He's done it all. You can't improve on the experiment he has undertaken. He's the greatest king, greatest architect, greatest judge, you name it, he was great at it. And it's still "vanity and a striving after the wind" (2:11). Work is limited and is not meant to satisfy us.

Work Doesn't Save

Ecclesiastes 2:13-15 | Then I saw that there is more gain in wisdom than in folly, as there is more gain in light than in darkness. [13] The wise person has his eyes in his head, but the fool walks in darkness. And yet I perceived that the same event happens to all of them. [15] Then I said in my heart, "What happens to the fool will happen to me also. Why then have I been so very wise?" And I said in my heart that this also is vanity.

You spend a lot of time at work. Keep your head on straight. Do it for the glory of God. Whether you are talking about your daily schedule at work, and all you do there, or the media contact you have with browsing the internet, watching the TV or the time you spend with family, church life—don't ever park your brain at the door. His philosophy is simply this, "It's better to have your eyes opened than your eyes shut." I don't think anyone wants to argue with that. I never met the guy who's like, "Man, blind people, they got it going on. Us sighted people, we're the ones who are all messed up." Philosophically, he's saying, "You

60

cannot afford to not pay attention to your life. You can coast on a lot of things; don't coast on this one."

WORK ITSELF ISN'T LASTING (2:16-23)

Getting your dream job is not the answer.

The Legacy of Work Does Not Last

Ecclesiastes 2:16 | For of the wise as of the fool there is no enduring remembrance, seeing that in the days to come all will have been long forgotten. How the wise dies just like the fool!

Solomon's "work" literally means his daily responsibilities. He had the best job in the world. He was the center of his own universe as king. He tried to get fulfillment and satisfaction out of his work. All the result of Solomon's exercise of his wisdom—his fantastic palace and gardens and building projects—he realized putting his hope in those things are vain, because they do not prepare him for death.

The best dream job cannot prepare you for death. Verse 14, "I myself perceived also that one event [*death*] happens to them all." Whether you are rich or poor, you are going to die. Wise or foolish, death is coming. Your dream job will not change that. Verse 16, "how the wise dies just like the fool." You can get your dream job, but listen to me, one day you are going to die. Whether you are picking up garbage, or you are the President of the United States, you are going to die. How is your dream job going to help you then. Your job is not your Savior. Jesus Christ is.

There are people that try to make work the very purpose of their life. That's never going to satisfy you. It's not enough to satisfy anyone's soul. Some people work for work itself. But ultimately, it's going to get old. It will not satisfy no matter how many dream jobs you have.

The Joy of Work Does Not Last

The best dream job cannot satisfy you. Your best dream job will never fulfill you for the long term. It my tantalize you for a year or so, but it will leave you empty.

Ecclesiastes 2:17 | So I hated life, because what is done under the sun was grievous to me, for all is vanity and a striving after wind.

Your dream job is not going to satisfy you. It can't. Go ahead and dream. Say, if only I could work the dayshift, then everything would be better. Wrong. If only I could work the night shift, then all would be better. Wrong. If only I had that promotion life would be better. Not true. If only I had my own business, I would be happy. Not true. If only I wasn't unemployed, then I would really be happy. Wrong again. If only, if only... Wrong, wrong, wrong, wrong. Happiness comes from Christ, not from your dream job. There is no dream job. It's a sham. It's a vain imagination. It doesn't exist. It cannot satisfy no matter how great it is.

Maybe you say, "Ok, I'll never be totally satisfied working, but I'm going to work my head off trying to get rich. My fantastic paycheck will make me happy". Wrong again.

The Reward of Work Does Not Last

If your goal for working is your paycheck, you're going to be quite disappointed. If your goal is a paycheck you are going to be depressed. Why? The reward of work does not last. But it does give a mirage of control.

Money Gives the Mirage of Power

Ecclesiastes 2:18-19 | I hated all my toil in which I toil under the sun, seeing that I must leave it to the man who will come after me, [19] and who knows whether he will be wise or a fool? Yet he will be master of all for which I toiled and used my wisdom under the sun. This also is vanity.

When you work hard you get paid well. There is this mirage of control. You don't care if you are wise or if you are a fool. Your measure isn't morality but money. Solomon said, "I will be the master of all for which I toiled." For this reason, this lack of power and control over how his money would be used was something so difficult he said, "I hated all my toil" (2:18). When we measure ourselves by control and money, we set ourselves up for unhappiness and misery. Time is ticking, and your paycheck will not always be yours. You get all this money, and then you die and leave it to someone else. Your paycheck cannot satisfy you because you can't take it with you. Remember the wisdom of Job.

Job 1:21 | Naked I came from my mother's womb, and naked shall I return. The LORD gave, and the LORD has taken away; blessed be the name of the LORD.

Money in this life quickly vanishes away. Solomon says that at times, it even sprouts wings!

Proverbs 23:5 | Suddenly it [*wealth*] sprouts wings, flying like an eagle toward heaven.

Other verses are similar. Jesus tells us to lay up treasure in heaven (Mt 6:19-21). Why? Because the world and all that is in it is fleeting.

1 John 2:17 | The world is passing away along with its desires, but whoever does the will of God abides forever.

1 Timothy 6:7 | We brought nothing into the world, and we cannot take anything out of the world

We want to feel like we are the master of our destiny, controlling our property, but the truth is, all that we have on this earth rusts and atrophies. Material things vanish away. We certainly can't control who gets our "stuff" when our life is over. We have control of very little in this life. Instead of imagining we are "master" over anything, we should adopt the attitude of a servant and a steward, laying up treasure in heaven. Trust in the one who "works all things after the counsel of his own will" (Eph 1:11).

Money Gives the Mirage of Prosperity

Ecclesiastes 2:19b | He will be master of all for which I toiled and used my wisdom under the sun. This also is vanity.

The rich person thinks he is truly prosperous, but he is mistaken. The truly rich person is the one who looks to Christ and is an "heir of God and joint heir with Christ" (Rom 8:17). Remember the words of the apostle James, pastor of the church in Jerusalem and half-brother of our Lord Jesus.

James 2:5 | Listen, my beloved brothers, has not God chosen those who are poor in the world to be rich in faith and heirs of the kingdom, which he has promised to those who love him?

Prosperity can be eternally dangerous because it can deceive a person into thinking they don't need the Savior. We are called to

contentment, valuing Christ above all else, and counting every competing affection as "dung" (Phil 3:8).

> *James 2:5* | If we have food and clothing, with these we will be con-
> tent. [9] But those who desire to be rich fall into temptation, into a
> snare, into many senseless and harmful desires that plunge people
> into ruin and destruction. [10] For the love of money is a root of all kinds
> of evils. It is through this craving that some have wandered away from
> the faith and pierced themselves with many pangs.

Money Gives the Mirage of Permanence

The reward of our toil does not last on this earth. Before we know
it we have to give it to another.

> **Ecclesiastes 2:20-21** | So I turned about and gave my heart up to des-
> pair over all the toil of my labors under the sun, [21] because some-
> times a person who has toiled with wisdom and knowledge and
> skill must leave everything to be enjoyed by someone who did not
> toil for it. This also is vanity and a great evil.

People who receive an inheritance normally do not toil for it. What
will happen to your work and wealth when you leave it behind? After
Solomon's death his son, Rehoboam, inherited all that the king had la-
bored for. But he did not have his father's wisdom, so the power and
wealth were soon dissipated.[23] The fact that Solomon was a wise busi-
nessman certainly gave him an amazing reputation as a king and a
ruler, but Rehoboam soon split the kingdom and many of the political
alliances were null and void. From a perspective solely focused on the
natural realm, it seems vexing and "a great evil" (2:21).

On a smaller scale, we see this repeated time and time again. You
see a man neglect his wife and children, skipping holidays, never available for his family because he's building his business. Suddenly he dies,
the business dies. What did he live for? He lived for that which is
earthly, which always disappears! We are called to have a heavenly
mindset.

> *Colossians 3:2* | Set your minds on things that are above, not on things
> that are on earth.

---

[23] Winter, *Opening up Ecclesiastes*, 44.

Hebrews 13:5 | Keep your life free from love of money, and be content with what you have, for he has said, "I will never leave you nor forsake you."

Money Gives the Mirage of Peace

People often say that once they hit the top, they will peace and rest. That's not how it works. Solomon was king. He had everything. But work is part of the creation mandate. We cannot exist in futility or purposelessness. When people stop working, they often give up and die. Solomon says here that the best he can strive for without Christ is a "hard day's night" as the song goes. It's a life that lives to toil, and then you die.

Ecclesiastes 2:22-23 | What has a man from all the toil and striving of heart with which he toils beneath the sun? [23] For all his days are full of sorrow, and his work is a vexation. Even in the night his heart does not rest. This also is vanity.

Is Solomon being extreme? A life full of work is "full of sorrow" and even "his work is a vexation." What's he saying? No one can be eternally happy who puts his trust in riches. In fact, every idol becomes a slave master, especially money. Remember the words of Jesus.

Matthew 6:24 | No one can serve two masters, for either he will hate the one and love the other, or he will be devoted to the one and despise the other. You cannot serve God and money.

There is a slavery to riches. "Even in the night," Solomon testifies, "his heart does not rest" (2:23). True happiness comes from knowing Christ. Riches don't last. "It is appointed unto man once to die, and after this the judgment" (Heb 9:27, KJV). Without Christ, all we can look forward to are "days" that "are full of sorrow" with work being a vexation. When we trust in that which can be easily taken away, it is idolatry, and those who trust in idols have their hearts filled with anger, anxiety, and despair. They fly to the world's addictions and earthly comforts for rest. As believers we know that rest comes from Christ alone (Mt 11:28-29).

Of course, that doesn't mean we shouldn't enjoy work as believers. The Bible affirms the dignity of work. Before the fall, Adam and Eve were commanded to execute their duties with the promise of being fruitful (Gen 1:28–31; 2:15–17; *cf* Ecc 3:13). But after the fall, work is toilsome (Gen 3:17–19). We no longer perform our tasks in the lush environment of a garden with full strength, unhindered by weariness, but now in the harsh conditions of a wilderness filled with thorns and thistles, failure, and frustration.

If your goal is a paycheck, you won't have rest, but a restless soul. Once you achieve your goal, you realize there is no ultimate purpose to all this work if there isn't a transcendent eternity attached to it. This goes for work and all of life. Without Christ, work can only bring you bitterness and "vexation of spirit." What you thought would satisfy you leaves you empty. What's the goal of work? Is it to be fantastically rich? Being fantastically rich will not help your soul. Knowing Christ will help your soul and often your paycheck as well! Now don't go to your employer tomorrow and say, "Here's my letter of resignation—my pastor says work's bad." I will not back you up if you do that. Work is good, but only if Christ is at the center. We should "seek first" Christ's kingdom, and then everything else "will be added to you" (Mt 6:33).

Truly only Christ can fully satisfy and bring us peace. He is the Prince of Peace (Isa 9:6). Knowing him is better than anything this life has to offer (Psa 63:3).

WORK IS AN OPPORUNITY TO WORSHIP (2:24-26)

It is estimated that a person will spend about 100,000 hours at employment in his lifetime, and that's only a 43-hour work week. Most of us work plenty more than that. But just on a 43-hour work week, that would be like working without stopping for over 11 years! We have much opportunity to turn our work into worship, because in our lives we are going to work a lot. The answer is not to work for work itself, but to worship God in your work. That is what Solomon says is truly satisfying.

Work occupies a lot of our life. Some might make the great mistake of separating their work from their worship of God. We need to understand how everything we do, especially our work, is our worship to God. In other words, worship is not just on Sundays and Wednesdays, but it is us valuing and honoring and adoring God every minute of every day. We serve Jesus Christ at church, at home, at work, and at play. Everything we do is worship, especially all the time we spend at work. It is working for the Lord that brings lasting enjoyment. Paul says as much in his letter to the Ephesians. He tells us we are to work not as people pleasers but for the Lord himself.

> *Ephesians 6:5-8* | Bondservants, obey your earthly masters with fear and trembling, with a sincere heart, as you would Christ. [6] Not by the way of eye-service, as people-pleasers, but as bondservants of Christ, doing the will of God from the heart, [7] rendering service with a good will as to the Lord and not to man, [8] knowing that whatever good anyone does, this he will receive back from the Lord.

Solomon says that there is nothing better in life than to be able to sit down and enjoy one's labor, but it's only through enjoying work as from the hand of God and part of his kingdom and loving rule over us.

> **Ecclesiastes 2:24-25** | There is nothing better for a person than that he should eat and drink and find enjoyment in his toil. This also, I saw, is from the hand of God. [25] for apart from him who can eat or who can have enjoyment?

Work is only eternally satisfying if it is done for the Lord. "Whatever you do, work heartily, as for the Lord and not for men" (Col 3:23). Some young Christians are idealistic. They think that if they could only be in ministry then all would be well. Every job you do is ministry. You are doing it for the Lord. God commands us to work quietly and faithfully. 1 Thessalonians 4:11, "

> *1 Thessalonians 4:11-12* | We urge you, brothers, to do this more and more, [11] and to aspire to live quietly, and to mind your own affairs, and to work with your hands, as we instructed you, [12] so that you may walk properly before outsiders and be dependent on no one.

God created work before the fall. God put man into the garden of Eden "to dress it and to keep it" (Gen 2:15). We must never separate our work from our purpose of living, that is, "to glorify God and to enjoy him forever." If your purpose of working is separated from glorifying God, you are going to be one miserable soul.

> **Ecclesiastes 2:26** | For to the one who pleases him God has given wisdom and knowledge and joy, but to the sinner he has given the business of gathering and collecting, only to give to one who pleases God. This also is vanity and a striving after wind.

The "sinner"—the unbeliever—is going to get only one thing ultimately from his work: vexation, vanity, and a striving after the wind.

Conclusion

The majority of human beings believe that people and circumstances exist to make them happy. So, when they're not happy, who's to blame? People and circumstances. So if you do not ascribe enjoyment as belonging to Christ and Christ alone, you almost ensure that your reality will be filled with bitterness, resentment and unforgiveness. Here's how it plays itself out over and over and over again. A man has a wife and children, and he's got a decent job. He's got a nice house, but something's still gnawing at his soul. So, what could it be? "It can't be that something's wrong with me. It has to be someone who's supposed to be making me happy is not making me happy." So he begins to look for imperfection in the circle that's around him, and he'll always find it. So then, this is the game we start playing. "I'd be happier if I had a bigger house. I wish I had a different wife. I'd be happier if they would honor me at work. They don't appreciate me there. They don't respect me here." And everything becomes about what everyone else is doing because you're asking people to fill a void that they can never fill. And this is Solomon's big argument. Only Christ can satisfy. He alone can fill the void, so you don't need a new wife, a new car, a new job, a new life. Christ is your life, and nothing compares to him. The greatest job you can imagine does not compare. Work by itself can only lead to the vexation of anger and anxiety and despair in our spirit. How vain and meaningless even the greatest careers and callings are without Christ at the center.

5 | ECCLESIASTES 3:1-15

TIME WITHOUT CHRIST IS MEANINGLESS

*He has made everything beautiful in its time. Also, he has put
eternity into man's heart.*

ECCLESIASTES 3:11

The prominent 20th century atheist Bertrand Russell once said,
"Unless you assume a God, the question of life's purpose is meaningless."[24] Russell taught, as all atheists do, that life is meaningless. This philosophy that life is meaningless is called "existentialism."
According to those who deny the supernatural realm, man exists with
no purpose. Life is completely arbitrary and without significance. How
sad! Yet many people live this way. God has laid out a different plan. In
God's universe, every moment matters. Time matters. All things work
according to the counsel of God's perfect will (*cf* Eph 1:11).

---

[24] Dr. Hugh Moorhead, *The Meaning of Life* (Chicago Review Press, December
1988). Dr. Moorhead, a philosophy professor at Northeastern Illinois University,
once wrote to 250 of the best-known philosophers, scientists, writers, and intellectu-
als in the world, asking them, "What is the meaning of life?" Their responses are pub-
lished in this book.

Isaiah 46:9-11 | Remember the former things of old; for I am God, and there is no other; I am God, and there is none like me, [10] declaring the end from the beginning and from ancient times things not yet done, saying, 'My counsel shall stand, and I will accomplish all my purpose,' [11] calling a bird of prey from the east, the man of my counsel from a far country. I have spoken, and I will bring it to pass; I have purposed, and I will do it.

We all live in a small window of time. God governs it all. God's governing over this time frame is so extensive that ravenous birds hunt because the Lord told them to. The hawk flies around hunting a mouse because God called him to do that. That's what this verse is saying. And then God says, "Unless you think you're not a part of that governance, a man moves from a far country to this present country because I called him to do that very thing." It was God's counsel that my grandfather moved from Scotland to the United States in March 1923 at Ellis Island, New York. He met my grandmother who was German, Charlotte Becker. They married and had children and grandchildren, including me! I'm glad God brought my grandfather to execute the counsel of God when he moved from a far country. That's what God is saying. It hits home.

Don't get me wrong. We do freely choose our way. But God works his way even through all the choices we make, both good and bad. It's what theologians call compatibilism. It's just as Joseph told his brothers, "You meant it for evil, but God meant it for good" (Gen 50:20). The Deists of old taught that God was like a watchmaker. He wound up the clock and walked away. The Bible, on the other hand, teaches that God is intimately involved in his creation. Amazingly, God is "mindful" of man (Psa 8:4). The apostle Paul even tells us that God picks the places that we live, and that God gives everyone breath to fulfill his plan. Listen to Paul as he speaks to the Athenians on Mars Hill.

Acts 17:24-28 | The God who made the world and everything in it, being Lord of heaven and earth, does not live in temples made by man, [25] nor is he served by human hands, as though he needed anything, since he himself gives to all mankind life and breath and everything. [26] And he made from one man every nation of mankind to live on all the face of the earth, having determined allotted periods and the boundaries of their dwelling place, [27] that they should seek God, and perhaps feel their way toward him and find him. Yet he is actually not far from each one of us, [28] for "In him we live and move and have our being."

This is an amazing passage of Scripture. It basically says that God is very close to all people. He has determined when and where they will be born, the language they would speak—which means ten trillion years ago—God said, "Matt Black will be born in 1974 near Chicago and be flown in a helicopter to Loyola University Medical Center in Maywood, and they'll save his life." Now my father will tell you that my sister and I were an accident, that we were the biggest surprise caboose in the history of the world. My oldest brother is 14 years older than me! So, my parents were like, "Oops!" But God was looking at my parents and perhaps said, "Watch William and Barbara's face when they find out they're having *twins*, and the second set of twins at that!" It was a surprise for my parents, but God planned it all along.

God planned that I would love Chicago and be born on the south side. I was raised in a school system that exposed me to the Spanish language. I got saved and met my sweetheart in Spanish class. All of this was ordained by God to prepare me for the mission field of Spain. He planned it all along.

We all made real choices, but God worked his will in all of them and ordained and weaved his will from before time began. What Paul is saying is we are all living in the allotted time period for your life. And not only that, but he's going to take it a step further and says—not only is the time period correct, but so is the place. Yet none of this has any meaning if you don't have God at the very center. Just as Bertrand Russell said, life is meaningless without God at the center. This is exactly what King Solomon says in Ecclesiastes 3.

Ecclesiastes 3:1-8 | For everything there is a season, and a time for every matter under heaven: [2] a time to be born, and a time to die; a time to plant, and a time to pluck up what is planted; [3] a time to kill, and a time to heal; a time to break down, and a time to build up; [4] a time to weep, and a time to laugh; a time to mourn, and a time to dance; [5] a time to cast away stones, and a time to gather stones together; a time to embrace, and a time to refrain from embracing; [6] a time to seek, and a time to lose; a time to keep, and a time to cast away; [7] a time to tear, and a time to sew; a time to keep silence, and a time to speak; [8] a time to love, and a time to hate; a time for war, and a time for peace.

Usually, when this list is mentioned, it is viewed as things that occur in life, things that happen in life. What this list really is, is not just a list of things that happen in life, but a list of things God sends. And this is hard for us. Think of this list as a list of ingredients that God mixes together to serve his purposes in your life, in your allotted time, in your set boundary. We tend to second guess events in our lives, don't we? But we have to remember with all these events that God has a purpose. They are meaningful if we understand God's plan.

THE PURPOSE FOR TIME (3:1-8)

Ecclesiastes 3:1 | For everything there is a season, and a time for every matter under heaven.

When you see everything from God's perspective, then everything has meaning, from the hardest things to the happiest things. We are not mere hedonists that live for pleasure and self. We can enjoy every season of life if we determine to live from God's perspective. Only then can every moment of time have meaning. Solomon regards God as "the absolute master of our destiny."[25] A parallel is Ephesians 2:10, where it is said that God created us in Christ Jesus for good works, which he has "prepared in advance for us to do."

The words of 3:1 suggest a "divinely ordained" time, not just an appropriate time.[26] He says for every event, there is a "season." In this sense a season is "a fixed time, a predetermined purpose."[27] Without realizing that the Lord at the helm of every event in our lives for our good and his glory, then life will be seen as no more than a mishmash of chaos—just a roll of the dice depending on "luck" and chance.

Solomon is clear: God has a predetermined purpose on which all things depend. Each human life has a span, and within its duration there are momentous events. Man may see them as random happenings, but the Bible teaches that God has a chosen purpose for everything (Rom 8:28-29). Man has mastered many things, but he has no control over time. Each moment is God appointed to bring people to

---

[25] *Wisdom in Israel and in the Ancient Near East* edited by M. Noth and D. W. Thomas, (Leiden, Netherlands: Brill Publishers, 1955), 140, 147.

[26] Robert B. Hughes and J. Carl Laney, *Tyndale Concise Bible Commentary*, The Tyndale Reference Library (Wheaton, IL: Tyndale House Publishers, 2001), 243.

[27] Charles Bridges, *A Commentary on Ecclesiastes* (1860; repr. Edinburgh: Banner of Truth, 1961), 48.

Christ and conform them to his image.[28] We can truly say with David, "I trust in you, O Lord.... My times are in your hand" (Psa 31:14–15). Everything has purpose. Solomon goes on to list all of seasons we have in life, and in all our seasons we realize God has a sovereign purpose for everything.

In fourteen statements, Solomon affirmed that God is at work in our individual lives, seeking to accomplish his will. All of these events come from God and they are good *in their time*. The inference is plain: if we cooperate with God's timing, life will not be meaningless. Everything will be "beautiful in his time" (3:11), even the most difficult experiences of life.[29]

God is Sovereign over Life Spans

Ecclesiastes 3:2a | A time to be born, and a time to die.

God is absolutely sovereign over when a woman gives birth, and when that child who is born will die, whether it be young or, hopefully, very old. God's plan is perfect, thought there are so many tragedies. Every death is a tragedy, yet we can rejoice that God is sovereign over our time of birth and our time of death, though we may not understand the "why" in this life. Instead of asking "why" we should be asking "who." In other words, in tragedy, we have to start with who God is— he is good, he is kind, he is all powerful. He does all things for my good and for his own glory, though we may not understand the "why" in this life. Matthew Henry reminds us that "just as there is *a time to be born and a time to die*, so there will be a time to rise again, a set time when those that lie in the grave shall be remembered."[30]

> *John 6:40* | This is the will of my Father, that everyone who looks on the Son and believes in him should have eternal life, and I will raise him up on the last day.

God is Sovereign over Success

Ecclesiastes 3:2b | A time to plant, and a time to pluck up what is planted.

---

[28] Winter, *Opening up Ecclesiastes*, 50.

[29] Wiersbe, *Be Satisfied*, 45.

[30] Matthew Henry, *Matthew Henry's Commentary on the Whole Bible: Complete and Unabridged in One Volume* (Peabody: Hendrickson, 1994), 1034.

God brings prosperity and poverty. He sovereignly guides the success and failure of all that we do. Being an agricultural people, the Jews appreciated the seasons. Men may plow and sow, but only God can give the increase (Psa 65:9–13). This is true in agriculture but also in people's lives. We plant the gospel and water it, but God must give the growth (1 Cor 3:6).

Plucking up is vital for agriculture. Dead branches must be pruned, and dead plants must be plucked up. This goes for all other areas of God's reign, from vineyards to kingdoms. God allows kingdoms and nations to be planted, only to be plucked up again (Jer 18:7-9). A successful farmer knows that nature works for him only if he works with nature. This is also the secret of a successful life: learn God's principles and cooperate with them.[31] Solomon call for obedience is a call to live life the way God designed it. "Fear God and keep his commandments, for this is the whole duty of man" (Ecc 12:13).

We lament everything from lost crops to lost business ventures, but we must realize that God allows something to be planted, God controls the growth, and he is sovereign over when something dies and needs to be pruned or plucked. As Job says, "The Lord gives, and the Lord takes away; blessed be the name of the Lord" (Job 1:21). Let us rest in this.

God is Sovereign over Disasters

Ecclesiastes 3:3a | A time to kill, and a time to heal.

This probably refers, not to war (3:8) or self-defense, but to the results of sickness and plague in the land (1 Sam 2:6). When God's judgements come and lay all waste; but, when he returns in ways of mercy, then is a time to heal what he has torn (Hos 6:1-2), to comfort a people after the time that he has afflicted them (Psa 90:15).

In these plagues and natural disasters, there is much mystery. God permits some to die while others are healed. I think of the tsunami that came through Indonesia at the beg, and in one day took the lives of 150 thousand people including children. This does not imply that we should refuse medical aid, for God can use both means and miracles to accomplish his purposes (Isa 38).[32]

---

[31] Wiersbe, *Be Satisfied*, 45.
[32] Ibid., 45–46.

God is Sovereign over Construction

Ecclesiastes 3:3b | A time to break down, and a time to build up.

Tearing down and building up, while involving plans for building development, also have both literal and metaphorical meaning.[33] God raises up buildings and cities. There are brilliant architects, but it is God who plans and allows all things. Solomon famously said in Psalm 127:1a, "Unless the Lord builds the house, those who build it labor in vain." God regulates the times of building and tearing down architecture, and the same could be said about all plans. God makes them successful, and he can stop them just as easily.

God is Sovereign over Circumstances

Ecclesiastes 3:4 | A time to weep, and a time to laugh; a time to mourn, and a time to dance.

Circumstances seem arbitrary and sudden, but they are not. They are all directed by God. Someone dies and there is great loss. We weep and mourn. A baby is born, and there is laughter. The weather is sunny for the outdoor wedding, and we dance at the news. So much seems random, but Solomon reminds us that it's not. God is guiding it all, making everything "beautiful" in its time (3:11).

God is Sovereign over Boundaries

Boundaries are quite important in life. Sometimes you need a fence to keep your beloved children in a safe place, and to keep unsafe influences out. Then there are times when there are no need for boundaries. Solomon describes these boundaries as gathering and casting away stones, since you needed a good number of stones in the ancient world to build a solid wall.

Ecclesiastes 3:5a | A time to cast away stones, and a time to gather stones together.

There is a *time to cast away stones*, by breaking down and demolishing defenses and boundary walls. When God gives peace within your borders, there is no more need for boundaries; but there is *a time to*

---

[33] J. Stafford Wright, "Ecclesiastes," in *The Expositor's Bible Commentary: Psalms, Proverbs, Ecclesiastes, Song of Songs*, ed. Frank E. Gaebelein, vol. 5 (Grand Rapids, MI: Zondervan Publishing House, 1991), 1161.

gather stones together, for the making of barriers of protection, as they would in Solomon's day.

God is Sovereign over Relationships

Ecclesiastes 3:5b | A time to embrace, and a time to refrain from embracing.

Bonds of friendships are powerful. People in the Near East openly show their affections, kissing and hugging when they meet and when they part. So, you could paraphrase this, "A time to say hello and a time to say good-bye." I remember sitting next to a Puerto Rican student in college chapel on our first day of classes as a freshman and little did I know he would become my best friend, get me interested in learning Spanish. Through him God would teach me how to evangelize, and I would eventually become a missionary to the country of Spain. All that based on a seemingly random seating assignment. Nothing is random with the Lord. He used that moment not only to build the embrace of friendship, but to lead my life. There came a time when I had to move on from college and refrain from that daily friendship and move on to marriage and the mission field.

This verse also enlightens us on the relationship of a husband and wife (Lev 15:19–31; and see 1 Cor 7:5).[34] There is a time to embrace in the conjugal freedom of marriage. To embrace with your lover before you marry them is like bringing the fire out of the fireplace and into the center of the living room: it can cause you to burn the entire house down. That's dangerous. Refrain from embracing with your love until you have vowed to one another before God and witnesses, with the approval of parents, God, and your local magistrates, and you will be blessed.

God is Sovereign over Resolutions

Ecclesiastes 3:6a | A time to seek, and a time to lose.

There is a time to seek. A man in his prime seeks his education while he can. He's single and freer to complete his studies. There is a time to seek something, and a time to give it up and call it a loss. A person may build up a business and lose it through collapse of the

---

[34] Wiersbe, *Be Satisfied*, 46.

financial market.[35] A person may seek a marriage and then suddenly lose their spouse. All of these times and occurrences are under the sovereign care and direction of our great God.

God is Sovereign over Possessions

Ecclesiastes 3:6b | A time to keep, and a time to cast away.

The next phrase gives biblical authority for garage sales: a time to keep and a time to clean house! The whole idea in the Preacher's mind is to put possession into context: gain, but be prepared to lose; keep, but be prepared to give away. As John Wesley saw the crowds of hurting people as Jesus saw them, and he designed ministries to care for them. His ministry became a financial success, and his annual salary grew to be the modern–day equivalent of $160,000. Wesley calculated the small sum that he really needed and gave the rest away. [36]

By no means was John Wesley against the idea of wealth; his problem was with "storing up treasures on earth" when wealth could be such a marvelous tool of ministry. He once preached a sermon in which he proposed the best attitude we can have toward wealth: "Gain all you can, save all you can, give all you can."[37] God gives you all your possessions so you can gain as much as you can to give it away for the kingdom of God.

God is Sovereign over Grief

Ecclesiastes 3:7a | A time to tear, and a time to sew.

This probably refers to the Jewish practice of tearing one's garments during a time of grief or repentance (2 Sam 13:31; Ezra 9:5). God expects us to sorrow during bereavement, but not like unbelievers (1 Thess 4:13–18). There comes a time when we must get out the needle and thread and start sewing things up![38] It may be a time of repentance. We do fail terribly at times in living in full awareness of God's presence. This is why we live a life of repentance. C.S. Lewis said states this truth so that we can appreciate it.

[35] Winter, *Opening up Ecclesiastes*, 53.

[36] See John Wesley, *Selections from the Writings of Rev. John Wesley* (New York: Methodist Book Concern, 1929), 232.

[37] John Wesley, *Sermons on Occasions*, volume 1, (1829; repr. Nashville, TN: Abington Press, 1984), 566.

[38] Wiersbe, *Be Satisfied*, 46.

> Fallen man is not simply an imperfect creature who needs improve-
> ment: he is a rebel who must lay down his arms...This process of sur-
> render...is what Christians call repentance.[39]

It may be a time of grief. Sorrow hits us suddenly. We tear our garments, so to speak. We stop. We take time. We reflect and ponder. It
may take quite a long time to get through the cycle of grief and recover.
This grief may come at the loss of a loved one, a job, or the committing
of sin. It all brings a loss that needs healing. God can and does heal, and
when he does, it's time to start sewing up the garment, a symbol of the
broken parts of our lives. We need to move on. We need to refocus, re-
fuel, and be recommitted.

God is Sovereign over Speech

Ecclesiastes 3:7b | A time to keep silence, and a time to speak.

God has designed times of silence and times of speech in our lives.
Restraint in speech is a recurring theme in Wisdom Literature. In Proverbs, a fool's speech brings trouble (Pro 18:6–7), while those who keep
their tongue avoid trouble (Pro 21:23).[40] James speaks of the taming of
the tongue (Jas 3:3–12), and Paul the need for grace in our speech (Col
4:6).

God is Sovereign over Affections

Ecclesiastes 3:8a | A time to love, and a time to hate.

Are God's people allowed to hate? There are some things that even
Christians ought to hate (2 Chron 19:2; Psa 97:10; Pro 6:16–19; Rev
2:6, 15). We are called to hate evil and to pray for evil doers to be
brought to justice. At the same time, we love them and believe God is
not wishing any should perish, but that all should come to repentance.
When we hear that a criminal has been incarcerated, because we hate
evil, we rejoice. When that same criminal is born again and transformed and perhaps released, we also rejoice. I think of Charles Colson
who was indicted and imprisoned because of his involvement in the
Watergate scandal of the 1970's Nixon White House. His removal and
imprisonment brought a sense of relief to the nation. And when Mr.

---

[39] Lewis, *Mere Christianity*, 59.
[40] John D. Barry et al., *Faithlife Study Bible* (Bellingham, WA: Lexham Press,
2012, 2016), Ec 3:7.

Colson came to know Christ and started his Prison Fellowship International ministry, all God's people rejoiced. There is a time to hate and a time to love, and God is sovereign over it all.

God is Sovereign over Politics

Ecclesiastes 3:8ba | A time for war, and a time for peace.

In a country like ours (the United States) with laws and standards, we might ask before we enter into war: is it a just war? The truth is, not all wars are just, but God is sovereign over all of them. Our Lord is sovereign over all kings and rulers. He rules over the entire geo-political realm.

In God's sovereign plan, we works all things together for good for his true people, the family of believers across the ages, to conform us to Christ (Rom 8:28-29). Indeed, we will see his point soon enough—he makes all things beautiful in his time (3:11).

THE REDEMPTION OF TIME (3:9-11)

We've just seen God's sovereign plan for everything, and now we are going to see God's purpose: to make it beautiful, all creation conformed to Christ. Solomon asks the question again, to see if you are listening. Is there a purpose? Is there any eternal profit in anything we do?

Trust God's Employment

Ecclesiastes 3:9-11a | What gain has the worker from his toil? [10] I have seen the business that God has given to the children of man to be busy with. [11] He has made everything beautiful in its time.

In all these sovereign events there seems to be a meaningless to at least some of it. So we have to ask some questions. What's the reason and purpose? What gain is there from a person's toil and work each day? Is there any rhyme or reason to it? Solomon has presented a question he's already answered. There *is* a purpose for everything. "To everything there is a season, and a time to every purpose under the heaven" (3:1). There's a purpose behind all of it, the joy, the sorrow, the mourning, the laughter. There's a deep abiding plan for good in the loving heart of God. Without God at the center of your work, all you do is worthless. But with him at the center, he gives even the littlest things we do purpose. Trust his employment. He's put you where you are for his plans and purposes.

Trust God's Timing

Ecclesiastes 3:11a | He has made everything beautiful in its time.

God is making all things beautiful in his time (3:11). This indeed is the greatest statement of divine providence in the entire Bible. In God's plan and with his vision, his ability to see, he is able to make everything beautiful in his time. This means every little step, every little sorrow, every little tear, every hurt, every joy, all goes into the bowl to bring about what is beautiful in the end.

You may be looking at some events in your life right now, and you are asking "What is the purpose?" I mean seriously, "I don't get it!" What Solomon is saying is: you are not supposed to always "get it" when you're going through it. Too often we find ourselves on the human side of time, with no ability to see or comprehend how this thing can be beautiful. But you can be encouraged that there is a purpose to it. God's going to make it beautiful in his time.

Think about life like a beautiful tapestry. When you look at the backside, all you see is loose strings and knots and messes. But turn it over and it is a beautiful work of art. Or how about the Grand Canyon? I've never been there, but some of you have. I'm told that if you take a hike from the bottom to the top, you feel like you are going down and up and sometimes you feel like you are getting nowhere, but once you get to the top it all makes sense. I think life is like that. When you are up close to the hills and trails, they don't make sense, and they might even look ugly. But when you look back, you can see your path and see how beautiful it is. "God will make all things beautiful in his time." That's the foundation of everything that happens in life. The only way to makes sense of it is to see all things working together for our good and for God's glory to conform us to the image of God's dear Son (Rom 8:28-29).

Trust God's Heart

Ecclesiastes 3:11b | Also, he has put eternity into man's heart.

God is focusing you on your unchanging, unmovable purpose for living: the glory of God. That's what verse 11 says, "He has set eternity in their heart." We know there's more than the here and now. All of these events—our joy and sorrow, mourning and laughter, our planting and harvesting, our living and dying and everything in between tells us that this can't be all there is. There is something far greater! Our goal is not to gain wealth and pleasure and knowledge. We must be a part of something larger than us. We feel like aliens in the world of time and yearn to be part of eternity.[41] This was put into our hearts by God. Our hearts are made to grasp the infinite and eternal. God put eternity in our hearts. Everything on this earth is just a fading shadow, filled with frustration! This can't be it. That's right. This is not it! God will make it beautiful one day, but if this were all there was, it would make no sense. God put this eternal purpose in our hearts.

Are you looking toward your eternal purpose in all the events of life? What is your eternal purpose? Paul said, "For me to live is Christ and to die is gain" (Phil 1:21). The catechisms put it another way: "the chief end of man is to glorify God and to enjoy him forever." Are you enjoying God in the uncertain ebb and flow of life? Are you living out your eternal purpose?

Trust God's Plan

Ecclesiastes 3:11c | He cannot find out what God has done from the beginning to the end.

Often when we look at the suffering and difficulties in our lives, we are nearsighted. We can't understand what God is doing. And here, Solomon says, we are incapable of finding out why and how God does what he does. Instead of asking "why," we should ask, "who." We know the "who" of God's character. He's good. He's great. He's trustworthy. God wants us to trust him through all the events in our life. We need to understand that God is God, and we are not! You cannot possibly understand all that God is doing in your life. You don't have to try to always figure it out. You need to trust God. We cannot understand the infinite mind of God with our finite minds.

Isaiah 55:8-9 | For my thoughts are not your thoughts, neither are your ways my ways, declares the Lord. ⁹ For as the heavens are higher

---

[41] Garrett, *Ecclesiastes*, 299.

than the earth, so are my ways higher than your ways and my thoughts than your thoughts.

Trying to understand the infinite God's mind is impossible, since his judgments are unsearchable.

Romans 11:33-36 | Oh, the depth of the riches and wisdom and knowledge of God! How unsearchable are his judgments and how in-scrutable his ways! ³⁴ "For who has known the mind of the Lord, or who has been his counselor?" ³⁵ "Or who has given a gift to him that he might be repaid?" ³⁶ For from him and through him and to him are all things. To him be glory forever. Amen.

His ways (lit. "footsteps") are inscrutable. They cannot be found or traced. So often we want to be God's counselor. Has God ever needed counsel? Do you think you are going to understand his ways in your life? He's God and you're not. You need to stop trying to figure every-thing out and simply trust him. We are told to "trust in the Lord with all your heart, and do not lean on your own understanding. ⁶ In all your ways acknowledge him, and he will make straight your paths" (Pro 3:5-6). How tempted we are to lean to our own understanding, but we must resist it and trust in God's heart when we cannot see or understand his hand.

THE ENJOYMENT OF TIME (3:12-15)

Solomon says you ought also to enjoy the good gifts that God sends your way, but enjoy them for his sake, not for the gifts themselves. God wants us to enjoy and worship him. We are not to worship the wrapping paper.

Solomon perceives two stark realities, the first of which cannot be seen (enjoyment of this life, 3:12-13) without the second (enjoyment of God himself, 3:14-15).

The Enjoyment of Life

Ecclesiastes 3:12-13 | I perceived that there is nothing better for them than to be joyful and to do good as long as they live; ¹³ also that everyone should eat and drink and take pleasure in all his toil— this is God's gift to man.

The first reality is that all of life is to be enjoyed. This seems to con-tradict his counsel to this point that all life is futile and vain and painful.

The secret to truly enjoying this life now is bound up in what Solomon has just said and is about to reiterate. God put eternity in man's hearts. That's why God can make all things beautiful in his time. All things will truly work together for good for God's purpose of conforming us again to his image in Christ (Rom 8:28-29). All the good things in life is God's gift to man. Family, work, food, etc. is to be enjoyed and celebrated.

The Enjoyment of God

Now comes the second reality. Life cannot be enjoyed without God at the center. We have to live life with a view toward eternity (3:11).

By Trusting His Sovereign Plan

Ecclesiastes 3:14a | I perceived that whatever God does endures forever.

"What God does," that is, his eternal decree, endures forever. It cannot be changed. We are called not to chafe against our life, but to trust God in it. Solomon acknowledges that the ability to enjoy life—both moments of recreation and labor—is a gift of God. The paradox is that one cannot genuinely face personal mortality and finitude without first facing God's immortality and infinite power.[42]

His decree of all things endures forever. Indeed, "all things work after the counsel of his will" (Eph 1:11). God sees the tapestry of life all at once and works it all together for good for those who love him (Rom 8:28). You won't see it until you get to heaven. Trust him in the meantime! Without him all the events of life are meaningless.

By Trusting His Sovereign Purpose

Ecclesiastes 3:14b | Nothing can be added to it, nor anything taken from it. God has done it, so that people fear before him.

Since we cannot change the immutable God nor his immutable plan, we are to accept it. "God has done it." It cannot be undone, so "people should fear before him." The concept of "fear" in the Bible is that of intentionally and consciously living in the presence of God, inviting him into all our thoughts, actions, motives, and plans. Another related concept is that of faith and trusting God. In other words, we are to live by faith in all of life, acknowledging that "God has done it"—he's

---

[42] Ibid., 300.

put all things into motion and designed every event, with all the pain and pleasure—so that we might fear him and know him. We are not to live life with the purpose of avoiding pain and pursuing pleasure in earthly things. We are to find all our pleasure on earth and in heaven in and through God, by fearing him and knowing him, and enjoying his infinite love.

By Trusting His Sovereign Providence

Ecclesiastes 3:15 | That which is, already has been; that which is to be, already has been; and God seeks what has been driven away.

In God's eyes, all things have already occurred, but this doesn't mean "what has been driven away" (i.e. the past and all its injustice) will be forgotten. God seeks it out; literally he "exacts it," "requires it," and he will "bring it to account" (*cf* NIV, NKJV, KJV, CSB). We can trust God because he stands outside of time. He will bring about perfect justice when we reach the end of time. Solomon will go into more detail about how injustice is dealt with in God's eternal decree in the last part of chapter 3.

Above all things, dear saints, we can trust God. For him, time itself is that which "already has been" because he exists outside of time. All time is like a past event for God. Therefore, you can trust his providence for your life even though there is often injustice and what seems like meaningless suffering. He has a beautiful and glorious purpose for it all. All that which takes place in time will have meaning, though we cannot see it yet from our finite earthly perspective. We have no better pathway than to trust God's providence and ordering of events for our lives, since he will work it out in the end. God will rectify the injustices in the world to come. Rest dear saint. When Christ came into the world perfect justice was satisfied. Therefore, even though you are a sinner, worthy of hell, you can rest in his perfect love and righteousness. He took our sin and gave us his perfect record of righteousness. Don't be afraid of mistreatment or insult. When evil comes against you, let it not be for your own wrong living, but as Christians we are to suffer for righteousness' sake. Let us shine the light of faith and trust in our sovereign God, his plan, his purpose, and his providence!

Conclusion

My mind goes back to the ugliest events in my life and how God has made them beautiful even in my lifetime. One traumatic event was when I was nine years old. My friends and I were confronted by Larry Huddle and his gang, probably five or six years older than us. I found some wood in a field, and we were gathering it when he came upon us. He and his gang wanted it for himself. He wanted to show some force, so his gang held me down while

Time keeps on ticking. And every moment matters in God's universe. He has a glorious purpose in all the events of life, whether happy or painful, but without him, the events of life are meaningless and confusing. God is making all things beautiful in his time. God is focusing you on your unchanging, unmovable purpose for living: the glory of God. We are called to fear God, seeing him in every event, watching his providence lead us to Christlikeness in our heart and life, preparing us for the eternity we seek in each of our hearts. Because of Christ, he will indeed make all things beautiful in his time. He makes all things new, in heaven and earth. We will one day be transformed into his glorious image and inherit the new creation. Then all the pain and suffering will be forgotten. He will wipe away all tears. And oh, how beautiful is the tapestry God is weaving with the threads of his love, and the colors of his mercy and kindness toward us.

6 | ECCLESIASTES 3:16-22

INJUSTICE WITHOUT CHRIST IS MEANINGLESS

I saw under the sun that in the place of justice, even there was wickedness, and in the place of righteousness, even there was wickedness. I said in my heart, God will judge the righteous and the wicked, for there is a time for every matter and for every work.

ECCLESIASTES 3:16-17

The great theme of social justice has been pulsating through our culture and the news cycle for the last several years. We have seen rioting in the streets, work strikes, and special days dedicated to this theme of justice.

The truth is injustice has always existed in all societies, including ours. We think we want fairness and justice. It sounds so noble, but at least in one sense, it can be misguided. If we all got divine justice, we would all suffer eternal condemnation. No one truly wants radical justice, but what we want is mercy and equity. This is what why Jesus entered the world. In the gospel, Jesus gets God's justice for our sin, and we get God's mercy and grace.

How do we deal with injustice on a cultural and individual level? Solomon pondered it in his day and gave us holy Scripture so that we can consider it in our day. Injustice hits us when a person or a people group are treated wrongly. If it's not dealt with through the perspective of God's word, you will be dealing with bitterness and hurt in your life. The question is not if, but how are you going to deal with the pain of being wronged and mistreated.

Are you battling with bitterness in your life? Some people live their whole lives eaten up with bitterness. As believers in Christ, we've been set free from the hurt and malignance of bitterness. We are to live in the freedom of God's peace through forgiveness and kindness. How do we live in freedom amidst so much injustice? Solomon just taught us that God orders all things, and he makes all things beautiful in his time (3:11). That includes the injustices we suffer. But we have to see even the worst evils and injustices from God's perspective. This will ultimately lead us to the cross of Christ where justice and mercy meet.

THE REALITY OF INJUSTICE (3:16)

Ecclesiastes 3:16 | Moreover, I saw under the sun that in the place of justice, even there was wickedness, and in the place of righteousness, even there was wickedness.

Solomon had just made an amazing statement earlier in the chapter: "God has made all things beautiful in his time" (3:11). But wait, even the worst things? Even the wickedness of injustice? Yes indeed. The greatest example of course is the greatest sin committed against God, the crucifixion of the Son of God. Peter said that when Jesus was crucified, they did whatever God's hand and "plan had predestined to take place" (Acts 4:28). Yet, at this point Solomon is presenting the reality that injustice takes place everywhere, every day, "under the sun." As we have seen before, the phrase "under the sun" describes "the futility and meaninglessness of life lived only for self and the moment, without gratitude to or regard for God and his ways."[43]

---

[43] T. M. Moore, *Ecclesiastes: Ancient Wisdom When All Else Fails: A New Translation and Interpretive Paraphrase* (Downers Grove, IL: InterVarsity, 2001), 11.

Injustice in the Law Courts

Ecclesiastes 3:16a | Moreover, I saw under the sun that in the place of justice, even there was wickedness.

The problem here is that even "the place of justice" is unjust. The very place where we most expect and most need to receive justice turns out to be a place of unfairness. Even the court system is corrupt. This is not merely a frustration, like some of the other problems we read about in Ecclesiastes, but a manifestation of genuine evil.[44]

Solomon was king and had full oversight of the places of justice, the law courts. Yet even there, wickedness was dominant. The injustice referred to was preferential treatment for those who could pay. Give a bit of money, and most judges, Solomon observed, would look the other way. Where you would expect justice, there was wickedness, and this is how life is "under the sun." That is, this is the common way life is experienced on this sinful, broken earth. Injustice is ever present, even where you would expect uprightness and fairness.

Injustice in the Heart

Ecclesiastes 3:16b | And in the place of righteousness, even there was wickedness.

In the place where there should be righteousness, there was wickedness. God made man upright, and yet, even there, especially there, was wickedness. This wickedness is rooted in the nature of fallen man, in his very heart. True justice cannot prevail on earth because true justice and judgment cannot be made without righteousness. In its place there is iniquity—lawlessness—in the heart of man. We are called to make judgments throughout our lives as to another person's character, abilities, actions, but these judgments will always be impaired in some way by our sin. Man is unrighteous, and therefore, our destiny is to face the judgment of God.[45] As we see our own unrighteousness and inability to attain justice, we should be driven to the perfect righteousness of Christ.

The problem Solomon presented so many thousands of years ago is front and center today. No one can get a just outcome unless the

---

[44] Ryken, *Ecclesiastes*, 100.
[45] Winter, *Opening up Ecclesiastes*, 56–57.

standard for justice is perfect righteousness in Christ. When people today talk about "social justice" their only solution is the "cancel culture." You become banished and cancelled from society. In other words, since humanity is setting the standards of righteousness, they get to create their own heaven (acceptance in culture) or hell (cancelled from influence in culture). You can be forever banished from culture in today's society. There is no mercy, only their version of eternal punishment by being banished and cancelled from society. This is unrighteous and unchristian.

God has a purpose for everything, even the worst things (3:11). God uses all things for his glory and our good. But what about evil? What about wickedness? There is a lot of injustice in the world. Every year, on average in the United States in the year 2010, approximately 10,000 murderers are put in jail. And every year another 10,000 go *unprosecuted*. How can we make sense of this? Solomon is telling the obvious. There's an incalculable amount of unchecked evil in the world. Are they getting away with it? What is the obvious answer to all the wickedness in the world? We may not be able to hold all the injustice to account, but God can and he will.

THE JUDGE OF INJUSTICE (3:17-21)

Ecclesiastes 3:17-21 | I said in my heart, God will judge the righteous and the wicked, for there is a time for every matter and for every work. **18** I said in my heart with regard to the children of man that God is testing them that they may see that they themselves are but beasts. **19** For what happens to the children of man and what happens to the beasts is the same; as one dies, so dies the other. They all have the same breath, and man has no advantage over the beasts, for all is vanity. **20** All go to one place. All are from the dust, and to dust all return. **21** Who knows whether the spirit of man goes upward and the spirit of the beast goes down into the earth?

If you want to live life without Christ and live how you want with no accountability, then you have to be able to live with totally unchecked, unjudged wickedness in the world. People are slandered every day with no justice. But as believers in Christ, we know justice is coming.

The Certainty of Judgment

Solomon saw all the injustice, and the unrighteousness of man's heart, and he found comfort in God who is the righteous judge.

Ecclesiastes 3:17 | I said in my heart, God will judge the righteous and the wicked, for there is a time for every matter and for every work.

Here Solomon sounds like one of the prophets. It is interesting that the king of Israel declares what the apostles declare in the New Testament. There is a day of judgment. All will appear before the tribunal of Christ. So many truths from Scripture confirm this.

Acts 17:31 | [God] has fixed a day on which he will judge the world in righteousness by a man whom he has appointed; and of this he has given assurance to all by raising him from the dead.

2 Corinthians 10:5 | For we must all appear before the judgment seat of Christ, so that each one may receive what is due for what he has done in the body, whether good or evil.

Revelation 11:18 | The nations raged, but your wrath came, and the time for the dead to be judged, and for rewarding your servants, the prophets and saints, and those who fear your name, both small and great, and for destroying the destroyers of the earth.

Revelation 22:11-15 | I saw a great white throne and him who was seated on it. From his presence earth and sky fled away, and no place was found for them. [12] And I saw the dead, great and small, standing before the throne, and books were opened. Then another book was opened, which is the book of life. And the dead were judged by what was written in the books, according to what they had done. [13] And the sea gave up the dead who were in it, Death and Hades gave up the dead who were in them, and they were judged, each one of them, according to what they had done. [14] Then Death and Hades were thrown into the lake of fire. This is the second death, the lake of fire. [15] And if anyone's name was not found written in the book of life, he was thrown into the lake of fire.

Matthew 25:31-33 | When the Son of Man comes in his glory, and all the angels with him, then he will sit on his glorious throne. [32] Before him will be gathered all the nations, and he will separate people one from another as a shepherd separates the sheep from the goats. [33] And he will place the sheep on his right, but the goats on the left.

Without the hope of judgment, when Christ rights every wrong at his second coming, life becomes meaningless, bitter, and hopeless, and we are put on the same plain as animals. Unchecked evil robs man of his humanity. Without God, human beings are as helpless as animals.

The Certainty of Death

Ecclesiastes 3:18 | I said in my heart with regard to the children of man that God is testing them that they may see that they themselves are but beasts.

If God has saved you, be thankful that God is restoring you back to his image. The farther we get away from God, the more we lose his image in us, and the more we act like animals. Animals have no element of self-control—only what might be imposed on them. They act according to raw instinct and desire. This is how humanity is without Christ. Without a God who holds us accountable for our actions, few can see themselves different than animals.

Ecclesiastes 3:19 | For what happens to the children of man and what happens to the beasts is the same; as one dies, so dies the other. They all have the same breath, and man has no advantage over the beasts, for all is vanity.

As far as physical dying goes, we have no advantage over the animals. Face it, you are as powerless as an animal to stop death. You are going to die. That's the point. God gives us all life, and he has ordained that we all expire. But if this is the only piece of the puzzle you have, you are actually going to live like an animal. You will live a meaningless life without seeing Solomon's main premise. "God will judge the righteous and the wicked" (3:17). We do have death in common with animals, but there is something after death that animals do not partake of: the judgment.

Hebrews 9:27 | And as it is appointed unto men once to die, but after this the judgment.

Solomon brings the logic of an unbeliever. If you remove God from your daily thoughts, you begin to think of yourself as an animal. As Solomon says, according to this philosophy, without God at the center of all of life then "all is vanity" (3:19). We all die and go into the ground! If that is the end, then life has no meaning! The only purpose in life is to stay happy and try to stay away from pain. This is where our society is today. Without God we begin living like animals.

Without living in the presence of God, a person will live according to raw instinct, emotion, and desire. How many times have we heard this? "If it feels good, do it!" People murder because it satisfies their hunger for vengeance at the time. People lie because it covers their shame of reality at the time. People abandon rational thought and the understanding of consequences and responsibility because they are abandoning God. And they, like animals live according to raw emotion and desire and set aside thinking capacities.

If we stray from God, we will become more and more addicted to evil, and be robbed of the image of God in us. As our love for God in society disappears, His image disappears from our culture. Why is there a rapid decline of reason, language, thoughtfulness, morality, ingenuity, creativity, imagination, aspiration, work ethic, and appreciation for beauty today? Because all these things remind us of the God who created us. Why do our children have no direction and no ambition? Because they are far from God. Animals have no ambition but to satisfy their natural cravings. They do not think. They act on pure instinct.

The Certainty of Life After Death

The understanding of God's bringing men into account cannot be attained by natural observation. We cannot see the spirits of animals and people. As many of us have sometimes thought we have seen a ghost, we must realize that the spirits of people are invisible. Therefore, we cannot know that there is something more, on our own. We need God's assistance.

Ecclesiastes 3:20-21 | All go to one place. All are from the dust, and to dust all return. [21] Who knows whether the spirit of man goes upward and the spirit of the beast goes down into the earth?

As far as the human eye is concerned, there is no one that can actually observe the souls of people or animals once they die. Solomon was told that the spirit of a man goes upward to God when the body lies below in the earth. But the spirit of a beast dies with the body in the earth. Yet Solomon has not experienced it himself, as Paul once did, going to the third heaven. Solomon could only speak by faith and by what the word of God says.

We must be careful not to misinterpret verses 20–21 and draw the erroneous conclusion that there is no difference between men and animals. Solomon merely pointed out that men and beasts have two things in common: they both die, and their bodies return to the dust (Gen 2:7; 3:19). Being made in the image of God, man has a definite advantage over animals as far as life is concerned; but when it comes to the fact of death, man has no special advantage: he too turns to dust. Of course, people who are saved through faith in Christ will one day be resurrected to have glorified bodies suitable for the new heavenly home (1 Cor 15:35ff).

The Bible says that death occurs when the spirit leaves the body (Jas 2:26; *cf* Gen 35:18 and Lk 8:55). In verse 21, Solomon indicates that men and animals do not have the same experience at death, even though they both turn to dust after death. Man's spirit goes to God (*cf* Ecc 12:7), while the spirit of a beast simply ceases to exist.[46] While the lost person with no observable evidence may doubt life after death, God says it's a certainty. You will live forever somewhere.

THE ANSWER FOR INJUSTICE (3:22)

Ecclesiastes 3:22 | So I saw that there is nothing better than that a man should rejoice in his work, for that is his lot. Who can bring him to see what will be after him?

If God is going to judge evil, how should we then live a meaningful life in the midst of all this evil? Is there any hope in this scenario?

A Healthy Vision of Life on Earth

Ecclesiastes 3:22a | So I saw that there is nothing better than that a man should rejoice in his work, for that is his lot.

Knowing that there can be no perfect justice on this earth, we look forward to the tribunal of Christ, where "each of us will give an account of himself to God" (Rom 14:12). Understanding that all things can only be enjoyed with God at the very center, the very best thing a believer can do is to "rejoice in his work, for that is his lot." God has established our gifts and abilities. He's predetermined our "lot" in life. He's determined that we should "inhabit the whole earth; and he marked out

---

[46] Wiersbe, *Be Satisfied*, 50.

[our] appointed times in history and the boundaries of [our] lands" (Acts 17:26). Indeed, every day of our lives is decreed in the mind of God before we are ever born.

> Psalm 139:16 | In your book were written, every one of them, the days that were formed for me, when as yet there was none of them.

The very best thing we can do is recognize that God has given us our lot and be content in him and thankful. Man should accept God's control over his life and live contentedly in those boundaries but live for that which is beyond this life.

Whatever happens in this present life, both good and evil, is allowed and established by God to manifest his love and bring forth his kingdom. Evil is endured by the righteous in this world in a redemptive way. We follow our Lord's example of forgiveness, when he says, "Father forgive them for they know not what they do" while hanging from a cross (Lk 23:34). We are not overcome by evil, but we give up our injustices to the justice and wrath of God (Rom 12:19-21). We never repay evil for evil.

The point the Preacher is making is without God our lives are no different than the beasts (3:19). If there were no divine justice, life would be completely vain. God is testing man so that he will see that death is inevitable. Our bodies all die like animals, but our soul will go to be with him. We will face judgment (3:17). We can trust in the justice of God. Since this is true, we should not get hung up on all the injustice on the earth. As believers we can move on with our lives and rejoice in the lot and work God has given us (3:22a). So many people get stuck with bitterness and unforgiveness, and it leaves them miserable with unrealistic expectations of meaningful justice on this earth. If all we have is earthly justice, then life is meaningless, and the human race would do what it wants and be extinct before sunrise tomorrow. No, our hope is in the justice of Christ who is coming "to judge the living and the dead" (1 Pet 4:5). You will be wronged. You yourself will at times wrong others. Seek forgiveness and reconciliation and move on. Rejoice in your work and in the lot God has given you. Be content, since we all deserve the wrath of God, but we've been granted forgiveness in Christ. We as believers should be the most joyous and content of all people. This is a healthy and happy vision for life.

A Heavenly Vision of Life Hereafter

Ecclesiastes 3:22b | Who can bring him to see what will be after him?

Solomon concludes with a provocative question as to how a broken sinner can actually see into the life hereafter. Is it even possible? The theme of the book is that it is not only possible, but life is vain unless you can see through to the great beyond. This life is not all there is, else it is completely meaningless. What fallen man needs is divine revelation: someone to show him the true reality of his position in the mind and heart of God; someone to show him his dignity and destiny. In asking the question, the Preacher leaves it open to us to pursue the answer, which is to be found clearly within the pages of the Bible.[47] Man cannot find God on his own. He is self-deceived. Man is incurably sick. He is beyond helping himself (Jer 17:9). God must be revealed to the lost sinner through the word of God since "faith comes by hearing and hearing by the word of Christ" (Rom 10:17).

Conclusion

When you observe evil, try to remedy it. Seek justice. Grant forgiveness. But we must remember sin is ultimately brought to account before God alone. He alone searches and knows the heart of mankind. What can you do? With God's help, endeavor to live a consistent Christian life in this dark world. Return good for evil. "Do not be overcome by evil but overcome evil with good" (Rom 12:21).

---

[47] Winter, *Opening up Ecclesiastes*, 57.

7 | ECCLESIASTES 4

RELATIONSHIPS WITHOUT CHRIST ARE MEANINGLESS

Two are better than one, because they have a good reward for their toil. For if they fall, one will lift up his fellow.
ECCLESIASTES 4:9

Relationships with friends, family, work, and within our culture and society are very important to us. The reason we love friendship is because we were created to exist in community. God has existed as a Trinity with love and communication and friendship. False religions have postulated that God created us because he was lonely. That's not true. God is not lacking in anything. He is self-sufficient and supremely satisfied in himself. Solomon is about to tell us another secret to happiness. Without a close walk with the living God, all our relationships are meaningless and unsatisfying.

THE PAIN OF HUMAN RELATIONSHIPS (4:1-3)

The Preacher begins by showing us how if all we have is this life, it's better that we are never born because life is so painful and oppression by fellow human beings is so common. We live in a broken world that brings deep trauma and suffering at the hands of those who take advantage of others.

The Prevalence of Oppression

Ecclesiastes 4:1a | Again I saw all the oppressions that are done under the sun.

Why didn't Solomon do something about this oppression? After all, he was the king. Alas, even the king couldn't do a great deal to solve the problem. For once Solomon started to interfere with his government and reorganize things, he would only create new problems and reveal more corruption.[48] Like an onion layer, everywhere Solomon looked was oppression.

The Pain of Oppression

There is pain with all relationships. Because we are all born depraved and selfish, there is the great possibility that we will all use the power and gifts and advantages that have been granted to us by the sovereign hand of God to our own self-exaltation and the oppression of others.

Ecclesiastes 4:1b | And behold, the tears of the oppressed, and they had no one to comfort them!

Look at the oppressed of this world! It seems like there is no one to comfort them. No one to dry their tears. Yet, this is why Jesus came into the world. He came to right every wrong and to bring us redemption and forgiveness. He came to give all of us as sinners and even oppressors a second chance by faith in Christ.

Jesus told us that in this life we will have tribulation and oppression and persecution, but we have nothing to fear with God at the center of our lives since Christ overcame the world's oppression through suffering the greatest oppression. Because of what Christ has done, one day he will wipe away every tear from our eyes. Until then, God guards all our tears and suffering in a bottle. He remembers them. He will make it right one day. At times there is no human comfort available, but our loving God will always comfort us. He will never leave us or forsake us (Heb 13:5).

---

[48] Wiersbe, *Be Satisfied*, 54.

The Power of Oppressors

Ecclesiastes 4:1c | On the side of their oppressors there was power, and there was no one to comfort them.

There is pain with all relationships. Because we are all born depraved and selfish, there is the great possibility that we will all use the power and gifts and advantages that have been granted to us by the sovereign hand of God to our own self-exaltation and the oppression of others.

The "power" spoken of in verse 1 are the God-given strengths and gifts and blessings and advantages that none of us have earned. It could be position or possessions or some kind of gifting. We all have a stewardship to use our gifts for the glory of God and for the good of others. Because of our innate selfishness, man without Christ, if he is not held accountable, he is prone to oppression and abuse. This reality is unmistakable in any culture. Find cultures that lack a political structure that provides accountability, and I will show you a poor nation that cannot survive its own corruption. It's true on a personal and family level as well. Those fathers and grandfathers that demonstrate love and equity and accountability will raise sons and daughters that live in the light of accountability. Good societies around the world are based on a Christian Judeo worldview, with a sincere belief that we will all stand before God and give an account. The more a society holds to this view, the more prosperous and loving and kind that society will be.

The Powerlessness of the Oppressed

Someone said, "Power corrupts; absolute power corrupts absolutely." Abuse can be so bad that it is better to be dead in Christ or never to have existed.

Ecclesiastes 4:2-3 | And I thought the dead who are already dead more fortunate than the living who are still alive. ³ But better than both is he who has not yet been and has not seen the evil deeds that are done under the sun.

Certainly, for those who reject Christ, it is better that they would never have been born. Without Christ, many relationships turn out to be painful in this life. Without the Lord at the center of life, there is a powerlessness and a hopelessness that is suffocating.

But with Christ, relationships can be redeemed and restored! But for the believer, Paul said "For to me to live is Christ and to die is gain" (Phil 1:21). It is true that for believers, "the dead who are already dead more fortunate than the living who are still alive." God's saints in heaven, our departed friends, are alive and well. Though their bodies have died and lay in the earth, they are more alive than ever and full of happiness.

For the unredeemed, it is truly better if they had never been born. The history of the human race is one of great abuse and oppression. Think of child prostitution today. Slavery and human trafficking is alive and well today. There are 600,000-800,000 trafficked internationally each year. The maximum sentence for human trafficking is only 20 years! 20,000 people a year are murdered in the US alone. Only 10,000 murderers are caught. If the only justice we have is earthly justice, then we are a miserable people, and there is no escaping that misery. From a purely humanistic perspective, life is so hard that it's better to have never existed.

True happiness and freedom are not found on this earth. Oppression is ever present here. Tears constantly flow in this broken world. The Christian's hope is not in money, marriage, health, security, or anything that is not guaranteed. Our hope is in Christ alone. All oppression will one day be judged by Christ himself. Though we may be powerless and oppressed, Christ will make it right when he returns. Solomon has already addressed life after death in chapter 3:17, "I said in my heart, God will judge the righteous and the wicked, for there is a time for every matter and for every work."

THE PROBLEMS WITH WORK RELATIONSHIPS (4:4-8)

Solomon now specifically mentions problems with work relationships. Certainly, our work relationships can be difficult. God created work for man before the fall. Work is good. It glorifies God. But if a person does not know Christ, then work becomes an idol, or a way of supplying money for all the idols in life. That's what verse 4 is talking about. Without Christ, we cannot have a proper perspective concerning our jobs.

Work Can Promote Envy

Ecclesiastes 4:4 | Then I saw that all toil and all skill in work come from a man's envy of his neighbor. This also is vanity and a striving after wind.

You see, work is not the problem. It is our heart that is the problem.

Mark 7:21-23 | For from within, out of the heart of man, come evil thoughts, sexual immorality, theft, murder, adultery, [22] coveting, wickedness, deceit, sensuality, envy, slander, pride, foolishness. [23] All these evil things come from within, and they defile a person.

The problem is, we bring our heart to work. The motives the lost person has for working, according to Solomon, are selfish. He wants to be envied.

Those without their life fixed on Christ are motivated by the competition to have the latest and the greatest and to outdo others. They are jealous and envious to have the number one place. And this envy can never ever be satisfied. That's why people who live without Christ are so unhappy. They can never work enough to have enough to satisfy what they really need. And what they need is Christ.

There was an article from the Wall Street Journal trying to figure out who the happiest people in America are. Their conclusion was that the people who are happiest are not people who have spent time, money and energy acquiring things. Those are some of the most unhappy people because possessions lose their luster and value after a while. Without Christ we have a temptation to make popularity our idol. We want people to envy us. This is the way of the world.

Young people see through this. You'll find that kids who are given everything from their parents so that they can actually be the envy of everyone else, really don't love their parents. Because they would rather have their parents love than have this empty envy and popularity. Deep inside popularity and envy do not satisfy.

So the parents work and work for toys for themselves and toys for their kids, and everybody hates each other. This is what life is without Christ. Here's another reason work is difficult.

Work Can Promote Laziness

Ecclesiastes 4:5 | The fool folds his hands and eats his own flesh.

Work relationships are difficult because of laziness. It's wrong to have too much ambition in life, but it is also wrong to have no ambition in life. Those with no ambition in life are simply *lazy*. Lazy people are people that don't want to work. You do all you can to get someone a job, and they quit and blame it on the manager. Lazy people don't care about relationships. They care about their comfort. They're life sucking human beings that require other people to feed them. As long as you are enabling someone not to take responsibility in life, you are hurting them and hurting yourself.

We have a generation of lazy young people. They have been enabled. They are at home until they're 30. They need to get to a point where they are so desperate that they are almost ready to eat their own flesh. Lazy people need to hit bottom.

One of the ways you can glorify God is by not enabling lazy people. They are usually in our own families. But if we are ever going to get through to their heart, they've got to hit rock bottom.

Work Can Promote Discontentment

Ecclesiastes 4:5-6 | The fool folds his hands and eats his own flesh. ⁶ Better is a handful of quietness than two hands full of toil and a striving after wind.

Many people do not live in the quiet contentment of what God has given them. It is estimated that a person will spend about 100,000 hours at employment in his lifetime, and that's only a 43-hour work week. Most of us work plenty more than that. Work occupies a lot of our life.

God created work before the fall. "The LORD God took the man and put him in the garden of Eden to work it and keep it" (Gen 2:15). We can be satisfied with work only if we are satisfied with God. "Now there is great gain in godliness with contentment" (1 Tim 6:6).

Most people are living for tomorrow—working and striving for something that doesn't exist. Verse 6, "Better is a handful of quietness than two hands full of toil and a striving after wind." People are dissatisfied. They are looking for some greener grass. I've said it before—if you want greener grass, start watering your own!

When my daughter was born, I couldn't wait for her to grow up. Now she's growing up, and I wish she'd slow down. I'm trying to enjoy every minute. We need to enjoy life right now. Each moment is precious. We all need that "handful of quietness." You may not have much, but you don't need much. There's a song I love— "Little is Much When God is in it."

Little is much when God is in it
Labor not for wealth or fame
There's a crown and you can win it
If you'll go in Jesus' name

The crown doesn't cost any earthly money. But it will take your heart focusing on treasures in heaven. Outside of Christ we can never be satisfied.

Work Can Promote Greed

Ecclesiastes 4:7-8 | Again, I saw vanity under the sun: [8] one person who has no other, either son or brother, yet there is no end to all his toil, and his eyes are never satisfied with riches, so that he never asks, "For whom am I toiling and depriving myself of pleasure?" This also is vanity and an unhappy business.

There are so many people who are so caught up in work, they never ask why they are working so hard. They are never satisfied, but they keep working, hoping to find satisfaction. The Greek philosopher Socrates said, "The unexamined life is not worth living." Most people never stopped long enough to ask himself: "For whom am I working so hard? Why am I robbing myself of the enjoyments of life just to amass more and more money?" What is my goal?

THE JOY OF HEALTHY RELATIONSHIPS (4:9-12)

The goal for the Christian, in work and in all things is *not* to please ourselves but to please Jesus Christ.

Healthy Relationships are Delightful

Right relationships in life bring trust and help and joy in Christ. Two are better when it comes to walking.

Ecclesiastes 4:9-10 | Two are better than one, because they have a good reward for their toil. [10] For if they fall, one will lift up his fellow. But woe to him who is alone when he falls and has not another to lift him up!

What we are talking about is accountability. Roads and paths in Palestine were not paved or even leveled, and there were many hidden rocks in the fields. It was not uncommon for even the most experienced traveler to stumble and fall, perhaps break a bone, or even fall into a hidden pit. How wonderful to have a friend who can help you up (or out). But if this applies to our physical falls, how much more does it apply to those times when we stumble in our spiritual walk and need restoration (Gal 6:1–2)? How grateful we should be for Christian friends who help us walk straight. What we are talking about is accountability.

Healthy Relationships are Beneficial

Ecclesiastes 4:11 | Again, if two lie together, they keep warm, but how can one keep warm alone?

Two are better when it comes to warmth. Solomon is not just speaking of a physical principle. It is true. But what he's talking about is encouragement.

I think we can make an application to us that when that spiritual winter comes for you, and it is coming for you, when it gets here, no matter how cold, being truly known by others will keep you warm. Somebody told me one of the reasons we have a warm church is because of testimony time.

We need that openness and warmth in our church. That's God's way for having relationships. We need to have that servant's heart in our church. If someone asks you to do something in an area of service you should really have a serious reason if you are going to turn it down, like you're going to have brain surgery or something.

Healthy Relationships are Protective

Ecclesiastes 4:12 | And though a man might prevail against one who is alone, two will withstand him—a threefold cord is not quickly broken.

Two are better when it comes to watch care. What Solomon is talking about here is community. It was dangerous for anyone to travel alone, day or night; most people traveled in groups for fellowship and for safety. If you start neglecting the fellowship of the saints, you are going to fall. You will start getting attacked by the "counsel of the ungodly", and then you'll "stand in the way of sinners" and then you'll "sit in the seat of scoffers" (Psa 1:1).

THE LETDOWN OF POLITICAL RELATIONSHIPS (4:13-16)

There is No End to Political Ambitions

Ecclesiastes 4:13-14 | Better was a poor and wise youth than an old and foolish king who no longer knew how to take advice. **14** For he went from prison to the throne, though in his own kingdom he had been born poor.

You would think the older king would be wise and helpful, but from the story, you can't depend on that. It is the youth in the story who started out poor and coming out of prison that through wisdom ascended to the throne. How is that possible? There are constant stories in politics that really "sell." Someone always has new ideas and new solutions that seem plausible.

We come to understand that political relationships are not dependable. There are some people who listen more to talking heads in the media than they do to their own pastor. We must understand that in our day, we can put so much of our emotional energy into political relationships that really make little difference for the kingdom of Christ. Solomon warns us to be careful because the political landscape is known to be quite unstable and constantly changing.

Political stars come and go. We need to be careful not to get Jesus' kingdom agenda mixed up with earthly agendas. Jesus said, "My kingdom is not of this world" (Jn 18:36). It's great to vote, to be informed, to voice God-glorifying opinions. But be careful. Almost always it is *not* your political connections that matter. We can spend so much time talking politics, watching the news, but what about spending time with your family, serving your church. Our agenda is much greater than anything congress is passing. Jesus commanded us to "Go...and make disciples of all nations" (Mt 28:19).

There is No End to Political Problems

Ecclesiastes 4:15-16 | There was no end of all the people, all of whom he led. Yet those who come later will not rejoice in him. Surely this also is vanity and a striving after wind.

Even though this previously impoverished young man had ascended to the throne with so many breathtaking ideas and solutions, and he led so many, yet he will quickly be forgotten. New problems will come along, and this ambitious young man will be scrapped in the dustbin of history. Why are his accomplishments seemingly vain, according to Solomon? I think we can fill in the blanks from what Solomon has already said and will repeat. Political accomplishments come and go as quickly as the politician, but the one who has God at the center of his life will endure forever.

Conclusion

Let's talk about the most important relationship of all. How is your walk with Christ? Are you meeting with him in his word? Do you hear his voice? All other relationships in your life will be vain if that one is not right. What good is any relationship if it is not connected to Christ? No matter who you are connected with, all relationships are meaningless if you're not right with the One who made you and loves you and died for you. Without accountability to Christ—without the "fear of the Lord" in our lives, we will be prone to every abuse in our relationships. Let's glorify God with all the people he's put into our lives!

8 | ECCLESIASTES 5:1-7

WORSHIP WITHOUT CHRIST IS MEANINGLESS

God is the one you must fear.
ECCLESIASTES 5:7

We all long for happiness. The Christian can say, "For to me to live is Christ" (Phil 1:21). The believer is genuinely consumed with Christ's love. We were made for worship. We cannot enjoy anything on earth until we first are enjoying our Creator. Unless we humbly experience God through faith and love, worship is man-centered and meaningless. How vital it is that we experience the living God. Acts of devotion are empty without an intentional awareness of God's presence.

It is for our good that we worship God alone. If you are not worshipping God, you'll be worshipping something that ultimately causes you misery. All idolatry fills us with anger, anxiety, despair, and addiction. We try to fill ourselves with stuff and relationships and security, but it all fails in the end. All other worship outside of the living God is slavery. You are not an independent being. You are hard wired for worship. Sadly, mankind has forsaken God and placed self at the center.

Our heart as Calvin said, "is an idol making factory."[49] The nature of the true worship of God is radical and all consuming.

Many people pay lip service to the worship of God, even in Christian churches. But most people want just a "little bit" of religion. People love to "play church" and "try God." If all else fails, maybe God will help me. What we are going to find out in Ecclesiastes 5, is that the God who created us and all humanity demands all or nothing. You are either his friend or his enemy. He will not be trifled with. Worshipping God in any way we please or approaching him with anything less than a serious heart is foolish and quite dangerous. How can we learn to worship God in a way that is meaningful, exhilarating, joyful, and life-changing?

We come to Solomon's wisdom on worship in Ecclesiastes 5. Here we have the final word on meaningful worship. What is the worship that God accepts? Worshipping God in a way other than what he has prescribed is meaningless, empty, and vain. We need to get this right since we were made to worship. Worship touches every part of our lives and emanates from our very inner being. We can't help but worship.

THE HEART OF WORSHIP (5:1-4)

The true worshipper is careful in his devotion: We need a heart for worship. It is more important to draw near to God with your heart than with your words. We can say all kinds of flowery things that mean nothing. It is better to be quiet and "be still and know that he is God" (Psa 46:10) than to offer the "sacrifice of fools." We are often not aware that we are sinning when we speak to God carelessly. We are to be engaged in our worship.

> **Ecclesiastes 5:1-4** | Guard your steps when you go to the house of God. To draw near to listen is better than to offer the sacrifice of fools, for they do not know that they are doing evil. [2] Be not rash with your mouth, nor let your heart be hasty to utter a word before God, for God is in heaven and you are on earth. Therefore let your words be few. [3] For a dream comes with much business, and a fool's voice with many words. [4] When you vow a vow to God, do not delay paying it, for he has no pleasure in fools. Pay what you vow.

[49] Calvin, *Institutes*, Ch XI, Para 8.

Be careful not to put religion in the place of God. Form and programs and structure is not our God. None of that makes us righteous with God. But God has given us form. He's given us the order of the local church. There are those who want no membership and no accountability to the local church. They are not following the Lord Jesus Christ. He established his church. He calls pastors and elders to shepherd local congregations. He even speaks to his churches individually in Revelation 2-3. But we must be careful to use the means of God's grace to meet with him. Be careful in your devotion to God! Solomon names three things that will poison your devotion to God: apathy, insincerity, and distraction.

Apathy Kills Our Worship

Ecclesiastes 5:1a | Guard your steps when you go to the house of God.

Apathy kills our devotion. Solomon was an expert on how to approach God; he built the Temple. It took him seven years to build it, so he knows a thing or two. This little phrase, "guard your steps," in the Hebrew literally means "to pay attention to your steps, pay attention to the direction of your feet."

Why is this so unbelievably important? Here's why. I have found that when difficult and dry times come and when sin grips us, the majority of us shut down the pursuit of God and fall into some sort of spiritual pouting hyper-Calvinism. Where all of a sudden, we go, "Well, this is hard, well I can't find God, so you know what I'm going to do? I'm going to do very little. And what I'm going to hope happens is that the pastor puts together the perfect service that will finally make all this go away.

Insincerity Kills Our Worship

Insincerity kills our devotion. You may not realize it, but insincerity and unengaged worship is sinful. It is the sacrifice of fools.

Ecclesiastes 5:1b | To draw near to listen is better than to offer the sacrifice of fools, for they do not know that they are doing evil.

Many people come to God without realizing who they are addressing. They come to Him offering the "sacrifice of fools." They are coming to him without understanding his holiness, his awesome power and majesty. We end up praying prayers with no meaning. They are all theologically correct, but they are not sincere. They are just empty words.

Matthew 7:7-8 | Jesus said: "And when you pray, do not heap up empty phrases as the Gentiles do, for they think that they will be heard for their many words. [8] Do not be like them, for your Father knows what you need before you ask him."

God doesn't want your eloquence – he wants your honesty! God wants your heart – He doesn't want your hot air! Be careful in your singing, in your prayers, in your attention to the message. Don't be insincere in your heart. Have you ever prayed without thinking? It's insincere! He wants your heart engaged.

Verbosity Kills Our Worship

Ecclesiastes 5:2 | Be not rash with your mouth, nor let your heart be hasty to utter a word before God, for God is in heaven and you are on earth. Therefore let your words be few.

Be careful and thoughtful when you come before God. Be careful how you pray! John Bunyan said when you pray "it is better to have a heart without words than words without heart." Remember, if you take prayer seriously, God will take you seriously. "The effectual, fervent prayer of a righteous man avails much" (Jas 5:16).

Distraction Kills Our Worship

Ecclesiastes 5:3 | For a dream comes with much business, and a fool's voice with many words.

Distraction kills our devotion. When we allow ourselves to be too occupied in life, we start daydreaming. Someone said that Solomon here is talking about mental "doodling." We are here but we are not here. We are not engaged. We are somewhere else.

It is so important when you are here to be all here. Jim Elliott, missionary martyr to the Auca Indians said, "Wherever you are, be all there! Live to the hilt every situation you believe to be the will of God."[50]

There are so many distractions in prayer and in worship. When you come to services, don't daydream. When we pray, don't be thinking

---

[50] Jim Elliott, *The Journals of Jim Elliot: Missionary, Martyr, Man of God*, ed Elisabeth Elliot (Grand Rapids, MI: Revell, 2002), 265.

about something else. God wants our whole heart, not mere superficial actions. We also wants the hands of serious commitment and service to him.

THE HANDS OF WORSHIP (5:4-6)

The true worshipper is careful in his commitments. We need to be good soldiers of the Lord Jesus Christ and press on with a radical determination to please God. Understand, all that we do in this life is ultimately a commitment to God. God is supremely worthy, and there needs to be a seriousness to our commitments in life.

The Danger of Shallow Worship

Ecclesiastes 5:4 | When you vow a vow to God, do not delay paying it, for he has no pleasure in fools. Pay what you vow.

Be careful how you pray. Solomon warns against the folly of rash vows which could cause a person to lose the fruits of his labor through God's destroying the work of his hands.[51] We live in a day of superficial commitments. We'd rather bail out than follow through. Whether it's a commitment to stay faithful in a marriage or a commitment of covenanting together in church membership, people are afraid of committing. Most people will make shallow promises and never follow through. Some young people I know have made a vow with God to remain morally pure until marriage.

The Delight of Serious Worship

Ecclesiastes 5:5 | It is better that you should not vow than that you should vow and not pay.

Serious worship is seen through a life of integrity. So many allow their words to multiply with promises and goals that are not realistic. A life of simple worship is careful with our words and commitments. Something changes when a person comes to know Christ. When you come to know Christ, your words begin to mean something. What does Jesus say about our commitment to him?

John 14:15 | If you love me, you will keep my commandments.

---

[51] Glenn, "Ecclesiastes" *BKC*, 988.

Matthew 10:37 | Whoever loves father or mother more than me is not worthy of me, and whoever loves son or daughter more than me is not worthy of me.

Luke 14:26 | If anyone comes to me and does not hate his own father and mother and wife and children and brothers and sisters, yes, and even his own life, he cannot be my disciple.

Matthew 13:44 | The kingdom of heaven is like treasure hidden in a field, which a man found and covered up. Then in his joy he goes and sells all that he has and buys that field.

Luke 9:62 | No one who puts his hand to the plow and looks back is fit for the kingdom of God.

True delight in the Lord does not have to pretend at commitment by way of loquacious words.

The Damage of Superficial Worship

You know that if you are not serious with God in your commitments, he's going to chasten you. He's called you to be serious about your walk with him. We have been sealed with the Holy Spirit, and we must be careful not to allow our mouth to lead us into sin. We must take God seriously, or he will purify you through his loving chastening.

Ecclesiastes 5:6 | Let not your mouth lead you into sin, and do not say before the messenger that it was a mistake. Why should God be angry at your voice and destroy the work of your hands?

Ultimately, our life's goals are worthless unless motivated by our affection for God. If our motive is wrong, God will correct us. He will destroy the works of our hands. For unbelievers, he will judge them. They fill up the cup of his wrath. For believers he will chasten them. "For the Lord disciplines the one he loves and chastises every son whom he receives" (Heb 12:6). A disobedient believer may even be given over to be harassed by Satan for a time. Paul says for any brother or sister who continues in sin that we are "to deliver this man to Satan for the destruction of the flesh, so that his spirit may be saved in the day of the Lord" (1 Cor 5:5). A true believer may even be taken home early if they choose to continue in sin. "That is why many of you are weak and ill, and some have died" (1 Cor 11:30).

THE HOPE OF WORSHIP (5:7)

The true worshipper's hope is not in mere outward words, but in God himself. The fear of God results in true love, faith and joy permeating the life of the surrendered believer.

Avoid Empty Words

Ecclesiastes 5:7a | For when dreams increase and words grow many, there is vanity.

Empty words cannot cover up true Holy Spirit conviction. Here's what he's saying. A dream is not reality, so here's what he's saying. "When your understanding of God becomes a dream and not based in reality and you cover up the fact that you don't know Him with your many theological words, that's all pretty much in vain, useless."

Enjoy Heartfelt Worship

Ecclesiastes 5:7b | But God is the one you must fear.

God wants us to fear him from a sincere heart. Fearing God means intentionally being aware of his presence in your thoughts, words, and actions. We are to live life on purpose in the presence of God.

Our hope is not in impressing people, but in enjoying God. Our happiness must not be based on the fear of man, which brings slavery, regret, anxiety, and exhaustion. We are called to be aware of the loving Father's guidance of all we do.

Reflect him and revere him in all you do. Theologian Greg Beale famously said, "What people revere, they resemble, either for ruin or for restoration."[52] Our fear, i.e., worship, and our affections right now are pointers to a future trajectory. Our worship is either aimed at our ruin, or our worship is aimed at our restoration, but we are one a pathway for one or the other. We are becoming what we worship. Thus the process of sanctification is the gracious redirecting of our worship and affections away from worldliness and toward God's image in Jesus.[53] As we look to Jesus, we are conformed to that image.

---

[52] Greg Beale, *We Become What We Worship: A Biblical Theology of Idolatry* (Downers Grove: Intervarsity Press, 2008), 16.

[53] Tony Reinke, "We Become What We Worship," Desiring God, August 22, 2012, https://www.desiringgod.org/articles/we-become-what-we-worship.

2 Corinthians 3:18 | We all, with unveiled face, beholding the glory of the Lord, are being transformed into the same image from one degree of glory to another. For this comes from the Lord who is the Spirit.

Conclusion

Solomon had experienced everything this earth had to offer, and his pathway to total happiness is found is something that transcends earth: the fear of God. Dive into the love and guidance of your heavenly Father.

9 | ECCLESIASTES 5:8-20
WEALTH WITHOUT CHRIST IS MEANINGLESS

He who loves money will not be satisfied with money, nor he who loves wealth with his income; this also is vanity.
ECCLESIASTES 5:10

D o you suffer from "back" problems? "Back" taxes, "back" rent, and "back" utility bills? Our faith is often tested by money problems. Whether you are wealthy or poor, we all have money problems. We all understand that we are stewards of all God has given us. Whether you are well off or barely making it, God has purposed special tests for you that involve money. He wants you to be faithful. Solomon shares some ancient wisdom with us about money. We ought never to put our trust in it. Money never solved any one's true problems. What is the answer to all our problems and worries? We must trust in God. Let's look at several tests of our faith.

DON'T TRUST GOVERNMENT FOR YOUR SECURITY (5:8-9)

Be careful not to put your ultimate trust in government. How many times have you gone to the polls to elect a new government official with high hopes of change for our country? We ought to be involved as good

116

stewards in government and elections, but truly, we ought not to put our ultimate hope in government. In fact, Solomon says that we shouldn't be surprised that bad government exists everywhere.

Don't Be Shocked at Bad Government

Ecclesiastes 5:8a | If you see in a province the oppression of the poor and the violation of justice and righteousness, do not be amazed at the matter.

We ought not to be surprised that corruption exists in the government. Power and money are a gift of God, but there are always people who will take advantage of their power for their own gain. People who are given power are prone to abuse it. God will take care of his people even though government corruption exists. There are so many kinds of injustice in society that we should never be surprised by sin. Unless there is "some Solomon to exhort and console him," said Martin Luther, "government crushes the man, extinguishes him, and utterly destroys him."[54] We need Solomon to encourage us and let us know that God is in absolute control even though government officials abuse their positions.

Trust in God's Power Over Government

Ecclesiastes 5:8b | For the high official is watched by a higher, and there are yet higher ones over them.

Even in the best of governments, there is corruption. Each level of government has a hierarchical system, where there are checks and balances, and yet corruption remains. Yet above the highest officials in our world, there is the Highest One—we will all stand before the Lord and give an account.

Acts 17:31 | [God] has fixed a day on which he will judge the world in righteousness by a man whom he has appointed; and of this he has given assurance to all by raising him from the dead.

We ought to pray for all our government officials, but our ultimate trust must not be in them, but in God. Afterall, God has placed each government in place, though they abuse his stewardship. He will do

---

[54] Martin Luther, "Notes on Ecclesiastes," in *Luther's Works*, trans. and ed. Jaroslav Pelikan, 56 vols. (St. Louis: Concordia, 1972), 15:5.

what he will despite their injustice. We should, therefore, submit as we are able with our ultimate trust and rest in God alone.

> *Romans 13:1* | Let every person be subject to the governing authorities. For there is no authority except from God, and those that exist have been instituted by God.

Pray for Good Government

Trusting in God's providence in our government doesn't mean we sit back and do nothing. We need to pray and work toward good government. Indeed, it seems the ideas of capitalism in the 21st century were found all the way back in Solomon's day.

> **Ecclesiastes 5:9** | But this is gain for a land in every way: a king committed to cultivated fields.

Take good care of landowners, and the poor will have work! We ought to pray for this. It is a great gain for a country to have leaders that promote prospering businesses. The Bible promotes these capitalistic principles. Everyone should work (2 Thess 3:10; Pro 13:4). People have the God-given right to own property through hard work. It was at creation that God the Creator committed the world and its resources to humanity (Gen 1:28-29). Private property ownership is assumed in the Decalogue itself (Exo 20: 15; Deut 5:21). God's gifting of people with various talents, skills, and abilities promotes the trades and entrepreneurial enterprise. No one should be left behind. Christian capitalism really demands that we look out for the poor and are generous with the needy (Deut 24:19-2; Lev 25:35-39). Indeed, "Whoever is kind to the poor lends to the LORD, and he will reward them for what they have done" (Pro 19:17). All should have the opportunity to work and be productive for the benefit of the entire society. Capitalism should always have checks and balances since man's heart is inherently depraved and deceptive (Jer 17:9). The fear of God must be brought into every part of life and government (Pro 9:10). Work must not be a savior; therefore, the Sabbath principle must be observed. God took one day out of seven to rest, and so should we (Exo 20:8-11). Proper rest, worship, vacation, and family time ought to be carefully observed. A good government promotes the principles of an ethical and compassionate capitalism. Along with this the government should promote laws that help to keep the nuclear of a mother and a father together and strong. A good government promotes multigenerational godliness as the foundational solution to all of society's problems. Much more could be said, but we can gladly can affirm: "Blessed is the nation whose God is the LORD" (Psa 33:12).

We should promote good government. Our children should be encouraged to get involved and engaged and not only vote but run for office and institute policy. Whether it is the day of Hezekiah or the day of Daniel, believers should be involved in making good policy and being a part of good government. Pray to that end. Take action.

What are you going to do when you are tested by bad government? Don't be surprised. Trust in God, and pray for good government. Good government is helpful for justice, but our ultimate accountability is the highest power, that is God himself.

DON'T TRUST MONEY FOR YOUR SECURITY (5:10-17)

Are you overcome when your financial security is threatened? Does it cause you anxiety? Let me ask you some questions. Do you think money can buy happiness? Do you think money will take all your worries away? Do you trust in riches to get you through problems? Do you ever live as if you could bring your riches with you after you die? Do you think money will allow you to suffer less, be less depressed, or less angry? If you answered yes to any of these questions, then it's time to readjust your focus. You can have all the money in the world, but if you don't have Christ, you will lose everything. Listen to Jesus.

Matthew 16:2 | What will it profit a man if he gains the whole world and forfeits his life? Or what shall a man give in return for his life?

Do you think money can buy happiness? Many people figure out far too late that money is not the solution to bringing a person happiness. It is virtually impossible for the average man to imagine immense wealth. Bill Gates, the creator of the Microsoft empire, is estimated to be worth 139 billion dollars, making him the richest man in the world. The children of Sam Walton, founder of Walmart, are reputed to be worth over 250 billion dollars. There is little doubt that, comparatively, Solomon was as wealthy as any multi billionaire of our generation. Money attracts money, so they say, and the Queen of Sheba, no pauper herself, brought him a fortune. But there has to be a point where wealth becomes so vast it renders itself meaningless.[55] Even if you have so much money, it takes away the little problems in your life, it cannot solve the ultimate problem. Happiness has never been found in money.

Money Can't Bring Happiness

Money is a tool with which to serve God, but it cannot bring happiness. Solomon has already told us that God has placed eternity in our hearts, meaning our hearts can be satisfied by God alone (3:11). The one who loves wealth will be sorely disappointed.

Ecclesiastes 5:10 | He who loves money will not be satisfied with money, nor he who loves wealth with his income; this also is vanity.

Money doesn't satisfy. It's not wise to love it because it cannot bring fulfillment. There is nothing wrong with those who have great possessions. But the "love of money" is the root of all kinds of evil (1 Tim 6:10). Solomon is warning of the false promises of greed and materialism. To the money-hungry, enough is never enough. Money can buy a certain level of physical comfort, but it cannot buy contentment for one's soul.

The Bible is clear that material wealth doesn't equate to happiness. Don't take my word for it. Listen to the richest people that have ever lived. W. H. Vanderbilt, famous for constructing America's railroads said, "The care of 200 million dollars is enough to kill anyone. There is no pleasure in it." John Jacob Astor of the Waldorf Astoria hotel fame, with all his money admitted: "I am the most miserable man on earth." John D. Rockefeller who made all of his money in the oil business, said later in his life, "I have made millions, but they have brought me no happiness." Andrew Carnegie said, "Millionaires seldom smile," and subsequently gave away his wealth. Another honest millionaire of the Detroit car industry fame, Henry Ford, confessed in his old age, "I was happier when I was doing a mechanics job." Heed the words of Jesus.

Luke 12:15 | Take care, and be on your guard against all covetousness, for one's life does not consist in the abundance of his possessions.

If you are living for that pay raise or for that perfect job, you are headed for heartbreak. Seeking happiness from money is a negative

---

[55] Winter, *Opening up Ecclesiastes*, 77–78.

investment. You get no return. Instead, we ought to seek the Lord wholeheartedly and trust in him to provide for our every need.

Matthew 6:33 | But seek first the kingdom of God and his righteousness, and all these things will be added to you.

Philippians 4:19 | My God will supply every need of yours according to his riches in glory in Christ Jesus.

Money doesn't satisfy, and it cannot remove our worries. In fact, it often increases anxiety.

Money Increases Worry

Ecclesiastes 5:11-12 | When goods increase, they increase who eat them, and what advantage has their owner but to see them with his eyes? **12** Sweet is the sleep of a laborer, whether he eats little or much, but the full stomach of the rich will not let him sleep.

A recent study showed that general satisfaction with life both emotionally and financially peaks when a person earns around $95,000. After that, the emotional and life satisfaction levels decrease. It's no secret that money can only go so far in helping lift the burdens of our lives.[56] Indeed, Solomon had already indicated this three thousand years ago (c. 931 B.C.). The person who loves money cannot be satisfied no matter how much is in the bank account—because the human heart was made to be satisfied only by God (3:11).

We all understand this don't we? I used to work at National Bullet Proof in Hickory Hills. I punched in at 7am, worked a punch press, or formed steel into doors and window frames all day, and then punched out. I didn't have to worry about any big-time decisions. On the other hand, as my boss's business grew, he had more employees to feed!

Ecclesiastes 5:11 | When goods increase, they increase who eat them, and what advantage has their owner but to see them with his eyes?

Who has the advantage as far as a peaceful life? Riches increase responsibility for those who are wealthy. When I was an iron worker, I could go home, relax, or take my wife and I out for a meal. My boss

[56] Andrew T. Jebb, Louis Tay, Ed Diener, and Shigehiro Oishi. "Happiness, Income Satiation and Turning Points around the World." *Nature Human Behaviour* 2, no. 1 (2018): 33–38. https://doi.org/10.1038/s41562-017-0277-0.

could have taken his wife to the classiest restaurant, but never had time to. The only advantage my boss had was to see his riches, but he was limited because of his responsibilities in his enjoyment of his riches.

Ecclesiastes 5:12 | Sweet is the sleep of a laborer, whether he eats little or much, but the full stomach of the rich will not let him sleep.

Have you ever talked to a small business owner? They work 24-7 because all the responsibility is on them. Be thankful when you work hard, but you get to come home and play with your kids and leave your worries at work. Then you can sleep!

John D. Rockefeller is an example of a man whose life was almost ruined by wealth. At the age of fifty-three, Rockefeller was the world's only billionaire, earning about a million dollars a week. But he was a sick man who lived on crackers and milk and could not sleep because of worry. When he started giving his money away, his health changed radically, and he lived to celebrate his ninety-eighth birthday![57] Without Christ at the center of our lives, riches are vain. Remember Jesus' wisdom on storing up riches on earth.

Matthew 16:26 | What will it profit a man if he gains the whole world and forfeits his life? Or what shall a man give in return for his life?

Money is Easily Lost

Do you trust in riches to get you through problems? The truth is wealth very often fails people when they need it the most. We have to be careful as believers that our motive for working is not simply to acquire wealth. If we think money can deliver us from all our troubles, then we have allowed money to take the place of God, and as you know money is a lousy Savior! It fails over and over again!

Ecclesiastes 5:13-14 | There is a grievous evil that I have seen under the sun: riches were kept by their owner to his hurt, **14** and those riches were lost in a bad venture. And he is father of a son, but he has nothing in his hand.

Solomon tells us a story. Here is a guy who works like a madman gaining all this money to his own hurt, to his family's hurt – just denying himself vacations, working like an insane man, and then in one day

---

[57] Wiersbe, *Be Satisfied*, 54.

through a bad venture he loses everything, and his children get no inheritance! When we hoard our money, we lose perspective and really hurt ourselves. We cannot trust in money. You see, money and investments are totally uncertain. You could hoard your money, and in one day lose it all in a bad venture. Remember what the Apostle Paul told to Timothy.

> *1 Timothy 6:17* | As for the rich in this present age, charge them not to be haughty, nor to set their hopes on the uncertainty of riches, but on God, who richly provides us with everything to enjoy.

Do you believe that God will give you everything you need to enjoy? Trust in God, not in uncertain riches. It is likely that Solomon is the author of Proverbs 23. He gives us a very realistic picture of money. Did you know your money has wings?

> *Proverbs 23:4-5* | Do not toil to acquire wealth; be discerning enough to desist. ⁵ When your eyes light on it, it is gone, for suddenly it sprouts wings, flying like an eagle toward heaven.

Think about how quickly money vanishes. Jill and I bought our house at the height of the housing market. At one point it listed as a hundred thousand dollars below purchase price. It's taken twenty-five years to come to a profit. You know what? I'm not terribly worried, because I am not hoping in riches. Money indeed has wings. It comes and goes. But our all-sufficient God is always with us.

Money Stays on Earth

Do you ever live as if you could bring your riches with you after you die? The truth is no one has ever brought their money with them beyond the grave. There are no U-Hauls behind hearses. I've never been to a funeral where the person being buried took anything with him. God is not going to ask us how much money we earned but what we did with the money he gave us.

> **Ecclesiastes 5:15-16** | As he came from his mother's womb he shall go again, naked as he came, and shall take nothing for his toil that he may carry away in his hand. **16** This also is a grievous evil: just as he came, so shall he go, and what gain is there to him who toils for the wind?

You can't bring money with you, but you can use it for the glory of God while you are here! If you don't utilize your resource for the kingdom of God and the glory of God, then Solomon tells us we are just "toiling for the wind." We want our treasure to be stored up in heaven.

Money Can't Cure Despair

Do you think money will allow you to suffer less, be less depressed, or less angry? The truth is rich people are not exempt from suffering, sickness, depression, and anger.

Ecclesiastes 5:17 | Moreover, all his days he eats in darkness in much vexation and sickness and anger.

Many rich people have so much money, and yet they are equally miserable. They suffer with the same bitter circumstances of life, the same illnesses, and unpredictable diseases. Certainly, there are thousands of ways life brings suffering to us. Without Christ, our riches cannot help us. But Christ can help us through all the uncertain difficulties of life. In Christ, all things work together for our good and his glory (Rom 8:28-30).

TRUST GOD ALONE FOR YOUR SECURITY (5:18-20)

The secret to contentment is trusting in God. Has God ever failed anybody? Who puts government and wealth and all things in place? Who made you and all things and keeps the world running? God. So we can trust in him. How are we to do that? Listen to Solomon.

Trust God by Enjoying God's Gifts

Ecclesiastes 5:18a | Behold, what I have seen to be good and fitting is to eat and drink.

We are to put God at the center of our lives, and then we can enjoy the good gifts he gives to us. The New Testament puts it this way:

1 Corinthians 10:31 | Whether you eat or drink, or whatever you do, do all to the glory of God.

Matthew 6:33 | But seek first the kingdom of God and his righteousness, and all these things will be added to you.

Without God, this verse could teach raw hedonism. Hedonism is pure self-indulgence. It is to get all the pleasure by all means possible.

124

Unadulterated hedonism is selfishly narcissistic and the absolute opposite of how God tells us to live our lives. We are called not to selfish hedonism but Christian hedonism in this verse. According to John Piper, the shortest description of Christian hedonism is that "God is most glorified in us when we are most satisfied in him." We are to seek pleasure in God first and above all in order to enjoy everything else. Enjoy God first so that you can enjoy his gifts and live in gratitude and generosity. Eat and drink, not for the pure enjoyment of consumption. How sad that would be. But eat and drink in gratitude for all that God has given you. Celebrate! Rejoice! You are made in the image of God. Acclaim his generous gifts.

Trust God by Enjoying Your Vocation

Trust God enough to enjoy your work.

Ecclesiastes 5:18b | And find enjoyment in all the toil with which one toils under the sun the few days of his life that God has given him, for this is his lot.

I believe every Christian should take pride in His work. For one thing we do not ultimately work for our employer, but for God. For another thing, accomplishing what God made you for is exhilarating. Whatever you do, do it with all your might for the glory of God! Enjoy your work.

Trust God by Enjoying Your Earnings

Trust God enough to enjoy the fruit of your labor. It is a gift of God. While you don't want to be wasteful with money, you don't want to just sit on it either. Enjoy it. Solomon says that "it is good and fitting...."

Ecclesiastes 5:19 | Everyone also to whom God has given wealth and possessions and power to enjoy them, and to accept his lot and rejoice in his toil—this is the gift of God.

One way you can enjoy what you have is to always be thankful for what you have.

Trust God by Enjoying Life

Trust God by storing up God-glorifying happy memories!

Ecclesiastes 5:20 | For he will not much remember the days of his life because God keeps him occupied with joy in his heart.

The Christian life is not always an easy life, but it is a joy-filled life, Amen? Isn't it wonderful to be a Christian and to know that we can trust God with our work and enjoy him? Through your work and enjoyment of life with your family and fellow brothers and sisters in Christ, God will give you keep you so busy with joy and happy memories.

When things are hard and difficult, life goes by slow, right? When things are good, life goes by fast. God commands us here to make an effort to enjoy our work and our time with our family and friends for the glory of God.

Conclusion

Let's be careful to make God the center of everything in our lives, and he will provide for us. Money cannot bring happiness, but as good stewards, we can enjoy the wealth God brings us by enjoying him first. Whether you pick up garbage for a living or manage money or wait tables or are a secretary, whatever you do, do all to the glory of God. Work for the glory of God. Live for the glory of God. Consider some wisdom from Warren Wiersbe, former pastor of the Moody Church in Chicago, Illinois.

> If we focus more on the gifts than on the Giver, we are guilty of idolatry. If we accept his gifts, but complain about them, we are guilty of ingratitude. If we hoard his gifts and will not share them with others, we are guilty of indulgence. But if we yield to his will and use what he gives us for his glory, then we can enjoy life and be satisfied.[58]

---

[58]Wiersbe, *Be Satisfied*, 54.

10 | ECCLESIASTES 6:1-12

THE MEANINGLESS PROMISES OF MATERIALISM

A man to whom God gives wealth, possessions, and honor, so that he lacks nothing of all that he desires, yet God does not give him power to enjoy them, but a stranger enjoys them. This is vanity; it is a grievous evil.

ECCLESIASTES 6:2

Materialism cuts directly against the gospel. Money is neutral, but if it is put in the place of God, it is an idol. That's what Jesus had in mind when he told us to renounce all material things.

Luke 14:33 | Any one of you who does not renounce all that he has cannot be my disciple.

I don't think anyone in America would adopt that slogan. Let me ask you, are you willing to be a follower of Christ, even if it costs you everything? We are not to lay up for ourselves "treasures on earth," but lay up "treasures in heaven" (Mt 6:20). Materialism is extremely attractive. Advertising has made it that way, but money cannot buy anyone happiness. Materialism promises much but delivers little!

A hundred years ago, young people started out dirt poor and through hard work and determination, slowly, perhaps by late middle age, they started to accumulate wealth. Most people saved their money, were frugal and careful with money. Ordinary people might have had three or four changes of clothing, and they things they purchased were not disposable. People in 1905 were not materialistic for the most part. People bought what they needed. Most of the colors of things were dark, and most things were simple and practical. They conserved what they could, and there was very little debt in society.

All of that changed with Edward Bernays. What Bernays did was set up propaganda departments in all of American retail companies and businesses. Propaganda was not a very friendly term, so he changed the term to "Public Relations." Bernays' most famous book is actually entitled "Propaganda." Then Bernays came on the scene and taught people that they should actually be more self-focused more concerned about the individual.

He got people smoking cigarettes first. In the 1920s, Bernays' began working for the American Tobacco Company. It was not at all acceptable for women to smoke at the time. He persuaded women's rights marchers in New York City to hold up Lucky Strike cigarettes as symbolic "Torches of Freedom." By relating things to freedom, he pushed women's liberation causes to the front—and women became more independent. No one could argue with women smoking now because he had successfully associated cigarettes and women's rights together with Freedom. There was one main motive in all this. It had nothing to do with freedom. It was *money*! Listen to what Bernays writes in his book:

> The conscious and intelligent manipulation of the organized habits and opinions of the masses is an important element in democratic society. Those who manipulate this unseen mechanism of society constitute an invisible government which is the true ruling power of our country. ... We are governed, our minds are molded, our tastes formed, our ideas suggested, largely by men we have never heard of. This is a logical result of the way in which our democratic society is organized. Vast numbers of human beings must cooperate in this manner if they are to live together as a smoothly functioning society.... In almost every act of our daily lives, whether in the sphere of politics or business, in our social conduct or our ethical thinking, we are dominated by the relatively small number of persons ... who understand the

mental processes and social patterns of the masses. It is they who pull the wires which control the public mind.[59]

From the time of Bernays on, Americans were told that they needed this and they needed that—"simple" and "practical" became outdated terms! People needed to be "in" and "fashionable." Bernays was the author of the idea of what we would call "The American Dream." He put the dream together. Everyone in America if they are anybody should have a car—a house with the three bedrooms and a picket fence. They shouldn't be simple and practical. That is outdated. The citizen of today is an individual. So cars and houses and clothes started coming out in every different colors and sizes. Fashions became big.

Now what was the point of all of this materialism? The bottom line was *money*. Any time more money needs to be made, you don't need to re-invent the wheel. You just need to change what is fashionable. And the more people began to serve "Mammon" the more they moved away from God.

Have you heard someone say to you—those clothes you're wearing are so 90s! The haircut of that person is so 60s. Why can we day that? Because Propaganda tells us that if we want to be happy, we need to be regulated by the fashion police. What is all of this? Living for what is "in" is idolatry. It's not wrong to be orderly and clean and modest and sharp. But materialism is Satan's way of dethroning God. Randy Alcorn put it this way:

> None of us can enthrone the true God unless in the process we dethrone our other gods. If Christ is not Lord over our money and possessions, then he is not our Lord.[60]

Is money a god in your life? Is money a savior? We need to be responsible; we need to be careful stewards of our work habits and be dependable people. But Christ is our Master, not money. C.S. Lewis said this,

---

[59] Edward L. Bernays. *Propaganda* (New York: Horace Liveright Publisher, 1928), 9.

[60] Randy Alcorn. *Money, Possessions, and Eternity: A Comprehensive Guide to What the Bible Says about Financial Stewardship, Generosity, Materialism, Retirement, Financial Planning, Gambling, Debt, and More* (Carol Stream, IL: Tyndale House Publishers, 2003), 5.

He that has God and has everything has no more than he who has God alone.[61]

THE APPEAL OF MATERIALISM IS FIERCE (6:1-2)

Even though we all know money cannot satisfy our deepest desires, there is a massive temptation to think that it will. And Solomon says this appeal is a very great evil.

Ecclesiastes 6:1-2 | There is an evil that I have seen under the sun, and it lies heavy on mankind: [2] a man to whom God gives wealth, possessions, and honor, so that he lacks nothing of all that he desires, yet God does not give him power to enjoy them, but a stranger enjoys them. This is vanity; it is a grievous evil.

Satan is the god of this world, and his advertising company is "Lies Incorporated." He wants you to believe that money will make you happy. You have to admit materialism's appeal is quite powerful. Everywhere you go, you are encouraged that if you can just buy health and happiness. But God has a different opinion. Those who trust in money are weighted down with a great evil. They can never enjoy their wealth or find ultimate satisfaction. God didn't make wealth to be worshipped. He is the One we are to worship. So Solomon tells us about a great evil of false worship regarding money. It steals away the heart from God.

Without God, Money Can Be Used for Evil

Ecclesiastes 6:1 | There is an evil that I have seen under the sun, and it lies heavy on mankind.

There is an evil that weighs all of us down—it is the idolatry of money. It's impossible to enjoy God's gifts without enjoying God first. Yet, the lie that weighs heavy on people that is so evil, is that if they just had enough money, it would solve all their problems. False!

What a tragedy it is to have all the resources for a satisfying life and yet not be able to enjoy them because God is not at the center of your life. The basic principle Solomon makes is that nobody can truly enjoy the gifts of God apart from the God who gives the gifts. To enjoy the gifts without the Giver is idolatry, and this can never satisfy the human heart. Enjoyment without God is merely entertainment, and it doesn't

---

[61] C.S. Lewis. *The Weight of Glory* (New York: HarperCollins, 1949), 34.

satisfy. But enjoyment with God is enrichment and it brings true joy and satisfaction.[62]

The lost live in the evil lie that money can satisfy. As if all we see with our eyes in this world is all there is. What deception. If your main goal in life is to make a lot of money, you are going to be part of a vast crowd of empty, frustrated, materialistic people. It's impossible to enjoy God's gifts without enjoying God first. Yet this evil weighs down heavily on all people. There is a temptation to only live for the here and now.

Money without God equals misery. Now don't get me wrong. Money is not evil. It is the "love of money" that "is a root of all kinds of evils" (1 Tim 6:10). Money is morally neutral. It is a means of payment. What you buy is not neutral. Jesus warns us in his Sermon on the Mount not to trust in earthly resources for our comfort and security.

Matthew 6:19-21, 24 | Do not lay up for yourselves treasures on earth, where moth and rust destroy and where thieves break in and steal, [20] but lay up for yourselves treasures in heaven, where neither moth nor rust destroys and where thieves do not break in and steal. [21] For where your treasure is, there your heart will be also.... [24] "No one can serve two masters, for either he will hate the one and love the other, or he will be devoted to the one and despise the other. You cannot serve God and money.

Where a person's money goes says a lot about a person. The majority of people in this world live as if this life is all there is. Those who try to find meaning and purpose in this world apart from God are going to be severely disappointed, frustrated, and miserable.

When a person puts money in the place of God, the Lord may give that person plenty of money, but he will take away their power to enjoy it. When we find our security in money, we become materialists. Jesus said that we "cannot serve God and money." Some older translations say "mammon" instead of money. Mammon is the demon-god of money and material prosperity. The demon-god of this world has blinded the masses and wants you to believe the lie that he has been promoting since his fall, that you can somehow be happy without God. If only you could win the lotto. So many people go to Vegas for a chance at instant money. What a lie! Money cannot produce joy in your life.

---

[62] Wiersbe, *Be Satisfied*, 74-75.

God is seen in this verse as the only one that can give us the power to enjoy wealth. So many people stake their happiness on money, and it is literally destroying their lives. We are told that half of all marriages end in divorce, and 80% of divorced people indicate that financial struggles played a major role in ending their marriage.

Without God, Money Cannot be Enjoyed

Money is a passing commodity.

Ecclesiastes 6:2 | A man to whom God gives wealth, possessions, and honor, so that he lacks nothing of all that he desires, yet God does not give him power to enjoy them, but a stranger enjoys them. This is vanity; it is a grievous evil.

Money comes from God. It wasn't meant to satisfy the soul. Therefore, God can give all of our riches to a "stranger." The word "stranger" means, "someone completely unrelated to you." Think about the treasures of King Tut. His treasures didn't do him very much good. We enjoy them today much more than he did. In other words, money is a passing commodity. Eventually, we will all die, and all that we have will be possessed and enjoyed by some stranger – someone we don't know.

THE ADD-ONS OF MATERIALISM ARE FUTILE (6:3-9)

Things don't satisfy, so we try to add on lots of other things: family, food, long life—even knowledge, but none of it will satisfy. People sacrifice everything for riches, and it doesn't satisfy, so they start adding other things to satisfy their longings—all to no avail.

Children Can't Fill the Void

Maybe if I have a lot of children to share my riches with, then I'll be happy! Solomon says that won't work!

Ecclesiastes 6:3 | If a man fathers a hundred children and lives many years, so that the days of his years are many, but his soul is not satisfied with life's good things, and he also has no burial, I say that a stillborn child is better off than he.

To have a hundred children (6:3) or live thousands of years (6:6) are oriental exaggerations. The three traditional conditions for happiness were wealth, long life, and many children.[63] Solomon says, no amount of children can bring ultimate joy, since that kind of joy comes from God alone.

No doubt, children certainly bring joy and are a gift from the Lord (Psa 127:3), but they also bring many added responsibilities (Pro 14:4) and even many heartaches. They can be thankless in light of their parents' generosity. Just like money can't take away depression, neither can children lift our frustrations. Many turn their dreams to a family. Some mothers who are childless think that if they only had children, they would be happy. Children are a great blessing from the Lord, but we are not made primarily to serve children but to serve God and glorify him.

If our ultimate happiness comes from anywhere outside of Christ, it is built on sinking sand. It is a cracked and crumbling foundation. Solomon says something astounding. For the one without a godly understanding of riches, it would be better if he had never been born. Solomon says a miscarried or stillborn child is better off than the one who trusts in riches, children, or anything else to bring satisfaction.

> **Ecclesiastes 6:3b-5** | I say that a stillborn child is better off than he. [4] For it comes in vanity and goes in darkness, and in darkness its name is covered. [5] Moreover, it has not seen the sun or known anything, yet it finds rest rather than he.

At least the stillborn child doesn't have the pain of living, but instead can rest in the presence of God. The void of not knowing God cannot be filled by children. Solomon says, it's better to be a stillborn child than to live this life without the Lord at the center of your life. The stillborn's name is "covered in darkness"—no one knows who they are but God, yet the stillborn is infinitely happier than the miserable person living this life without Christ. The stillborn has true "rest" in the Lord rather than the richest man with a hundred children.

Long Life Can't Fill the Void

I know! What about long life? That will work! I will have lots of money, lots of children, and long life. Listen, because we live on a sin cursed earth, long life will just multiply your sorrows.

---

[63] Garrett, *Ecclesiastes*, 315.

Ecclesiastes 6:6 | Even though he should live a thousand years twice over, yet enjoy no good—do not all go to the one place?

Living long will not help because we all have to go to that "one place"—the grave. We all have to face death. Solomon of course is not addressing our eternal destiny. He already covered that earlier.

Ecclesiastes 3:17 | I said in my heart, God will judge the righteous and the wicked, for there is a time for every matter and for every work.

People are doing everything today to stay alive and live longer healthier lives. Of course, it is important to be good stewards of our bodies, but America's obsession with fitness does not have God in the equation. People want to save the earth, legislate what you eat, and they are even trying to find ways to genetically alter our DNA to take away predispositions to inherited diseases.

While all of that is noble, the motive is really to conquer or put off death as long as possible. The truth of the matter is that death is coming, and when that happens, all the money, and all the good life, and all the children will not help you.

Don't get me wrong, long life is a blessing from God if you know the Lord. But if you don't know the Lord, your life is just more vanity added onto vanity. In eternity, it will hurt, not help if you lived longer.

The point that Solomon is making is that we are all going to die. The pleasures and pains of this life will soon be forgotten. For those who trust in their money, it would be better that they would have miscarried in their mother's womb. Those who trust in riches have their reward on this earth, and much of it is money that they cannot enjoy with children they do not enjoy and a life they do not enjoy. How sad it is to live without Christ!

Food Can't Fill the Void

Why do we work so hard for all this money? We work so that we can eat and enjoy life. Well, Solomon reiterates the same problem. Food doesn't satisfy.

Ecclesiastes 6:7 | All the toil of man is for his mouth, yet his appetite is not satisfied.

Scholarship Can't Fill the Void

What if I add scholarship and knowledge to all my prosperity? Still there is no advantage.

Ecclesiastes 6:8-9 | For what advantage has the wise man over the fool? And what does the poor man have who knows how to conduct himself before the living? [9] Better is the sight of the eyes than the wandering of the appetite: this also is vanity and a striving after wind.

The uneducated poor man is in a better position if the Lord is at the center of his life. The poor saved man is content, but the lost person is never satisfied no matter how much money or education he has. The wise rich man has no advantage over the poor and uneducated. The fool is wiser than the scholar if he is content with what he sees, resting in God's providence.

The rich and educated may have much, but they have a "wandering of the appetite" that can never be satisfied. They are striving "after the wind"—after something they will never catch!

THE ESCAPE FROM MATERIALISM IS BY FAITH (6:10-12)

Man cannot escape this "rat race" without faith. Material wealth without God is futile. Without God, all men are pursuing their own way, and it always ends up in frustration. Life is unsatisfying apart from God, and all the money and material resources in the world cannot take away that fact. What can bring meaning from the futility of earthly riches? First, we need to consider the richness and comfort of God's providence.

Study God's Providence

Slow down and stop trying to use money to change your circumstances. Instead of living with riches at the center of our lives, we are called to surrender to God who has all power to direct the events of your life. We can rest in his glorious providence, that indeed "all things work after the counsel of his will" (Eph 1:11).

Ecclesiastes 6:10a | Whatever has come to be has already been named, and it is known what man is.

This is a bit of an obscure verse, but most believe the one stronger than man is referring to God. If that is the case, then this verse is talking about the providence of God bringing to pass "whatever has come to be." It's "already been named by God." Remember God has "put eternity in man's heart," and in his providence, he makes "all things beautiful in its time" (3:11). God knows who man is. Man is the creature, and he can never dispute with the One who is stronger than him, namely God. We can dispute all day long that life is not fair. But truly all that we struggle with, we've brought on ourselves. The only solution is to turn to the Lord and to surrender to him and *stop* disputing!

Surrender to God's Power

We've got to stop disputing with the Lord almighty. That's a dangerous and futile activity. Multiplying words gives man no advantage at all.

Ecclesiastes 6:10b-11 | And that he is not able to dispute with one stronger than he. [11] The more words, the more vanity, and what is the advantage to man?

No matter how many books we write trying to improve our lives through money, through children, through the obsession with long life, it's all a vain dispute. We need to submit to our Creator. We need to live in loving union with him and his ways and his plans for us. Arguing with God is an exercise in futility. It's useless!

Seek God's Partnership

You'll never find satisfaction apart from the Lord! You certainly cannot find it on your own. You need to seek the one who knows the future and has your future in his sovereign hand.

Ecclesiastes 6:12 | For who knows what is good for man while he lives the few days of his vain life, which he passes like a shadow? For who can tell man what will be after him under the sun?

A mere human being cannot know what is good for him. He looks at all the temporary things and tries to satisfy himself with all this world has to offer. But this world is quickly passing away. And all the money, family, and long life he can get will not make his life satisfying. He's still going to be "grasping after the wind"! He needs God to guide him to "what will be after him under the sun." As we live "under the sun" on this broken earth, we need the Lord to tell us where to go, what to do, and how to live life the way he designed it. Solomon has wisely taught us that we should aspire to a happy and holy life in God whether we are rich or poor.

Matthew 6:33 | But seek first the kingdom of God and his righteousness, and all these things will be added to you.

The truly wealthy person is the one who has put his trust in God!

Conclusion

The boxer Muhammad Ali was known as "the champ," arguably the most famous athlete of his generation. He was on top, and his entourage of trainers and various helpers shared the adulation with him. But after Ali's last fight, the party ended. Some of his close confidants were disillusioned that they could be at the center of the spotlight, and suddenly, it all disappears. Ali himself, so articulate at one time in his life was now halting in speech and uncertain in his movement. At the end of the day, he said, "I had the world, and it wasn't nothin'."

We can't put our trust in riches. "Whoever trusts in his riches will fall" (Pro 28:11). We will put our trust in the living God. Christ himself is all the eternal riches we could ever ask for. We are granted "every spiritual blessing" in him (Eph 1:4).

11 | ECCLESIASTES 7:1-6

WITHOUT CHRIST, DEATH IS OUR ENEMY

A good name is better than precious ointment, and the day of death than the day of birth. ² It is better to go to the house of mourning than to go to the house of feasting, for this is the end of all mankind, and the living will lay it to heart.

ECCLESIASTES 7:2-3

We are a culture that is fixating on living long, curing disease, and abolishing death. Death is such a depressing subject, that the majority of people simply get fixated on the here and now and forget about the fact that death is coming. Ten out of ten people die. It's the ultimate statistic. What if you could read your own obituary? How do people really see you? Here is the story of a man who did.

One morning in 1888 Alfred Nobel, inventor of dynamite, awoke to read his own obituary. The obituary was printed as a result of a simple journalistic error. You see, it was Alfred's brother that had died, and the reporter carelessly reported the death of the wrong brother. Any man would be disturbed under the circumstances, but to Alfred the shock was overwhelming because he saw himself as the world saw him. The "Dynamite King," the great industrialist who had made an immense fortune from explosives. This, as far as the general public was concerned, was the entire purpose of Alfred's life. None of his true intentions to break down the barriers that separated men and ideas for peace were recognized or given serious consideration. He was simply a merchant of death. And for that alone he would be remembered. As he read the obituary with horror, he resolved to make clear to the world the true meaning and purpose of his life. This could be done through the final disposition of his fortune. His last will and testament—an endowment of five annual prizes for outstanding contributions in physics, chemistry, physiology or medicine, literature, and peace (the sixth category of economics was added later)—would be the expression of his life's ideals and ultimately would be why we would remember him. The result was the most valuable of prizes given to those who had done the most for the cause of world peace. It is called today, the "Nobel Peace Prize."[64]

What is your legacy? Without Christ, you will be eternally forgotten, but with Christ you will have a good name for eternal ages to come. For the Christian, death is not extinguishing your light; it is putting out the candle because the dawn has come. Alfred Nobel changed his legacy. It's not too late to change yours, as Solomon explains.

Ecclesiastes 7:1-6 | A good name is better than precious ointment, and the day of death than the day of birth. [2] It is better to go to the house of mourning than to go to the house of feasting, for this is the end of all mankind, and the living will lay it to heart. [3] Sorrow is better than laughter, for by sadness of face the heart is made glad. [4] The heart of the wise is in the house of mourning, but the heart of fools is in the house of mirth. [5] It is better for a man to hear the rebuke of the wise than to hear the song of fools. [6] For as the crackling of thorns under a pot, so is the laughter of the fools; this also is vanity.

The truth is that none of us knows just when we are going to meet God. It can come very suddenly. It can come without warning, and suddenly you are standing in the presence of God to be judged. There are two types of people at the judgment. Jesus says you are either a sheep or a goat. You are either saved or lost. Death is unpredictable. None of us have a guarantee on life. None of us knows if we are going to make

---

[64] Edoardo S. Miciano, *The Faith Factor: Living Out What We Believe* (Eugene, OR: Wipf & Stock Publishers, 2016), 21.

it until the end of the day. Death is all around us. This year, it is likely that someone you love will die.

Hebrews 9:27 | And just as it is appointed for man to die once, and after that comes judgment.

People don't like to talk about death unless they know Jesus Christ. Why is that? As we will see, death is a biographer, telling us that one day our lives will end. Death is also an evangelist, urging us to surrender to the God who we will meet when death comes for us. Finally, we will see that death is a wise sage that teaches us how to live life the way God designed it, preparing us for life eternal with Jesus.

DEATH IS THE GREAT BIOGRAPHER (7:1)

Death is the great biographer. When death comes for you, your story is finished, and the story of your life speaks, either for the good or the bad. For better or worse, your life will warn sinners to run to Christ. Listen to Solomon.

Ecclesiastes 7:1 | A good name is better than precious ointment, and the day of death [*is better*] than the day of birth.

It's better to have a good name of knowing and humbly walking with Christ, since that will demonstrate the way of salvation for poor, undeserving sinners like us. But it can be said that every funeral is better than every other day, since the casket is a warning to all. Death is coming! Run to Christ! Your life will tell a story, for better or worse, that it is best to run to Christ while you are living since once death comes for you, your fate is eternally and unalterably sealed.

The funeral of a lost person will shout a message: "It would have been better to prepare for eternity than for you to waste your life." The funeral of the saint will preach: "Oh the joy of eternal bliss because this poor, wretched sinner believed on Christ, and they are now eternally saved."

A Good Name is like Perfume

Death is the great biographer, telling us that there will be an end to our lives. Since death is coming, wise Solomon warns us to remember that a good name and reputation will be a fragrant aroma long after you are gone from this earth.

Ecclesiastes 7:1a | A good name is better than precious ointment.

When you die, someone else writes your obituary. Will they say you had a good name? Your funeral could happen today. It's a serious thing to realize that your life has consequences on people around you. How you live matters. What will the aroma and fragrance of your legacy be after you die? What is your legacy?

A good name is better to have than costly perfume. Why is a good name compared to costly fragrance? In Solomon's day, there was no running water. People did not bathe every day. They did not wash their clothes often. Costly oils were very valuable and made a person pleasant to be around.

Do you realize that after you die, you will leave a fragrance for all to evaluate? We are to be the "aroma of Christ" while we live on this earth.

2 Corinthians 2:15-16 | For we are the aroma of Christ to God among those who are being saved and among those who are perishing, [16] to one a fragrance from death to death, to the other a fragrance from life to life.

Are you leaving behind the legacy of a Christian concerned with holy living? As Christians we are to seek to have the mind of Christ and to live the life of Christ. We are to "be holy" as he is "holy" (Lev 20:26; 1 Pet 1:16).

Often people live for the moment, selfish lives for the here and now, and they miss the fact that each one of us is leaving a legacy. The Scripture is clear that those who know Christ will leave a legacy that is a blessing.

Proverbs 10:7 | The memory of the righteous is a blessing, but the name of the wicked will rot.

How will you be remembered? Do you have a good name? Is your life and heart leaving the aromatic presence of the Holy Spirit everywhere you go?

A Good Name is Precious

No one can measure the worth of having a powerful Christ-centered legacy. It's more valuable than all the money in the world.

Proverbs 22:1 | A good name is to be chosen rather than great riches, and favor is better than silver or gold.

Your legacy is more important than your job or how many friends you have or how much money you make. It influences people more than silver or gold. Death is the great biographer. It puts the period at the end of your life. Your legacy will be evaluated by others.

A Good Name Preaches

For believers in Christ, the day of one's death is better than the day of one's birth. Then Solomon says something amazing, astounding.

Ecclesiastes 7:1b | And the day of death [*is better*] than the day of birth.

You will preach more effectively on the day you die more than any other day of your life, so that day is better than any other day, from an evangelistic standpoint. Why? Because that day is forward looking. We are all going to live somewhere forever and ever. On that day of your death, your legacy is cemented. A period is placed on your life. Your life is over. If you followed Christ, people will realize that no matter what trial or tribulation, what weakness or times of failure. But listen, if Christ was at the center of your life, people will see that and want to follow Christ. If your life was empty and worthless, that will preach too! Whatever worldly gains were obtained through the empty life of sin will be revealed as utterly worthless.

Death is the great biographer. Do *you* have a good name? When death came for Elijah, Elisha said, "Where is the God of Elijah?" (2 Kgs 2:14). What about your sons or daughters? Will they be saying when you die, "Where is the God of my Daddy and my Mama"?

Death will bring a period to your legacy. It could be today. People without Christ don't want to think about this. It's a serious thing to realize that your life has consequences on people around you. Your life also has consequences on your eternity. For better or worse, the day of your death will preach Christ better than any other day of your life. for the Christian, the words are certainly true. At birth we are brought into a world of sin and sorrow; at death we are delivered from it! The apostle Paul writes, "For to me, to live is Christ, and to die is gain" (Phil 1:21).[65]

---

[65] Winter, *Opening up Ecclesiastes*, 94.

DEATH IS THE GREAT EVANGELIST (7:2-4)

Death is the great evangelist. You may notice, most people get uncomfortable when they are evangelized. Death tells us that there is an end – that we will all meet our Maker. Listen to Solomon.

Ecclesiastes 7:2 | It is better to go to the house of mourning than to go to the house of feasting, for this is the end of all mankind, and the living will lay it to heart.

When you walk into a funeral home, the greatest preacher is the deceased loved one. Though they are silent, they are shouting that one day, you too will die. Your life will certainly end. It may be today. While many people like to attend a church where they are entertained, this not at all good for them. It may very well condemn their soul. There was one thing that stirred Solomon up, and that was people who did not take death seriously! What do we learn from Solomon? Considering our death and our own mortality is good because it focuses us on "our end" – we are all going to live forever somewhere.

Death Preaches Accountability

The day of one's death is good because it causes the living to ponder eternity. Unless the Lord returns first, one day our lifeless bodies are all going to be in the box at the front of the church or funeral home.

Ecclesiastes 7:2 | It is better to go to the house of mourning than to go to the house of feasting, for this is the end of all mankind, and the living will lay it to heart.

Take every opportunity to ponder your own mortality. Are you ready to die? If your car was hit head-on by a drunken driver or you went to the doctor and received news of your imminent death, would you be ready? Would you know where you are going? Ponder this. Solomon later says that no man can avoid the ultimate statistic: ten out of ten people die.

Ecclesiastes 8:8 | No man has power to retain the spirit, or power over the day of death.

Are you ready? It could happen anytime. Ponder your mortality. Solomon says, it's better to go to a funeral home than to a party because at the funeral you can consider in your heart the true meaning of life. Unless Christ is at the center of your life, then your life is meaningless.

Death Pleads for Repentance

Considering our own mortality is good because it urges us to seek the Lord with brokenness of heart and sadness for sin and not to put it off with the distractions of laughter and foolishness.

Ecclesiastes 7:3 | Sorrow is better than laughter, for by sadness of face the heart is made glad.

If sorrow is focused in the right direction—if it leads us to soul searching, it can make our heart glad. We will search until we find the solution. What is the cause of all our sorrow in this life? Sin is the ultimate culprit. Before sin there was no sorrow in the universe.

Sorrow in your life lead can lead you to the solution to all pain and death and suffering. "The wages of sin is death, but the gift of God is eternal life through Jesus Christ our Lord" (Rom 6:23). Our problem in life is our own sin. We need to settle that through Jesus Christ. When it comes down to it, do you have a settled certainty that you will enter into the glory of heaven?

Sorrow and seriousness help focus the heart on eternity, which will make the heart glad! Sorrow gets us to start soul-searching. It gets us to consider that all might not be well with our soul and to seek for an eternal solution. Sadness is meant to lead to gladness in the Lord.

For the Christian, God often uses times of crisis to change our heart, so sadness is often turned into gladness. Have you had a time of deep sorrow where a loved one died, and God drew you close, and it made you glad? Often the difficult times of our life are the best teachers.

Death Points to Wisdom

Considering death is good because it causes believers to focus on what is most important.

Ecclesiastes 7:4 | The heart of the wise is in the house of mourning, but the heart of fools is in the house of mirth.

Ultimately all that we see is going to pass away, so we believers choose wisdom over folly. We appreciate the funeral home much more than the fair. Carnivals distract us from the reality of what's coming for all: ten out of ten people die. The reality of death points us to numerous truths of wisdom. First, we are going to give an account to God! Second, that means that everything we do in this life matters. Third, there is mercy and grace in God, so when we fall, we should keep going, and not check out in the "house of mirth." Believers, if given the choice, we focus our interests on that which is serious and eternal over that which is silly and temporary.

DEATH IS THE GREAT SAGE (7:5-6)

Only the fool avoids the serious subjects of life. Some of course, take this too far—they morbidly focus on sin and death. Now understand that Solomon is not telling us never to laugh or lovingly tease our children. Christianity is not morbid, but it is the "good news". Solomon is not telling the believer to morbidly focus on sin and death. Christianity deals with sin and death but focuses on God's love in Christ and the joy of His forgiveness. But though we as believers laugh and enjoy life – our goal and our god is not pleasure. Our goal is to please God! At the core God's people are serious minded people!

The Wise Appreciate Faithful Rebuke

Wise people appreciate rebuke and correction.

Ecclesiastes 7:5 | It is better for a man to hear the rebuke of the wise than to hear the song of fools.

God's people profit from people giving them a truthful, loving rebuke. We are to admonish one another as Christians. It is our responsibility. Those without Christ are prone to avoid the truth through foolish entertainment.

The Wise Avoid Folly

Wise people will avoid laughter that forgets God. This is the laughter of fools. It is meaningless with no good purpose.

Ecclesiastes 7:6 | For as the crackling of thorns under a pot, so is the laughter of the fools; this also is vanity.

You can hear this crackling laughter from most of the sitcoms and late-night TV. It's vain and useless. It doesn't help us. We have to be careful to avoid foolish laughter and crude silliness. We cannot disobey God or make light of him for the sake of a joke. We cannot make light of anything sinful. Sin is serious. We ought to grieve at this kind of humor. Anything that makes light of God or laughs at sin is "crude joking." Of course, Paul tells us that "filthiness and crude joking" are forbidden (Eph 5:4). This eliminates many of the stand-up comics today.

I have often missed an opportunity to address the issues of someone's soul because I allowed myself to be drawn into silliness. There is a time for laughter and silliness. It can be used to calm someone down or to let someone know you are their friend. It can glue you together with a friend. But it must never distract from what is most important.

Sadly, the lost are laughing themselves right to hell. All the laughter of the lost is only to numb the pain of the present and future consequences of sin. Their laughter is vain and empty. There is no substance to it. The saved use laughter for comfort and for edification.

Many people use laughter like a drug to keep their mind off of important things. Laughter in this way can distract the heart from what is most important. It is easy to get caught up in the laughter and hilarity of our day. Solomon says, for this reason, it is better to choose to go to a funeral home than to a bar-b-que. In the end what good does all the good times do if we miss Christ? "For as the crackling of thorns under a pot, so is the laughter of the fools; this also is vanity" (3:6).

Truly, it is always God who has the last laugh. He "sits in the heavens laughs; the LORD holds them in derision" (Psa 2:4). The idea that anyone can avoid accountability with God is truly the laughable thing.

We ought to be known as people filled with the joy and gladness in Christ. In Christ there is a joy in Christ that is "unspeakable and full of glory" (1 Pet 1:8). True peace and contentment come through knowing Christ! What can pry a person from vain silliness to a joy and contentment in Christ? The pondering of their own mortality can lead a person to consider Christ.

Conclusion

Death puts everyone on the same page. We are all going to face God very soon. A hundred years from now, we will all be in eternity. That is a fact. By the end of this year, there may be one or more of us that are in eternity.

When a loved one near me was diagnosed with cancer, I asked her the question, what is the chance that you won't make it? You know what her answer was? It's 100% that she was going to die. It's just a matter of when. We are all going to die. Without Christ, death is your enemy.

But for all who know Christ, death is not your enemy. Death is the door to eternal life. There is sorrow in death, but our sorrow is only temporary, and it is only on this side of eternity. When we reach the other side, God will wipe away all tears. What joy! What wisdom!

Charles Ward had this kind of wisdom. Ward served in the Union Army as a sergeant with the thirty-second Massachusetts Volunteers. In one of his last letters home, he wrote, "I hope I may come home again but life here is uncertain." The soldier was right about the uncertainties of life and death because a few days later he was mortally wounded in the bloody wheat field at Gettysburg. Although he lingered for a little while, Ward died within the week. In his last letter home he wrote, "Dear Mother, I may not again see you but do not fear for your tired soldier boy. Death has no fears for me. My hope is still firm in Jesus. Meet me and Father in Heaven with all my *dear friends*. I have no special message to send you but bid you all a happy farewell. Your affectionate and soldier son, Charles Ward."

If we are wise, we will follow Ward's example. By laying death to heart and looking ahead to what God has planned for us in Christ, we will live wisely ... and die well.[66]

---

[66] Ryken, *Ecclesiastes*, 159.

12 | ECCLESIASTES 7:7-29

FOUNDATIONS FOR A MEANINGFUL LIFE

All this I have tested by wisdom. I said, "I will be wise," but it was far from me. That which has been is far off, and deep, very deep; who can find it out?

ECCLESIASTES 7:23-24

In 1991, a yet-to-be-identified flea market enthusiast discovered a simple picture frame to his liking. Securing the purchase, the shopper returned home only to discover an ancient document hiding inconspicuously behind the frame. Thinking little of the discovery, he continued about his life. Two years later, a friend stumbled on the document and investigated its origin. The rest is history. The four-dollar frame had hidden a first edition copy of the Declaration of Independence worth $2.4 million dollars.[67] We might consider a find like that incredible, wonderful, and breathtaking. But there is something far more valuable than any treasure on earth. Christ is the most precious treasure of every believer.

---

[67] Eleanor Blau, "Declaration of Independence Sells for $2.4 Million." *The New York Times.* 14 June 1991.

Living with Christ at the center makes life meaningful no matter what the circumstances of life may be. He makes everything else worthwhile. We all want to have a meaningful, Christ-centered life. If you are married, you want to grow old together. If you have children, you want to see your children and grandchildren follow Christ. You want to make a difference for Christ. Living the "good life" is not about how much money or pleasure or knowledge you have. It's about wisdom, that is, being conformed to the image of Christ in covenant with God. Wisdom is the ability to make practical decisions in a way that is in line with God's will—the ability to live life the way God designed it. Solomon tells us how important wisdom is in the book of Proverbs.

Proverbs 4:7 | Wisdom is the principal thing: Get wisdom, and whatever you get, get insight.

How do we get wisdom? We need "the fear of the Lord"—the awe and reverence for God in every moment—in order to have wisdom.

Proverbs 9:10 | The fear of the LORD is the beginning of wisdom, and the knowledge of the Holy One is insight.

Who are the wise? Believers! When the Bible talks about the "wise" it is talking about believers, plain and simple. Without knowing the Lord personally and intimately, we may think we know what is right, but it leads to destruction.

Proverbs 16:25 | There is a way that seems right to a man, but its end is the way to death.

Clearly the New Testament teaches us that ultimate wisdom cannot be found apart from knowing Jesus Christ.

1 Corinthians 1:24 | But to those who are called, both Jews and Greeks, Christ the power of God and the wisdom of God.

Christ is called the word (Jn 1:1) and the truth (Jn 14:6). He is wisdom!

Key Thought: To know Christ and to fear him and to live with him as the center of your life is *wisdom.*

Ecclesiastes points us to the Treasure of all treasures: Jesus! The wise mirror Christ's character, treasure Christ above all, and live in Christ's love. Believers who live in wisdom will experience Christ's favor and influence in all of life. In short, choose Christ and you will be conformed to him, living life with him at the center.

THE CHARACTER OF THE WISE (7:7-10)

People who treasure Christ have incredible character. The Bible calls this kind of moral excellence: virtue. Fearing God leads believers to despise corruption and shady dealings of all kinds.

The Wise are Principled

The righteous carefully guard their integrity, wanting God's moral excellence in everything they say, think, and do. They should not be intimidated or bought but are influenced by the indwelling Spirit. But sometimes, Solomon says, oppression is so powerful, even the wise can be driven to foolishness and madness. Be careful! Don't be sucked into the power and politics of life.

Ecclesiastes 7:7 | Surely oppression drives the wise into madness, and a bribe corrupts the heart.

Even the wise and godly person can be tempted by the madness of money and power. The idea of "oppression" and "bribes" are specifically in the context of someone in a place of power, whether in politics or leadership. It's easy to oppress and neglect the sheep under one's care if that leader is self-centered.

When a wise man is in power, he must be very careful not to play favorites for favors, kickbacks, or bribes. We must have the highest integrity. Power and politics can turn a wise man into a fool.[68] The truly wise follower of Christ will not be corrupted by power and money. True virtue loves what is good and shuns compromise.

Ephesians 5:9 | The fruit of light is found in all that is good and right and true.

A truly wise person insists on integrity and accountability. When you hold them up to the light, they are sincere people. For them to live is Christ. We walk in the light with other Christians, living a life of faith and repentance, determining to be blameless in our inner heart and outer walk. Let's see something else about the character of believers. They are patient.

---

[68] Glenn, "Ecclesiastes" *BKC*, 992.

The Wise are Patient

The righteous are patient and humble in tribulations because they are looking to the "end," and that means they trust in the sovereignty of God and his direction of all events.

The Legacy of Patience

Ecclesiastes 7:8a | Better is the end of a thing than its beginning.

If the child of God is patient, they will finally see that moral integrity is indeed the better way.[69] The way to have a patient spirit is to look at the end goal and work backward. When you see the end, you see that God is your judge, and there is no need to huff and puff about people's opinions of you. Trust in the Lord; focus on him. That's where the peace of patience comes from.

The Superiority of Patience

Ecclesiastes 7:8b | And the patient in spirit is better than the proud in spirit.

Patience is the ability to rest in God's control, and to suffer long. The opposite of that is foolish, sinful anger. The child of God is filled with the Spirit of God, the fruit of which is patience.

Galatians 5:22 | But the fruit of the Spirit is love, joy, peace, patience...

Patience is always better than pride! Pride protects the kingdom of self and is willing to cross lines and be foolish and sinful in order to preserve self. The growing child of God is going to yield to God and die to the temptations of pride and arrogance. We need to have thick skin and a big heart. That only comes through humility and seeing yourself as small and unworthy. With humble patience there are no regrets. It's so much better than pride which always leaves a disaster of foolish words and actions behind.

The Morality of Patience

Ecclesiastes 7:9 | Be not quick in your spirit to become angry, for anger lodges in the heart of fools.

---

[69] Garrett, *Ecclesiastes*, 320.

A wise hearted person has the power of patience. Fools gets angry easily. They are shortsighted, self-centered, and overly sensitive. Those who have their focus off of Christ lose patience easily. They are focused on self or others or circumstances. This is why "anger lodges in the heart of fools." The wise are focused on God himself.

Do you take what people say personally and get angry? Anger demonstrates that a person is "proud in spirit." Sinful anger demonstrates a distrust in God's wisdom, plan, and control of all things. The wise trust in God no matter what circumstances appear to be. The wise know that all things both good or bad, are working toward the redemption of all things (Eph 1:10).

The Wise Trust God's Providence

What is it that drives the virtue and patience of the righteous? Their trust is in the sovereign control of God over all things to bring about all things for his own glory and for our good. The wise trust God's providence over all circumstances, but the unwise are controlled by the events and happenings of life, jerked by the chains of the ups and downs of life. The wise can rest secure in any circumstances. The unwise are often filled with angst and longing for better days.

Ecclesiastes 7:10 | Say not, "Why were the former days better than these?" For it is not from wisdom that you ask this.

Do you get depressed when you see life going up and down? Are you controlled by circumstances? God's people take the long view. Merely asking for "better days" from the past is not wisdom, but worldly, thinking only of the here and now. We as Christ followers can suffer long if there is something worth suffering for! Christ is our treasure! We long to see him! It doesn't matter how we start, but how we finish! "Better is the end of a thing than its beginning..." (7:8).

THE TREASURE OF THE WISE (7:11-15)

Above all things, believers treasure Christ. We can be patient, peaceful, and full of joy because our treasure is Christ. We place our hope and trust and happiness in the one who can never be taken away from us. In this way, knowing Christ brings a wisdom to us that is far more valuable than riches.

The Wise Treasure God's Wisdom

Wise people count the wisdom of God as more valuable than money. They treasure the wisdom that comes from walking with Yahweh.

Ecclesiastes 7:11-12 | Wisdom is good with an inheritance, an advantage to those who see the sun. [12] For the protection of wisdom is like the protection of money, and the advantage of knowledge is that wisdom preserves the life of him who has it.

Even the wise prefer prosperity to poverty. If one is blessed with a large inheritance, it's vital to have wisdom. Those who possess both money and wisdom are under the protection of both.[70] Yet, Solomon indicates that wisdom is more advantageous than even the protection of money, since wisdom "preserves the life."

Think of those with much money who die young because they have no wisdom. The wise have Christ as their master, and they "cannot serve God and money" (Mt 6:24). They treasure eternal life! Have you ever seen a wise person become very rich through their wisdom, and then you notice their children who do not have a clue? Riches are fine, but a greater advantage is wisdom.

Truly wise people have something that is a protection better than riches. Riches can protect us from many things on a superficial level. It can get us good health insurance; it can buy us a house in a secure neighborhood. We can get a security system. But wisdom is better because it gets eternal spiritual protection.

Mark 8:36 | For what does it profit a man to gain the whole world and forfeit his life?

The goal of the wise is not earthly comfort, but Christlike character. Our focus is not on the here and now but the eternal redemption of the world. Job's focus, even on his worst days, was on Christ's plan of redemption.

Job 19:25-26 | For I know that my Redeemer lives, and at the last he will stand upon the earth. [26] And after my skin has been thus destroyed, yet in my flesh I shall see God, [27] whom I shall see for myself, and my eyes shall behold, and not another.

---

[70] Keil, *Commentary on the Bible*, vol 6, 730.

We are only temporary citizens of this earth but eternal citizens of heaven (Phil 1:21). We "lay up treasure in heaven" by knowing Christ, our great treasure and "Pearl of Great Price" (Mt 13:46). Everything else compared to knowing Christ is nothing but dung and excrement (Phil 3:8). Let us "press on toward the goal for the prize of the upward call of God in Christ Jesus" which is to know him and be perfected in his image (Phil 3:12-14)!

The Wise Treasure God's Sovereignty

Wise people treasure the will of God more than worldly peace and prosperity. The wise don't think everything has to go their way. Some people are all about making their life happier by straightening out their circumstances. They are tossed about by the crazy circumstances of life. Instead, the wise consider God and yield to his sovereign control over all things.

Ecclesiastes 7:13 | Consider the work of God: who can make straight what he has made crooked?

God sometimes makes our days crooked. By "crooked" Solomon is not saying morally crooked. God could never be the author of evil. He is talking about difficulty. Isaiah speaks of God's complete control over all events, both blessing and calamity.

Isaiah 45:7 | I form light and create darkness; I make well-being and create calamity; I am the LORD, who does all these things.

Or consider the words of Amos.

Amos 3:6b | Does disaster come to a city, unless the Lord has done it?

There are times when things are going along just fine, and *boom*, we are brought to a crooked, calamitous place. What should our response be to the difficulties that are part of God's will? What are we to do? We are to trust God completely, knowing he is good and right.

Ecclesiastes 7:14 | In the day of prosperity be joyful, and in the day of adversity consider: God has made the one as well as the other, so that man may not find out anything that will be after him.

The reason God sends adversity, disaster, and calamity into your life is so that you will become dependent on God. You are a mere human being and cannot "find out anything that will be after [you]." You cannot know the specific plans God has for you. Your only option is to trust God. Consider the good result of adversity: God is drawing you nearer by showing you your powerlessness over all events. You will never be like God in knowing what tomorrow brings. Stop worrying about your situation (Mt 6:34) and accept the adversity as a pathway to draw near to God. The healthy, growing Christian will submit to the sovereign, loving hand of God. Like Jesus said, "It is vain for you to kick against the pricks" (Acts 26:14). God has a long pointy stick that is prodding you in the right direction. Don't resist it. It may hurt, but it's guiding you to the right place.

The Wise Treasure God's Justice

What about the seeming unfairness of life that sometimes effects God's people? Solomon has an answer for that as well.

Ecclesiastes 7:15 | In my vain life I have seen everything. There is a righteous man who perishes in his righteousness, and there is a wicked man who prolongs his life in his evildoing.

We all wish we could straighten out the injustices in this life. But understand we are all going to stand before the Lord. The sheep and the goats will all give an account. Injustice is ultimately against God, and he will settle it. Be wise and trust in Christ! The wicked will seem to prosper except when we lay to heart what is coming. Asaph had a similar dilemma when he considered the prosperity of the wicked in Psalm 73.

Psalm 73:12-13; 16-19 | Behold, these are the wicked; always at ease, they increase in riches. [13] All in vain have I kept my heart clean and washed my hands in innocence.... [16] But when I thought how to understand this, it seemed to me a wearisome task, [17] until I went into the sanctuary of God; then I discerned their end. [18] Truly you set them in slippery places; you make them fall to ruin. [19] How they are destroyed in a moment, swept away utterly by terrors!

Even in the worst, most unjust moment in our lives, the wise can be at peace because we do not expect any sort of final justice in our lifetimes. Justice will flow when Jesus returns! Then we can say with Amos:

Amos 5:24 | Let justice roll down like waters, and righteousness like an ever-flowing stream.

It is only when we live with Christ at the center of our lives that injustice has an ultimate answer. When Jesus comes, there will be no more unresolved mysteries or unsolved murders, There will be no more cold case crimes. There will be no more injustice. He will wipe away all our tears. Hallelujah! Let us treasure the only one who brings final justice!

THE BALANCE OF THE WISE (7:16-18)

Believer ought to be reasonable, balanced people. There is a predictability with them. They don't go off on tangents. The Amplified Bible puts it this way:

Ecclesiastes 7:16-17, AMP | Be not [morbidly exacting and externally] righteous overmuch, neither strive to make yourself [pretentiously appear] overwise—why should you [get puffed up and] destroy yourself [with presumptuous self-sufficiency]? ¹⁷ [Although all have sinned] be not wicked overmuch or willfully, neither be foolish—why should you die before your time?

Solomon tells us: avoid the extremes of legalism on one side and license on the other. Be balanced by loving God! These verses point us to a mild and moderate lifestyle, avoiding both overzealous righteousness and overindulgent sinfulness.[71]

The Wise Avoid Legalism

Don't be legalistic. God wants us to be righteous in every way, and that comes from the heart. Our real problem is thinking that we are more righteous than we really are.[72]

Ecclesiastes 7:16 | Be not overly righteous, and do not make yourself too wise. Why should you destroy yourself?

Solomon was not saying we should not be righteous and morally holy. He was not discouraging righteousness but condemning self-righteousness.[73] Solomon was telling us to avoid being the overly

---

[71] Glenn, "Ecclesiastes" *BKC*, 994.
[72] Ryken, *Ecclesiastes*, 166.
[73] Whybray, "Qoheleth", *Israelite Wisdom,* 191–204.

zealous individual who is so concerned about externals and legalistic rules. God is concerned about the heart. Don't be known as a "goodie two shoes" but as a humble, broken sinner turned saint, who loves God.

We all struggle with legalism. Perhaps you really like to talk about your knowledge of the Bible—it's so stimulating, but there are serious flaws in your character you are not willing to deal with. You love the Bible, but you love your anger or your porn or your gossip. You are overly righteous in the outward, but not you are seeing meaningful change within. You may be glad to serve at church in outward right-eousness, but are you willing to serve at home? You may love studying the Bible, but you have a hard time talking about it without arguing.

The idea is don't be overly outward in your righteousness. Don't wear it on your sleeve. Instead, serve God when no one sees. Love him when no one but him knows. Deep humility moves a person to be mod-erate, measured, and even broken.

The Wise Avoid License

To review, we've learned we cannot live a life that is "overly right-eous" or we might say, merely externally righteous. But that doesn't mean we should be very diligent about our walk. We can't be sloppy either and live a life of lawlessness. Christians, as God's covenant peo-ple, don't live a life of license, excusing our sins.

Ecclesiastes 7:17 | Be not overly wicked, neither be a fool. Why should you die before your time?

If we sin, God is gracious, and his love abounds in forgiveness to his children. Paul rightly asked the question, "Should we continue in sin that grace may abound?" If you do that, you may very well "die be-fore your time" (vs 18). Indeed, the Christian is no longer comfortable living in sin because of his fellowship with God (cf 1 Jn 1:7-2:2).

Christians should live in the freedom of the Holy Spirit. There is leeway within various cultures and families. Some may choose never to drink alcohol and others may allow themselves to celebrate with a toast or a glass of wine. But to indulge in alcohol is sinful since "no drunk-ard... will inherit the kingdom of God" (1 Cor 6:9). We have liberty in many things, but we must not use our liberty to pursue the world. We must never use grace to allow ourselves to follow after sin (Psa 1:1-3; Rom 6:15).

Galatians 5:13 | For you were called to freedom, brothers. Only do not use your freedom as an opportunity for the flesh, but through love serve one another.

We also must never push our liberty on anyone. Each one should live before God in blamelessness, according to their own conscience.

Romans 14:5 | One person esteems one day as better than another, while another esteems all days alike. Each one should be fully convinced in his own mind (*cf* Col 2:16).

Above all, never allow your liberty to cause another brother to stumble.

Romans 14:13-15 | Therefore let us not pass judgment on one another any longer, but rather decide never to put a stumbling block or hindrance in the way of a brother. [14] I know and am persuaded in the Lord Jesus that nothing is unclean in itself, but it is unclean for anyone who thinks it unclean. [15] For if your brother is grieved by what you eat, you are no longer walking in love. By what you eat, do not destroy the one for whom Christ died.

We must never use grace to allow ourselves to follow after sin (Psa 1:1-3; Solomon then warns that God may take you home early if you use God's grace and forgiveness as a license to sin more. Abraham dies "full of days" (Exo 23:26), but those who play with wickedness often die young—*before their time.*

The Wise Aim for Love

What is the answer for right living? It's not legalism. It's not license. Both of those may lead to death. The answer for solid, stable, balanced living is loving and fearing God.

Ecclesiastes 7:18 | It is good that you should take hold of this, and from that withhold not your hand, for the one who fears God shall come out from both of them.

There is a way to avoid both of these extremes of rules on one hand and riotous living on the other: it's a relationship with God—we are to live in the fear of God.[74] Live in the face of God and in the fear of God and you will escape both legalism and license. Don't ever let go of living

---

[74] Ryken, *Ecclesiastes*, 167.

in the presence of the Lord, and you will be delivered from both legalism and license.

THE POWER OF THE WISE (7:19-29)

Wise people are powerful influencers of their families, and collectively they can transform their community and society as a whole. They may be quiet and certainly humble, but God's powerful hand is upon them. God opens doors and gives favor to the wise.

From a Christian point of view, Jesus Christ is the embodiment of wisdom since he is indeed the "wisdom and power of God" (1 Cor 1:24). When we grow in our walk with Jesus, we are going to be growing in wisdom. It's powerful to protect and guide us in a number of ways, according to wise Solomon.

The Power of Shelter

The mark of a true believer, a person who has the wisdom of God dwelling in them by the Holy Spirit, is the shelter that the person of Christ provides us.

Solomon now paints a picture of the wise as one who has incredible "strength" which can also mean a "stronghold, safe retreat, or protection."[75] The wisdom of the wise is a strong refuge and shelter.

Ecclesiastes 7:19 | Wisdom gives strength to the wise man more than ten rulers who are in a city.

Through wisdom we have the fortress of a city and the understanding of the wisest city council. These ten rulers may also be referring to ten generals—heroes, or commanders, at the head of their forces, to whom the defense of the city is entrusted.[76]

A wise person is better than ten generals who would guard the city. How? Think about the wisdom that transformed society as a whole after the Reformation and the first and second great awakenings. No army can hold back the truth. Remember the words of Jesus.

John 8:32 | You will know the truth, and the truth will set you free.

---

[75] Carl Friedrich Keil and Franz Delitzsch, *Commentary on the Old Testament*, vol. 6 (Peabody, MA: Hendrickson, 1996), 735.

[76] Thomas H. Leale, *Ecclesiastes*, The Preacher's Complete Homiletic Commentary (New York; London; Toronto: Funk & Wagnalls, 1892), 95.

Wisdom can set free whole societies of people, better than any army. Wisdom through the fear of God, walking in the presence of God and by the word of God can change whole families. It can break the awful cycle of generational sin. It can turn the addict into a worshipper of Jesus, free from the idolatry and cravings of the flesh.

The Power of Single-mindedness

Another mark of a true believer is a single-minded focus on Christ. Growing in the wisdom of Christ will provide a single-minded focus. It's so easy to become distracted in life. We must not get our guidance from fallen people, since there is not a truly righteous person on the earth.

First, *we must not focus on people.* People are fallen.

Ecclesiastes 7:20 | Surely there is not a righteous man on earth who does good and never sins.

Wisdom comes from a single-minded focus on God, fearing and loving him. If you begin to look only outwardly at self or others, you will quickly be discouraged. Why? Because the entire human race is fallen and depraved. There is no one who "never sins."

No one can trust external righteousness, since there is not even one righteous man on the earth. Even the truly righteous are not sinless, but they look to Christ for righteousness in brokenness and humility. We cannot look to self or others, since it is there that we see Adam's sinful race. The only way out of this fallen mess is by being justified by grace through faith in Christ alone (Rom 5:1; Eph 2:8-10; 2 Pet 1:1).

Because the entire human race is fallen, wisdom teaches us not to expect that those we deal with should be completely faultless. We ourselves are not sinless. If we said we were, we'd be lying (*cf* 1 Jn 1:8). Not even the best of people is without sin.[77] So don't focus on fallen people.

Second, we must not focus on people's words. What people say about you ought not to have a great impact on you as a believer.

Ecclesiastes 7:21-22 | Do not take to heart all the things that people say, lest you hear your servant cursing you. [22] Your heart knows that many times you yourself have cursed others.

---

[77] Henry, *Commentary on the Whole Bible*, 1044.

People's words must not define us. God's word defines us. People say all kinds of things. You have said all kinds of things you regret. When you hear your reputation slandered, try to move on quickly. We dare not trust in what mere human beings say about us.

Jeremiah 17:5 | Thus says the LORD: Cursed is the man who trusts in man and makes flesh his strength, whose heart turns away from the LORD.

Finally, do focus on the Lord. You are wise if you do not allow people to control your outlook on life. Don't trust in man, but in the Lord.

Jeremiah 17:7-8 | Blessed is the man who trusts in the LORD, whose trust is the LORD. ⁸ He is like a tree planted by water, that sends out its roots by the stream (*cf* Psa 1:1-3).

People make their own choices. We cannot control the choices of other people. We need to have a single-minded focus and devotion to the Lord.

The Power of Sobriety

The wise are not overly proud but realize they have not arrived. Without God, true wisdom is unattainable, far beyond the grasp of the greatest and most intelligent of people.

Solomon was sober about his own *limited intellect* and ability to have wisdom.

Ecclesiastes 7:23-24 | All this I have tested by wisdom. I said, "I will be wise," but it was far from me. ²⁴ That which has been is far off, and deep, very deep; who can find it out?

Solomon now openly admits what has often been implicit: his own limited wisdom is insufficient for the task of "testing" all things.[78] There is a real humility with wise people. They realize that God is so vast and so great and so amazing, that we all end up saying with Solomon, the wisest man in the world, "I want to be wise, but it's humanly unattainable." The implication is that only through fearing and knowing God can a person be truly wise.

---

[78] Max Rogland, "Ecclesiastes," in *Psalms–Song of Solomon*, ed. Iain M. Duguid, James M. Hamilton Jr., and Jay Sklar, vol. V, ESV Expository Commentary (Wheaton, IL: Crossway, 2022), 1083.

The king was sober about own *limited perspective*. What Solomon expresses is "the epitaph of every philosopher."[79] He says, "I tried to understand, but it is beyond me!"

Ecclesiastes 7:25 | I turned my heart to know and to search out and to seek wisdom and the scheme of things, and to know the wickedness of folly and the foolishness that is madness.

Has any man ever made a more serious attempt to understand the meaning of life than King Solomon? He tried to understand the theodicy of evil, the problem that God is good yet evil exists. He tried to understand and search out true wisdom and how the universe operates. Solomon implied, but silent answer is that he realizes he's just a man. At the end of all his questing he had to admit—very reluctantly—that he had failed to find the wisdom he had been seeking all his life.[80] In Ecclesiastes' searching out of wisdom and folly, Solomon's mere humanity is showing. This kept Solomon sober and humble.

The Power of Self-Control

The wise are not controlled by passion and pornography but are chaste and self-controlled.

Ecclesiastes 7:26 | And I find something more bitter than death: the woman whose heart is snares and nets, and whose hands are fetters. He who pleases God escapes her, but the sinner is taken by her.

Solomon recalls "the strange woman" whose temptations lead to hell as did in Proverbs 1–9. An adulterous woman (or man) is worse than fetters and cages (*cf* Pro 9:13–17; Zech 5:7–8).[81] Solomon tells us the path to joy and satisfaction in marriage is monogamy: being completely devoted to your spouse for the entirety of your life.

Proverbs 5:25-29 | Drink water from your own cistern, flowing water from your own well. [16] Should your springs be scattered abroad, streams of water in the streets? [17] Let them be for yourself alone, and

---

[79] Derek Kidner, *The Message of Ecclesiastes: A Time to Mourn, and a Time to Dance*, ed. J. Alec Motyer and Derek Tidball, The Bible Speaks Today (England: Inter-Varsity Press, 1984), 71.

[80] Ryken, *Ecclesiastes*, 174–175.

[81] Glenn, "Ecclesiastes" *BKC*, 995.

not for strangers with you. ¹⁸ Let your fountain be blessed, and rejoice in the wife of your youth, ¹⁹ a lovely deer, a graceful doe.

God invented romantic love. The fire should remain in the fireplace, not in the middle of the living room. Take it out of the fireplace, and you will burn down the house. So it is with romantic love. Guard it and save it for your wedding night. Enjoy it all your married life.

The Power of Standing Alone

Solomon was willing to stand alone in holiness. The wise understand that very few people in the human race are truly wise and consistent in living a life of wisdom. Does anyone truly live a life of wisdom?

Ecclesiastes 7:27-29 | Behold, this is what I found, says the Preacher, while adding one thing to another to find the scheme of things— **28** which my soul has sought repeatedly, but I have not found. One man among a thousand I found, but a woman among all these I have not found. **29** See, this alone I found, that God made man upright, but they have sought out many schemes.

Solomon testifies that among his fellow men, he only knew of one in a thousand that were truly wise and feared the Lord. It is not just that there is not a righteous person who never sins (7:20), but that there are very few righteous men in existence.[82] Since he was much less familiar with women, they were a closed book to him—he didn't even know one godly woman, especially since many ungodly women had turned his heart away from the Lord. As verse 18 says, it is "the one who fears God" who will live out wisdom through a righteous life.

What Solomon was certain of was this one thing alone: that God made man upright but that all humanity everywhere had fallen. After all his study of wisdom, more than anything he saw the reality of mankind's fall from the "upright" state in which God had created him.[83] Mankind is corrupt and in need of a Savior! We need Jesus.

Even when all are corrupt around us, we must be willing to stand alone for the Lord. Solomon, much later in life, has come to this

---

[82] Richard P. Belcher Jr., *Ecclesiastes: A Mentor Commentary*, Mentor Commentaries (Ross-shire, Great Britain: Mentor, 2017), 285.
[83] Rogland, "Ecclesiastes," 1084.

conclusion. But for a time, as an older man, he joined in the corruption of those around him.

> *1 Kings 11:1-4* | King Solomon loved many foreign women, along with the daughter of Pharaoh: Moabite, Ammonite, Edomite, Sidonian, and Hittite women, [2] from the nations concerning which the LORD had said to the people of Israel, "You shall not enter into marriage with them, neither shall they with you, for surely they will turn away your heart after their gods." Solomon clung to these in love. [3] He had 700 wives, who were princesses, and 300 concubines. And his wives turned away his heart. [4] For when Solomon was old his wives turned away his heart after other gods, and his heart was not wholly true to the LORD his God, as was the heart of David his father.

After failing and falling from his faith in the Lord, Solomon returned and wrote Ecclesiastes. Don't follow that example. Instead, be willing to stand alone. But even if you have failed, be bold in your repentance like Solomon. Even in his old age, he repented and turned back to the Lord.

Conclusion

What is the essence of wisdom? Solomon's conclusion is that true wisdom comes with God at the center of your life. Paul said, "For me to live is Christ and to die is gain." Do you fear the Lord? Do you live for him? Is he the very center of your life? We will not find the answers among human philosophies. Satisfaction comes by knowing God alone. It's not about accumulating knowledge since even "unlearned fisherman" were the wisest men that walked the earth. If you want to be wise, seek Jesus Christ! He is the "wisdom and the power of God."

13 | ECCLESIASTES 8:1-8

THE GLORY OF A MEANINGFUL LIFE

*A man's wisdom makes his face shine, and the hardness of his
face is changed.*

ECCLESIASTES 8:1

I'm not much into superhero movies outside of Superman. But I do love the story behind Captain America. It is 1941 and here is this young man, Steve Rogers, in the throes of World War II who has a massive heart and courage. Young Steve wants to do his part and join America's armed forces, but the military rejects him because of his small stature. Finally, Steve gets his chance when he is accepted into an experimental program that turns him into a super soldier called Captain America. One of my favorite scenes is when Steve goes into the super machine as a scrawny, pitiful, but courageous young man, and he comes out, a foot taller, with the body of a superhero.

God's word can't make us a physical super soldier, but it can make us a spiritual super soldier, empowered to do supernatural things. That's what Ecclesiastes 8 is about. We are called to be like Christ. Our super serum is the wisdom from applying of God's word. While it is true that we are predestined to be conformed to his image and likeness (Rom 8:28-29), yet the means to that end is the wisdom that comes from walking in the word. You have everything you need for life and godliness in Christ (*cf* 2 Pet 1:3), but without wisdom you have no idea how to apply it.

What we find in this passage is that the wise person is the one who lives his life in submission to God and focused around Christ. Focusing on the Lord and his character and his will for us is the essence of wisdom. Wisdom is found in Christ alone. And we ought to go after him with all our might.

Proverbs 4:7 | Wisdom is the principal thing: Get wisdom, and whatever you get, get insight.

What is wisdom? Wisdom is knowing how to live right, but it is not only that. It is also right living for the right reason. It is right living for the Lord's sake. When the Bible talks about the "wise" it is talking about believers, plain and simple.

Proverbs 9:10 | The fear of the LORD is the beginning of wisdom, and the knowledge of the Holy One is insight."

It doesn't matter what seems right to us. Indeed, "there is a way that seems right to a man, but its end is the way to death" (Pro 16:25). Clearly the New Testament teaches us that ultimate wisdom cannot be had apart from knowing Jesus Christ.

A New Testament summary of King Solomon's argument that wisdom is the principle thing is in our Lord's Sermon on the Mount.

Matthew 6:33 | Seek first the kingdom of God and his righteousness, and all these things will be added to you.

The essence of wisdom is to put Christ at the center of everything in life. Paul informs us that "Christ the power of God and the wisdom of God" (1 Cor 1:24). Christ is called the Word (Jn 1:1) and the Truth (Jn 14:6). He is the supernatural expression of perfect wisdom! To know him and to fear him and to live with him as the center of your life is wisdom.

The passage before us addresses the counselors to kings to showcase the advantage of wisdom. Wisdom is so vital and important to living in the fullness God designed, that the wise are a commodity that kings seek after.

Keep in mind that Eastern rulers in that day held the power of life and death in their hands and often used that power capriciously. They were not elected by the people nor were they answerable to them. Some leaders ruled as benevolent dictators, but for the most part rulers in the ancient East were tyrannical despots who permitted nothing to stand in the way of fulfilling their desires.

Solomon described an officer in the royal court, a man who had to carry out the orders of a despotic ruler. The officer had to have wisdom; in fact, it showed on his face.[84] We learn in 1 Kings 4:29–34 of the great wisdom of Solomon, so even as the wisest in the world, he still understood the absolute necessity of wise counselors.[85] So how can we lay a foundation for a full, meaningful life in Christ? You can always pick them out. The Bible says their face shines!

THE RADIANCE OF THE WISE (8:1)

Those with the insight to give true explanations (or "interpretations") of reality are hard to find.[86] Solomon declares that the thoughts and motives of our heart can is reflected in one's face or appearance.[87]

The Wise are Rare

Ecclesiastes 8:1a | Who is like the wise? And who knows the interpretation of a thing?

Who has the answers to real life problems? Only those who have the Lord at the center of their lives can know the interpretation of a thing. Those who look to the author and fountain of wisdom are truly wise, and they are so very rare.

Where, asks the Preacher, is the man who discerns his way through all the problems detailed in the first part of the book, and who will interpret aright the mysteries of providence?[88] Who's going to tell us why life without Christ is vain and meaningless? Who will tell us that life without Christ is joyful and satisfying? Only the wise person who trusts in the Lord completely (Pro 3:5-7). Yet the truly wise person in today's society of compromise is so rare. It's so rare that someone can speak with competence about the complex problems of life. But the child of God is competent because he has the word of God.

---

[84] Wiersbe, *Be Satisfied*, 96.
[85] Belcher, *Ecclesiastes*, 292.
[86] Rogland, "Ecclesiastes," 1087.
[87] Glenn, "Ecclesiastes" *BKC*, 996.
[88] Eaton, *Ecclesiastes*, 134.

Those who apply the Scriptures to their heart and life are wise like no one else. They have more insight when it comes to understanding the complicated situations of life. Those skilled at wisdom are like a sharp blade compared to a dull blade (10:10). They are not common in society, but rare, hard to come by. Remember the words of Jesus.

Matthew 7:14 | The gate is narrow and the way is hard that leads to life, and those who find it are few.

Indeed, the wise are truly rare! The way of the wise is narrow and unpopular.

The Wise are Radiant

Ecclesiastes 8:1b | A man's wisdom makes his face shine, and the hardness of his face is changed.

Moses had to hide his face after he met with God. His countenance was so radiant that he had to where a veil over his face because the glory was so bright from his face, it was uncomfortable for people (Exo 34:33; *cf* 2 Cor 3:13). His face broadcast the peace and glory of his relationship with the Lord.

To be wise is to know Christ, and our countenance is informed! This is very similar to the Levitical blessing from Numbers where the shining face denotes Yahweh's favor.

Numbers 6:24-26 | The LORD bless you and keep you; [25] the LORD make his face to shine upon you and be gracious to you; [26] the LORD lift up his countenance upon you and give you peace.

Those who know the Lord are wise. Even the demeanor of the face of the Christian changes. We are "changed into the image of Christ" as we look to him (Rom 8:29). The shining *face* speaks of his love and favor for the child of God (*cf* Num 6:25).[89]

In 1835 German chemist Justis von Liebig devised a process for coating plates of glass with metallic silver. This was the beginning of the mirror as we know it today and helped it become a common household item.[90] It helped the person to see themselves clearly. So it is with the mirror of God's word. Paul tells us that the faces of the wise will

---

[89] Eaton, ibid.

[90] Kerry K. Karukstis and Gerald R. Van Hecke, *Chemistry Connections: The Chemical Basis of Everyday Phenomena* (Amsterdam: Elsevier Science, 2003), 143.

shine. As we gaze into the mirror of God's word, we don't have to veil their faces like Moses. We are transformed by looking at Christ.

2 Corinthians 3:18 | We all, with unveiled face, beholding the glory of the Lord, are being transformed into the same image from one degree of glory to another.

We ought to all be making spiritual progress in our lives, having our faces enlightened by the word of God. As you are saturated with the joy of Christ as you find him in the Scriptures, you will be changed. There is a joy about the countenance of every believer who is right with God. The peace and joy that comes from true wisdom is physically evident to those who observe the wise.

THE RELIABILITY OF THE WISE (8:2-4)

Wise counselors are always in demand. They don't waver, even in the presence of kings and princes. They are reliable people. They understand who is really in control. Every knee shall bow before Yahweh, and the wise understand this. It's what makes them wise.

Ecclesiastes 8:2-5 | I say: Keep the king's command, because of God's oath to him. ³ Be not hasty to go from his presence. Do not take your stand in an evil cause, for he does whatever he pleases. ⁴ For the word of the king is supreme, and who may say to him, "What are you doing?" ⁵ Whoever keeps a command will know no evil thing, and the wise heart will know the proper time and the just way.

Solomon now gives the example of real wisdom in the context of a counselor in the court of a king, like Daniel or Joseph or even Esther.

They Model Surrender

Ecclesiastes 8:2 | I say: Keep the king's command, because of God's oath to him.

The wise model surrender to God's sovereignty. They have the right attitude toward authority, since they recognize God's sovereignty over all governments and authorities. Solomon says: "Submit to the king." Why? God, by his sovereign decree and oath, puts all governments in place. We can say the same thing today. Submit to the government. Pay your taxes. Obey the laws. The king's or government's office exists to serve the sovereign purposes of God. Indeed, all authority comes from God. Paul tells us what our attitude should be.

> *Romans 13:1-2* | Let every person be subject to the governing authorities. For there is no authority except from God, and those that exist have been instituted by God. ² Therefore whoever resists the authorities resists what God has appointed, and those who resist will incur judgment.

Peter tells us the same thing.

> *1 Peter 2:17* | Honor everyone. Love the brotherhood. Fear God. Honor the emperor.

Peter tells us to honor, or literally prize, the emperor. This is written by a man that was eventually crucified upside down by the king (Nero) he is writing about. Nero was destroying Christians everywhere, yet Peter tells us to honor the authorities God has put in place, including the emperor.

How are we to honor authority? In the family, Moses and Paul say we are to honor father and mother (Exo 20; Eph 6:1-3). In marriage, we are told to submit to one another (Eph 5:21) as well as the wife submitting to her husband (Eph 5:22). In our employment, we are to submit to our employer as we "would unto Christ" (Eph 6:5). In government, as I mentioned above, Paul tells us to submit to governmental authorities. The powers "that exist have been instituted by God" (Rom 13:2). Truly, your attitude toward authority reveals your heart's attitude toward God. Civil disobedience is always permitted if the laws or decrees of a government are unjust since we must obey God rather than man.

They Model Seriousness

Ecclesiastes 8:3a | Be not hasty to go from his presence.

To go from someone's presence' elsewhere signifies disaffection or disloyalty (*cf* Hos 11:2).[91] The fifth commandment has to do not only with honoring mother and father but all authority. The wise are not hasty to disregard a command they have heard from authority. They don't go away quickly and forget what was said. They take it seriously. They are reliable because they are faithful and serious.

---

[91] Eaton, *Ecclesiastes*, 135.

The wise have great reverence for authority since it is delegated by God to those who have it. It's vital we have allegiance for the political sphere God has placed us in.

They Model Sanctity

Ecclesiastes 8:3b | Do not take your stand in an evil cause, for he does whatever he pleases.

At the same time, while the wise have great reverence for authority, they are not willing to violate their conscience for "an evil cause." We must never be fearful to "obey God rather than men" even though the king or other authorities may do whatever they please (*cf* Acts 5:29). Every knee will bow to Christ, even the greatest and most powerful of kings and presidents will bow. Therefore, the wise should not be afraid to follow and obey Christ even if it contradicts the desires of the most powerful authority. A wise man will not take their stand with "an evil cause." Yet even in civil disobedience we must have the meekness of Daniel and Joseph.

Here's the main point: as mature and wise believers in Christ, it ought to be our intention to carry out the desires of those in authority over us. We should want to immediately do what those in authority desire, as long as it is not defying God in any way.

They Model Self-Control

While the wise have a humble and submissive attitude toward authority, they are also patient and wise in their timing of offering advice.

Ecclesiastes 8:4 | For the word of the king is supreme, and who may say to him, "What are you doing?"

Royal power cannot be challenged. Such power with its potential of abuse caused the prophets to resist the monarchy (1 Sam 8:10–18).[92] Daniel is a good example of what patience as the king's advisor looks like. He did not compromise with his food, even though he was the king's cupbearer. He exercised his conscience at the proper time and in the proper way and became beloved to several of the greatest kings of his time.

---

[92] Carl Schultz, "Ecclesiastes," in *Evangelical Commentary on the Bible*, vol. 3, Baker Reference Library (Grand Rapids, MI: Baker Book House, 1995), 445.

THE REASONABLENESS OF THE WISE (8:5-8)

Wisdom is a safety and protection for the child of God. We do not fear calamity or what people can do to us.

Ecclesiastes 8:5-7 | Whoever keeps a command will know no evil thing, and the wise heart will know the proper time and the just way. ⁶ For there is a time and a way for everything, although man's trouble lies heavy on him. ⁷ For he does not know what is to be, for who can tell him how it will be? ⁸ No man has power to retain the spirit, or power over the day of death. There is no discharge from war, nor will wickedness deliver those who are given to it.

The Wise Understand God's Protection

The wise know that living in submission brings stability. Calamity and evil are rare in the lives of the wise. Wisdom is actually a protection for the godly.

Ecclesiastes 8:5 | Whoever keeps a command will know no evil thing, and the wise heart will know the proper time and the just way.

Evil here means calamity or trouble. The wise counselor of a leader does not need to fear the troubles of political consequences. No matter what happens, God will work all things for his glory and our good (Rom 8:28-29). The wisdom of the wise will guide him to make the proper and righteous decisions at the proper time. We don't have to fear what calamity or "evil thing" the government can do to us. Remember the Psalmist's reason for not being afraid?

Psalm 118:6 | The LORD is on my side; I will not fear. What can man do to me?

The child of God is under the sovereign protection of God, predestined for all things to work out for the good of being conformed to Christ (Rom 8:28-29). The Christian has a moral responsibility to obey "the powers that be" since they are indeed "ordained by God" (Rom 13:1). This does not mean we are to carry out everything our government says. Submission is not to be blind passivity.[93] The wise person does not render a thoughtless obedience, as if *every* command

---

[93] Eaton, *Ecclesiastes*, 136.

proceeding from merely human authority must be obeyed without questioning.[94] Especially with the world and her leaders, we follow the wisdom of our Lord Jesus.

Matthew 11:16 | Be wise as serpents and innocent as doves.

We remember how Joseph, Daniel, and Esther were placed in positions of prominence by God and were given discernment that would enable them to fulfil God's will for their people. But their obedience to the king was always subject to their obedience to God.[95]

If you are wise and follow authority generally speaking, God is going to protect you. Yet even if God indeed does allow trouble in your life, we can rest with the wisdom of the three Hebrew children before the fearsome king of Babylon. Remember what they said when threatened with death for obeying Almighty God?

Daniel 3:16-18 | O Nebuchadnezzar, we have no need to answer you in this matter. [17] If this be so, our God whom we serve is able to deliver us from the burning fiery furnace, and he will deliver us out of your hand, O king. [18] But if not, be it known to you, O king, that we will not serve your gods or worship the golden image that you have set up.

It doesn't mean all wise people are going to always have peace and prosper. It is a general rule that those who obey authority live long, avoid trouble, and have far more stability in their lives.

This doesn't mean life will always be peaceful. Remember the words of Jesus: "In the world you will have tribulation" (Jn 16:33a). Look at Paul—he suffered (*cf* 2 Cor 11:23-27). He told Timothy to "endure hardness" (2 Tim 2:3). But these men were blessed by God. They saw God work. Any evil (or *troublesome*) thing that came their way was put there by God for their good.

The Wise Understand Godly Principles

The wise avoid calamity for the governor or king they are working for because they understand proper timing and righteous policy.

Ecclesiastes 8:5b | And the wise heart will know the proper time and the just way.

---

[94] Leale, *Ecclesiastes*, 120.
[95] Winter, *Opening up Ecclesiastes*, 106.

The child of God is wise and principled. Much skill, discretion, and good sense are needed to help a king or a great leader. The skill of a humble, meek tongue is vital. There is a proper time and a good and right way to give counsel to a leader. If you want to say something to anyone, whether it be a friend, your spouse, your employer, how you say it is just as important as what you say. We see also that the wise person is not prone to talk back to authority. He doesn't question for no reason and say: "What are you doing?" (8:4).

The wise understand that there is a proper time and way to approach authority. It is never right to make an accusation against any authority without evidence and witnesses. We see this in regard to a pastor or elder in Paul's first letter to Timothy.

1 Timothy 5:19 | Do not admit a charge against an elder except on the evidence of two or three witnesses.

I believe this ought to be our practice toward all authority. We need to be very careful how we talk about those who are in authority over us. This includes our parents, our employers, our church leaders, and our secular government.

The Wise Understand Godly Priorities

The wise also know how to balance priorities.

Ecclesiastes 8:6a | For there is a time and a way for everything.

Life's responsibilities and troubles can be so heavy. The wise know how to balance the responsibilities of life. Life can be *crazy*. You've got family responsibilities, church obligations, friends, work, etc. How do you know who to put first? You will know because you have a wise heart. You are studying God's word. Wisdom does not come from you; it comes from God! If you are in God's word, you will know how to balance priorities! I can say: "your word is a lamp to my feet and a light to my path" (Psa 119:105). It gives me wisdom that not only lightens my load, it lightens my path.

The Wise Understand God's Providence

Ecclesiastes 8:6b-7 | Although man's trouble lies heavy on him. [7] He does not know what is to be, for who can tell him how it will be?

The wise understand the providence of God. So many times, we are tempted to stew about things we cannot control. There is so much trouble that "lies heavy" on all of us. Providence is the doctrine that God is working out all things personally in your life for his glory and your good. The hard thing about God being in control is that we don't know how it's going to turn out. I love the question: "Who can tell him how it will be?" I know the answer. Only God knows how things will turn out. He "works all things according to the counsel of his own will" (Eph 1:11). God tells us in his word in Romans 8 how his providence works.

Romans 8:28-29 | We know that for those who love God all things work together for good, for those who are called according to his purpose. [29] For those whom he foreknew he also predestined to be conformed to the image of his Son.

Life is difficult and unpredictable, yet the wise, those who center their lives on Christ, know how to navigate those rough waters. We are not controlled by what people or circumstances bring. We do what is right and trusting that God is growing and changing us to be like Christ. Don't be surprised by the trouble in your life. You'll have it. Trust God's good plan to use that trouble in his providence for your good.

The Wise Understand God's Power

The wise live with a readiness to meet their Lord and Savior. God alone has power over life and death.

Ecclesiastes 8:8a | No man has power to retain the spirit, or power over the day of death.

A wise person lives in the full reality of his own mortality. A person can put off thinking about death through wickedness, but death is coming. Just as there is no discharge from war, we are all going to die, and a person who tries to ignore it by going after wickedness will not be delivered.

When you see the drug culture or the sensuality in all the media and all around us, remember, people are trying to put of death. But just as a general calls a soldier for service, God is going to call each one of us to himself. A wise person is always ready for death. I'm not saying you should be morbidly thinking about death, but you should live with an urgency as if today where your last.

Jonathan Edwards as a young man wrote about this in his famous resolutions. Two of them jumped out at me, and I think Edwards was hitting upon what Solomon was saying.

> 7. Resolved, never to do anything, which I should be afraid to do, if it were the last hour of my life.

> 17. Resolved, that I will live so as I shall wish I had done when I come to die.

Are you living as if today could be the last day of your life? Are you living with an abandon to God. We cannot keep our soul in our bodies when God calls us home, so we ought to live in a way that we will not be ashamed when we see him!

The Wise Understand God's Placement

It matters where God places us in our lives and callings, even if it means we have to give our life in that calling. It does us no good to fight against it or to give ourselves to wickedness to get around it. Solomon uses military service as an example of trusting God.

Ecclesiastes 8:8b | There is no discharge from war, nor will wickedness deliver those who are given to it.

The Bible generally regards military service as a noble calling. For example, John the Baptist told soldiers in the Roman army(!) not to quit their post but to honor God in the way they did their duty (Luke 3:14). Of all the things that a government commands people to do, the most demanding is to defend our country. It is also the duty that brings the most danger, and with that danger, the most uncertainty about the future. A soldier in wartime deals with the real possibility of death at any moment. He of all people knows that he does not have knowledge of the future or power over the day of death.[96]

Even life on a battlefield matters to the wise. They're going to perhaps die, but the wise do not turn to wickedness, but they trust God.

Conclusion

If you are wise, you will build your life on the platform of God's authority, submitting to him and his word and to those he puts in

---

[96] Ryken, *Ecclesiastes*, 188.

authority over us. God's word is our strong foundation—those who build their lives on it and building on a rock foundation and not on the sand.

One of the things I love about Captain America is his shield. Think about it: his only weapon is a special shield made from an indestructible alloy capable of absorbing kinetic energy. Not even Thor's hammer or Hulk's fist can penetrate the shield.

We as believer has a greater shield: the shield of faith. Walking in wisdom requires a total surrender to God's word as supreme, sufficient, and wise. It is only when we choose that surrender in the Spirit to God's word that we can be untouched by the enemy's fiery arrows.

14 | ECCLESIASTES 8:9-17

A CONTENT LIFE

I know that it will be well with those who fear God, because they fear before him. But it will not be well with the wicked, neither will he prolong his days like a shadow, because he does not fear before God.

ECCLESIASTES 8:12-13

Life has many ups and downs. Prosperity and adversity, good times and difficult times are all part of the plan of God. Do you know how to remain content in the Lord through all of it? Do you see God's hand in the past. Do you trust God's hand in your future?

> *Philippians 4:11-13* | I have learned in whatever situation I am to be content. [12] I know how to be brought low, and I know how to abound. In any and every circumstance, I have learned the secret of facing plenty and hunger, abundance and need. [13] I can do all things through him who strengthens me.

If I were to ask you, do you know how to be content in life? God gift wraps trials for you. He gift-wraps mountain top experiences for you. Life is not all one trial, neither is it all adversity. It's a mixture. The question is do you know how to be content in Christ? Have you learned how to keep your heart content?

What we find in this passage is that Solomon is in the midst of all this human misery. People doing wrong—even professing believers being wicked and doing evil—and wrong and trouble happening to God's people. Not only that but prosperity and happiness are happening to people who could care less about God. Happiness does not come from solving the problem of evil. It's already solved. Christ came and died, indeed he rose again! Without seeing life through that lens, nothing can be enjoyed.

With our tastebuds, we enjoy all kinds of food. It nourishes us, but it we also appreciate all the savors and aromas of food. Remember when the corona virus swept through our land and some people lost their sense of taste and smell. People still had to eat food because they were hungry, but it was not enjoyable. They had to eat for nourishment, but the food tasted like metal. They have to eat but it's not satisfying and enjoyable. This is what it's like to be lost. They are hungry all the time, feeding themselves, but they are never satisfied. Solomon's point is if you know Christ, your job is to keep your eyes on him in faithfulness, fearing him, and finding joy in Christ.

How can you live to please God and be content, and not be distracted or jaded by the ups and downs in life and by the depravity of people? The meaningful life is a life of contentment in knowing Christ, not based in circumstances or emotions, but based on a fulfilling relationship with Christ through his Spirit and his word.

Key thought: Contentment comes from knowing and following Christ. Every other source of happiness is a false savior and an idol of misery.

Those who live a life of joy and contentment are first and foremost faithful to the Lord.

BE FAITHFUL TO THE LORD (8:9-11)

We should determine to remain faithful to the Lord, regardless of the wicked world we live in. Often the cruelty, hypocrisy, and immorality of the world can leave us jaded. In our deep desire to live holy lives, there is a danger of becoming overly focused on politics and culture. It's common for modern Christians to become overcome with fear instead of faith. We must keep our eyes on the Lord to keep a contented spirit.

Ecclesiastes 8:9-11 | All this I observed while applying my heart to all that is done under the sun, when man had power over man to his hurt. [10] Then I saw the wicked buried. They used to go in and out of the holy place and were praised in the city where they had done such things. This also is vanity. [11] Because the sentence against an evil deed is not executed speedily, the heart of the children of man is fully set to do evil.

Solomon esteemed those who feared God amidst a great current of wickedness. In verse 12 he said, "Though a sinner does evil a hundred times and prolongs his life, yet I know that it will be well with those who fear God, because they fear before him." It should be the central desire of your life to be faithful to the Lord and to fear him, regardless of what others do. All is well in the inner being of those who love the Lord. They fear him, not people, and not circumstances.

Faithful in the Midst of Cruelty

God's people are faithful in the midst of cruelty. It is easy to become disillusioned when we see cruelty around us. It seems everyone is pushing for their own way. Solomon observed this too.

Ecclesiastes 8:9 | All this I observed while applying my heart to all that is done under the sun, when man had power over man to his hurt.

So often we observe cruelty and oppression on this earth. We see people abusing other people. We wake up one day, and a person that we've trusted, a friend, a professing believer seems faithful, but then they turn. They hurt others. They do wrong to others.

There is of course racism. America is supposed to be a melting pot, but we have a crisis of major proportions for the Black community in our country. Racism has often resulted in the killing of innocent humans in our history. Between 1882 and 1968, 3,446 Black people were lynched in America.[97] Today more black babies are killed by white abortionists every three days than all who were lynched in those years. The black population in America in 1790 was almost twenty percent. Today it is thirteen percent. It should thirty percent or higher today. Eighty percent of all Planned Parenthood abortion mills are in minority

---

[97] Walter A. Hazen, *American Black History* (St. Louis, MO: Milliken, 2004), 40.

neighborhoods, mostly in black communities.[98] This is a crime. This is genocide. This is racism in its most oppressive and brutal form because it is murder. Listen to the words of Jesse Jackson in 1977 who was then pro-life.

> Politicians argue for abortion largely because they do not want to spend the necessary money to feed, clothe and educate more people. Here arguments for inconvenience and economic savings take prece-dence over arguments for human value and human life... Psychiatrists, social workers and doctors often argue for abortion on the basis that the child will grow up mentally and emotionally scarred. But who of us is complete? If incompleteness were the criterion for taking life, we would all be dead. If you can justify abortion on the basis of emotional incompleteness, then your logic could also lead you to killing for other forms of incompleteness — blindness, crippleness, old age.[99]

We must find our contentment in an oppressive, criminal society by being faithful to the Lord. We are happy to serve the Lord and to stand against whatever he stands against. We have the solution. What is the solution for racism and oppression of all kinds? Is it the cancel culture? No. That's not good news. That's a message of unforgiveness and bitterness. We need the gospel of Jesus Christ. We have a message that reconciles all ethnicities. Every tribe, tongue, people, and nation worship him! Listen to the words of Pastor Tony Evans.

> Racism isn't a bad habit; it's not a mistake; it's a sin. The answer is not sociology; it's theology.[100]

We live among sinners who are bent inwardly. We proudly prefer our own culture, our familiar families, and we can be racist toward others and preferential to our own culture. We have seen some awful abuses of power. The wise person is not intimidated by the abuse of power, but we as believers know the solution. The gospel gives us courage to confront evil. It also brings redemption to the worst of enemies who come to know Christ. This is joy and contentment. We put our

---

[98] Star Parker, ed., "Policy Report: The Effects of Abortion on the Black Community," Library of Congress (Center for Urban Renewal and Education, June 2015).
[99] Jesse Jackson in Daniel K. Williams, *Defenders of the Unborn: The Pro-Life Movement Before Roe v. Wade* (New York: Oxford University Press, 2019), 176.
[100] Tony Evans in Daniel York, *I Keep Asking* (Warrenton, OR: Norseman Ventures, 2001), 126.

trust in the Lord. We are faithful regardless of the faithlessness around us!

Faithful in the Midst of Hypocrisy

Ecclesiastes 8:10 | Then I saw the wicked buried. They used to go in and out of the holy place and were praised in the city where they had done such things. This also is vanity.

These are surprising verses. Not that the wicked are buried, for all people die. The wicked will have their day before God. The surprising thing is that wicked used to go to the temple in Jerusalem. They looked righteous on the outside—they were among those who worshipped the Lord. They look the same as believers. They even had good reputations and received the praise of men, but they are the tares among the wheat.

A wise person observes much wrong and hypocrisy in life, but it doesn't taint him. The wise are not jaded by hypocrisy. You are going to see people who go in and out of the holy place be admired, and yet in their private lives you find out they are wicked. What a vain thing it is to praise men. We ultimately know no one's heart. Many will come to Jesus at the day of judgment and proclaim that they know him and preached in his name, but Jesus will say to them, "Depart from me you lawless people, I never knew you" (Mt 7:21-23). We need to be faithful despite the many accounts we hear of people we thought we knew, turning from God back to sin.

It can be disheartening. The social media revolution reveals where many people's hearts are. Many professing Christians boast about their sinful, worldly escapades. It makes you want to blush. What are we to do? Be discouraged? No, we need to be faithful. We need to remember what God's word tells us about the wheat and the tares.

God will judge the wicked. They will be buried. When they are released from their earthly tabernacle, they will meet God. There will be a separation of the wheat and the weeds. Jesus reminds us that the wicked will have their day with God. They can fool people, but they cannot fool God. Jesus could judge them now, but he says, let them live their lives. Let them grow together even in the churches, but judgment day is coming.

Matthew 13:30 | Let both grow together until the harvest, and at harvest time I will tell the reapers, Gather the weeds first and bind them in bundles to be burned, but gather the wheat into my barn.

God will sort out the hypocrites at the judgment. They will be burned in the lake of fire. God will bring justice to all hypocrisy very soon. As believers, we are to be faithful and content in Christ even amidst so many people's hypocrisy.

Faithful in the Midst of Immorality

Every day we see the immorality of our culture: drugs and substance abuse, fornication and pornography and the sex trade, the disintegration of the family, filthy language, and open homosexuality. Our society is normalizing all sorts of sin, so the culture is becoming more and more evil. People, and even Christians, are boasting in their tolerance for sin and sinful behavior.

Ecclesiastes 8:11 | Because the sentence against an evil deed is not executed speedily, the heart of the children of man is fully set to do evil.

Some people seem to literally get away with murder. Every year 200,000 murders are committed in our country, and half of them go free. People steal and think they can get away with it. People think they can live any way they want to and because nothing happens immediately, that they are going to get away with it.

Solomon says "the heart of the children of man is fully set to do evil" for the sheer reason that they can get away with it. Not only are we not prosecuting sin "speedily"—we aren't prosecuting it at all. We are changing our laws to protect the guilty and leave the innocent at risk. But we know that even if people get away with everything on this earth, there is a pay day, someday. There is a day of judgment. We can live in contentment because when we are wronged, we can submit ourselves to the Lord. He is just and will judge rightly at the right time.

Peter says that Christ "when he was reviled, he did not revile in return; when he suffered, he did not threaten, but continued entrusting himself to him who judges justly" (1 Pet 2:23). As believers we understand that ultimate justice is coming.

Hebrews 9:27 | It is appointed for man to die once, and after that comes judgment.

The wise are faithful among outright evil around them. Despite all the evil, we can remain pure, unjaded, and unspotted from the world.

Jesus says we are the light of the world. Paul says we are to live without blemish in the midst of this depraved generation.

Philippians 2:15 | That you may be blameless and innocent, children of God without blemish in the midst of a crooked and twisted generation, among whom you shine as lights in the world.

The wise are faithful even amidst constant evil around us. We know that the wicked will be judged. Though "the sentence of death" for sin is "not executed speedily," it will most definitely come. The early church father, Origen gave this warning.

Let all know that God's people shall be advanced to a higher state, and that the wicked shall be delivered over to sufferings and torments, in punishment of their licentiousness and depravity, their cowardice, timidity, and all their follies.[101]

God is patient, not wishing anyone to perish (2 Pet 3:9), yet once the final number of the elect come in, swift destruction will come to pass, so much so that the people under his judgment will beg the mountains and say, "Fall on us!" (*cf* Lk 23:30; Rev 6:16; Isa 2:10; Hos 10:8).

FEAR THE LORD (8:12-14)

We should fear the Lord if we are to be content. Contentedness comes from beholding the beauty of our Creator and being full and satisfied in him. Fearing him sets us free from all other fears. Only when we fear God can we experience the infinite peace of God that passes all understanding.

The Virtue of Fearing God

Ecclesiastes 8:12-13 | Though a sinner does evil a hundred times and prolongs his life, yet I know that it will be well with those who fear God, because they fear before him. **13** But it will not be well with the wicked, neither will he prolong his days like a shadow, because he does not fear before God.

---

[101] Origen Adamantius, "Origen against Celsus," in *Fathers of the Third Century: Tertullian, Part Fourth; Minucius Felix; Commodian; Origen, Parts First and Second*, ed. Alexander Roberts, James Donaldson, and A. Cleveland Coxe, trans. Frederick Crombie, vol. 4, The Ante-Nicene Fathers (Buffalo, NY: Christian Literature Company, 1885), 659.

188

The definition of fearing God. What does it mean to fear God? It means to recognize God as God, all powerful creator and sustainer of every breath. That's something to fear. It can bring dread, but it can also bring fear in the sense of something more wonderful than you can comprehend. It brings a dread of displeasing him and a realization of his greatness and power. Think of how people in the Bible have trembled and feared at the sight of angels, which are mere finite beings (Jdg 13:22; Mt 28:4; Mk 16:5-6). How much more should we fear the infinite God.[102] The fear of the world makes us paralyzed, but the fear of God sets us free so that if you fear God, you need not fear anything or anyone else.

The desperation of those who do not fear God. Solomon says those who lack virtue try to prolong their days. They live in misery but all they have is this life. They have nothing more, so they do everything they can to prolong their misery. But for those who fear the Lord, we know that it will be well.

The delight of fearing God. The lost live for the fleeting, futile moments of misery on earth. But those who fear the Lord know that even the best things on earth are misery and "dung" (as Paul says) compared to the knowledge of Christ (Phil 3:8).

The destiny for those who fear God. Is your focus on this life or the life to come? For those who fear God, "it will be well" for them, not only in this life, but for eternity. But not so for the wicked. "It will not be will with the wicked" neither in this life or the life to come. No amount of money or fame or relationships can bring satisfying and meaningful joy. Yes, there are many wicked people that seem to have everything go their way. They prolong their life. Yet the best this life can offer is misery compared to knowing the forgiveness of sins and the beauty of God's presence and love. The wicked will not live forever. One day we are all going to meet God. Live with that in mind, and you will be wise. "Seek first the kingdom of God and his righteousness" (Mt 6:33). Solomon knows that contentment comes from walking closely with God. Yet how vain a life people live who do not fear the Lord.

[102] John Bunyan, *The Fear of God* ((London: The Religious Tract Society, 1839), 5.

The Vanity of Not Fearing God

Ecclesiastes 8:14 | There is a vanity that takes place on earth, that there are righteous people to whom it happens according to the deeds of the wicked, and there are wicked people to whom it happens according to the deeds of the righteous. I said that this also is vanity.

The randomness of life. Without the lens of faith in the Lord, this life looks so random and cruel and truly vain. The prosperity and blessing that should come to the righteous often happens for the wicked. And the cursing and poverty that should come to the wicked often overcome the righteous. If all you have is this life, then it doesn't make sense. Think of our Lord Jesus Christ. His death made no sense to the disciples, but there was a resurrection day! Don't lean to your own understanding. Trust God!

The redemption of life. Though it is unstated here, Solomon's premise is that the person who dreads God's majesty and is comforted by his beauty can see God's purpose in the chaos. God will redeem the worst of circumstances, tragedies, and injustices.

Ecclesiastes 12:13-14 | The end of the matter; all has been heard. Fear God and keep his commandments, for this is the whole duty of man. [14] For God will bring every deed into judgment, with every secret thing, whether good or evil.

The unfairness of life. Those people who walk away from the faith do so because they do not fear the Lord and will not trust the Lord for ultimate justice. They are hurt by the pain of life, and they blame God. I know so many people who have built their lives around a bitterness or an injustice. It seems whenever there is a family reunion, I find out that there is deep pain from the faults of parents. And some people live their whole lives bitter about some serious disappointment or injustice that has happened to them. The wise don't live that way. They know it is vanity to live that way! God will judge. Better yet, God forgives! Without a God focus we are forced to carry the pain of all the injustice. We are unable to forgive until we find forgiveness ourselves from the Father.

What's your focus? Are you worried or angry about things you cannot control? People and circumstances ought not to control you. Focus on God. Sometimes godly people die as if they were wicked and the wicked prosper. Yet, God is in control to bring all things to pass for our good and his glory (Eccl 3:11; Rom 8:28-29; Eph 1:11).

FIND JOY IN THE LORD (8:15-17)

We should determine to find our joy in knowing Christ. How does a person truly find joy? This is very practical. Sometimes our view of serving God is from a Roman Catholic view. It's like we have to take a vow of poverty to really serve God. Actually, if you are poor or rich you can serve God. The key is enjoying the use of God gifts for his glory.

Enjoying God by His Gifts

The wise person knows how to enjoy the gifts God sends him. Solomon commends us to be joyful in all that God gives us!

Ecclesiastes 8:15 | And I commend joy, for man has nothing better under the sun but to eat and drink and be joyful, for this will go with him in his toil through the days of his life that God has given him under the sun.

Some people feel bad enjoying the gifts of God. For others God's gifts become idols, taking the place of God. There are two extremes: to think to be godly you must be rich, or you must be poor. There is no prosperity gospel or poverty gospel. We are to find contentment in whatever state we are in, knowing that it all comes from God. Be happy with what God has given you. We are commended to enjoy God's good gifts!

James 1:17 | Every good gift and every perfect gift is from above, coming down from the Father of lights with whom there is no variation or shadow due to change.

Amidst the toil and hard work of this life, we are commended and commanded to enjoy God's gifts and not think that through our vexation we can solve the problem of evil.[103] The believer is to live in constant praise to the Lord for the "life that God has given him."

In no way is Solomon advocating hedonistic indifference to injustice and suffering, but he would have us come to terms with the limits of our ability to explain (much less eliminate) unjust suffering.

---

[103] Garrett, *Ecclesiastes*, 329.

Unending vexation over this problem is pointless.[104] Living in an ungodly environment is a constant exercise of faith in the Lord, trusting him to guide all things for his kingdom. Whether good or evil, God will make good out of all things (Rom 8:28-29; Eccl 3:11).

Enjoying God by His Work

Solomon studied how to enjoy work, and the first thing he found out was, there is no joy in work without God.

The Tediousness of Work Without God

Without the fear of God, there is only weariness and exhaustion.

Ecclesiastes 8:16 | When I applied my heart to know wisdom, and to see the business that is done on earth, how neither day nor night do one's eyes see sleep.

The wise person knows that ultimate joy does not come from our work and plans, but God's work in and for us. We are not the master of our own destinies.

The Pointlessness of Work Without God

What does work get you after this life? For the most part, people won't remember what you did from day to day. It's a mystery. They don't care that you made a great sale, or that you changed that one policy that needed to be changed. All of that is well and good, but people won't remember that. They may remember what your vocation was: plumber, preacher, schoolteacher, mom, dad, etc. But whatever God does through you lasts forever.

Ecclesiastes 8:17 | Then I saw all the work of God, that man cannot find out the work that is done under the sun. However much man may toil in seeking, he will not find it out. Even though a wise man claims to know, he cannot find it out.

Set your heart to do God-sized work. Even the most wise people on the earth cannot know a tiny percentage of what God is doing. He is infinite in his capacity, and when he's doing one thing in your life that you can see, he's doing a thousand things that you cannot see. Without

---

[104] Ibid.

192

that perspective on work and life, then all our labors are pointless and vain.

Contentment is found in Christ! Nothing can be truly enjoyed without Christ at the center. Work and pleasure are meaningless unless we can see the reflection of Christ in all we do. For those who fear the Lord, we see the beauty of his holiness in all we do.

Conclusion

Are you content? Contentment is impossible with your life being vitally connected to Christ. Are you surrendered to God's direction of your life in your place of employment, your place in life (single or married), your personality, abilities, and gifts? Do you trust that God has given you all things for your good and his glory? Do you fear him in all these things? Can you enjoy the life that he has given you? This is a great challenge in this life "under the sun." It would be so much easier to be with him in glory, but he's called us to find our contentment in his fear. Without the fear of God, nothing can be enjoyed.

How do we find joy in the midst of a sin-sick world? There's so much depravity and evil. Are we to merely be culture warriors, trying to chase down all the lies? Many who do that become jaded and cynical. How do we avoid that? There is a better way. We need to go to the source.

Enjoying life is like being able to take in nourishment and thrive. That's only possible if you are connected to Christ, in union with him. Think about how trees get nourishment. They have good fruit because they have good roots. If a tree is not growing, or it is sick, you must realize if there is a problem with the fruit, there is a problem with the root. If the roots are not deep down and growing and stabilized, the tree has no hope of surviving.

According to science writer Hope Jahren, if a seed takes root, the roots can go down 50 feet, 100 feet, 150 feet, and the results are powerful. The tree's roots can "swell and split bedrock, and move gallons of water daily for years, much more efficiently than any pump yet invented by man."[105] If the tree's root system becomes established, then the tree becomes all but indestructible: "Tear apart everything

---

[105] Hope Jahren, *Lab Girl* (New York: Knopf Doubleday Publishing Group, 2016), 52.

aboveground—everything—and most trees can still grow rebelliously back from just one intact root. More than once. More than twice." [106]

Solomon's message is similar to Paul's in Ephesians: "Be rooted and grounded in Christ" (Col 2:7). Be vitally connected to Jesus, like a tree's roots are connected to the water source. "Grow up in every way into him who is the head, into Christ" (Eph 4:15), and you will be able to enjoy all the fruit and work of life despite the seemingly indestructible bedrock. The best way to break the bedrock of miseries and hardships and sins in this life and find your fountain of nourishment in Christ and teach others to be connected to him!

---

[106] Ibid.

15 | ECCLESIASTES 9:1-10
A PURPOSEFUL LIFE

*Go, eat your bread with joy, and drink your wine with a
merry heart, for God has already approved what you do.*
ECCLESIASTES 9:7

Some of us are going to live to be 95. Some of us are going to die at
35. But with the limited amount of time that we've been given, Solomon is pleading with us not pursue earthly comfort, but to pursue
meaning, significance, beauty, and depth as we live in the fear of God.
How can we pursue a meaningful life that will count when we see Jesus
Christ? Jesus said if we abide in him and he in us, we will bear "much
fruit" since apart from him we "can do nothing" (Jn 15:5). Solomon lets
us in on the joyful, purposeful, meaningful life in Ecclesiastes 9.

Those who live life without Christ are unable to truly enjoy the richness and beauty of life. They live to satisfy their flesh, which is impossible to satisfy. Only the godly can truly enjoy life. It's been reported
that after the Dallas Cowboys won their first Super Bowl, legendary
football coach Tom Landry observed, "The overwhelming emotion—in
a few days, among the players—was how empty that goal was. There
must be something more." And there is something far deeper and more
satisfying than the highest award in any sport, or the most glorious living arrangement or fame or fortune.

I think of the pop star Madonna who said that once she finally made her first million, she was more miserable as a millionaire than when she was poor. The "material girl" said, "I've learned ultimately material things won't bring you happiness. Most very wealthy people are not happy."[107] Money doesn't bring meaning or happiness to life. Life is deeper than success and mere earthly comfort. The actor Jim Carrey said, "I think everybody should get rich and famous and do everything they ever dreamed of so they can see that it's not the answer."[108]

What is the answer? What does bring meaning to life? How can we as believers break through the slavery to earthly comfort, earthly security, and the rat race for possessions, power, and pleasure as we live life "under the sun"? Solomon tells us that we have to learn to live in the fear of God, under his providence, and enjoying his provisions for his glory. We live for eternal fruit, not for temporary happiness or self-centeredness.

> Key thought: It is only when we enjoy God, that we can enjoy all his gifts.

Meaningful living begins with seeing God's purpose in everything.

THE PURPOSE FOR MEANINGFUL LIVING (9:1-6)

The godly person understands that God is sovereign over life and death. Life is not always pretty for the godly, but it is guided by God. The godly are able to see through all the difficulties, sins, and madness of this present world and understand that no matter what happens, they live for the God who is guiding us to a higher purpose, above happiness or sadness.

Consider the Purpose of Life

Some think everything needs to go right to have a good and meaningful life. Not true. A meaningful life will include both good and bad, but all is guided by God. The Lord sovereignly guides the lives of his

---

[107] Mark Shanahan, "Despite Living Quiet Life, Madonna Has a Lot to Say," Boston.com (The Boston Globe, June 9, 2005), http://archive.boston.com/ae/celebrity/articles/2005/06/09/despite_living_quiet_life_madonna_has_a_lot_to_say/.

[108] Jim Carrey in Kyle Cease, *The Illusion of Money* (Carlsbad, CA: Hay House Publishers, 2022), 27.

people. His purposes reach beyond love and hate, or we might say happy or sorrowful circumstances.

Ecclesiastes 9:1 | But all this I laid to heart, examining it all, how the righteous and the wise and their deeds are in the hand of God. Whether it is love or hate, man does not know; both are before him.

Whether hateful circumstances or happy circumstances, life is guided by the Lord. The vital thing is to realize that there is a purpose beyond happiness and sorrow. In fact, you cannot use good and bad events as criteria to decide whether God loves you or hates you. Your future may be a mixture of two. When trouble comes, it is easy to ask, "What have I done to deserve this?" It is less easy to ask the same question when happiness comes.[109] The wise person know God's sovereignty over all things. Solomon put it best in his Proverbs.

Proverbs 16:9 | The heart of man plans his way, but the LORD establishes his steps.

Nothing befalls the children of God that doesn't first pass through God's hands. The goal is not the good life, but the godly life! God's purpose is to conform us to the image of Jesus Christ. We are predestined to that purpose (Rom 8:28-29). God doesn't spare the righteous from the flood or fire, but he promises to take us through the flood and the fire.

Isaiah 43:2 | When you pass through the waters, I will be with you; and through the rivers, they shall not overwhelm you; when you walk through fire you shall not be burned, and the flame shall not consume you.

The child of God may feel like he's alone emotionally, but God promises never to leave or forsake us. He's with us in the fire and the flood. He is there to take us through our falls and failures.

Proverbs 37:23-24 | The steps of a good man are ordered by the Lord, and he delights in his way. [24] Though he fall, he shall not be utterly cast down.

One of the things I love about the three-thousand-year-old book of Ecclesiastes is that it does not pretend that life is always nice or fair.

---

[109] Wright, *Ecclesiastes*, 1181.

But God is sovereign in all of life to bring about a greater purpose than happiness or sorrow. That purpose is to glorify him, but "whether it is love or hate, man does not know." Glorifying God is something that goes far beyond love or hate, happiness or sorrow.

The truth is, when you obey God, he may or may not bless you with a happy life on this earth. Think about the saints of God. Jeremiah gets beat up, stripped naked, and thrown into a ditch. Isaiah is sawn in two and dies. Consider what God says about the greatest saints of the Old Testament era.

> *Hebrews 11:35-40* | Some were tortured, refusing to accept release, so that they might rise again to a better life. [36] Others suffered mocking and flogging, and even chains and imprisonment. [37] They were stoned, they were sawn in two, they were killed with the sword. They went about in skins of sheep and goats, destitute, afflicted, mistreated— [38] of whom the world was not worthy—wandering about in deserts and mountains, and in dens and caves of the earth. [39] And all these, though commended through their faith, did not receive what was promised, [40] since God had provided something better for us, that apart from us they should not be made perfect.

The great saints did not get the promises while on this earth, but instead got the opposite. They died, and some were tortured waiting for it. Joseph suffered much in the pit and the prison and in Potiphar's house in slavery. Yet, we read in Genesis 50:20, Joseph's words to his brothers, "As for you, you meant evil against me, but God meant it for good." Joseph's brothers did whatever was in their deceitful hearts, but God worked it all for Joseph's good. And think about our Lord – he was crucified—and this was God's will.

Don't be surprised that a very fulfilling, meaningful life includes both fantastic times and fantastically awful times. Both love and hate are before you—you will experience both as a child of God. What matters is that our heart is submitted to God, that we have an unwavering confidence that all we do is "in the hand of God." A meaningful life goes far beyond the happy and sad times of life. The life of faith is guided by the sovereign hand of God to a higher purpose of glorifying God.

Consider the Taker of Life

The Lord guides the lives of the godly, but all will pass from this earth. Ten out of ten people die. It is the ultimate, unavoidable statistic. Sometimes the good die in awful ways. The evil and wicked often die with great honor. What is true is that a godly, meaningful life will often end in the same way as those who live a meaningless life. Death may happen the same for all.

Ecclesiastes 9:2-3a | It is the same for all, since the same event happens to the righteous and the wicked, to the good and the evil, to the clean and the unclean, to him who sacrifices and him who does not sacrifice. As the good one is, so is the sinner, and he who swears is as he who shuns an oath. **3** This is an evil in all that is done under the sun, that the same event happens to all.

God watches over his children. He guides them through thick and thin. He leads them through the valley of the shadow of death. We don't know what tomorrow will bring. But we do know this. There is coming a day when we will all die. The only thing we can all be sure of is that we are closer to death right now than a minute ago.

Solomon concludes that death is "an evil" (9:3), not simply a natural phenomenon. It is the outworking of rebellion and sin against God. Thankfully the gift of God is eternal life through Jesus Christ (Rom 6:23). Humanity has been cut off from the tree of life. The astonishing thing, however, is that instead of reckoning with the meaning of death, humans fill their lives with the distractions of a thousand passions and squander what little time they have to immediate but insignificant worries.[110]

The redeemed are wise and prepare for death. Yet, do not be surprised if you as a believer die in the same way as the wicked. The righteous and the wicked both die of cancer; both are crushed in hurricanes and tsunamis. Both die alone at times, and both die at times with family surrounding them. Both may die in prison or in freedom. Death is the evidence that something has gone cataclysmically wrong in the universe. Praise the Lord that God has sent his Son to put things right again (Eph 1:7-10).

Consider the Madness of Life

The madness and insanity of sin excludes this life from ever bringing anyone real meaning and purpose in life. If all we have is this life, then truly this is evil and insanity.

---

[110] Garrett, *Ecclesiastes*, 331.

200

Ecclesiastes 9:3b | Also, the hearts of the children of man are full of evil, and madness is in their hearts while they live, and after that they go to the dead.

The most insidious problem of humanity is in the dar, fallen heart of man (Jer 17:9). We are born totally depraved, unable to do that which is truly good. We are unable to live selflessly for God, but instead are selfish beings from our mother's womb (Isa 51:5). This is why death comes to all. People commit acts of lawless violence, like killing police officers. They pursue self-destructive addictions, like sex and drugs. They hurt the people they love the most and need the most, including the members of their own families. We are living in a mad, mad, mad, mad world.[111] This is why without the Lord we are all doomed.

After a life of sinful madness, death levels the field. Death is the great leveler. No matter who we are or how well we live, our time on earth will end in death— "the universal obliterator."[112] In the words of one bumper sticker, "Eat well, stay fit, and die anyway." Death is therefore a predictable and universal event that comes only once upon a person (9:5–6; *cf* Heb 9:27).[113] The believer is ready for that great day when we see the Lord because we know "all things work together for good" (Rom 8:28). Even death is good for the believer because it is the entrance into the eternal kingdom!

Consider the Hope of Life

With such hopelessness in death, where can we find hope? Where there is life there is hope. While we live, we can live for the eternal, not for that which is temporal and "under the sun." We can live meaningful lives of hope and change for the Lord. For those who die without the Lord, they will "forever" have "no more share in all that is done under the sun."

Ecclesiastes 9:4-6 | But he who is joined with all the living has hope, for a living dog is better than a dead lion. **5** For the living know that they will die, but the dead know nothing, and they have no more reward, for the memory of them is forgotten. **6** Their love and

---

[111] Ryken, *Ecclesiastes*, 206.
[112] Kidner, *The Message of Ecclesiastes*, 82.
[113] Rogland, "Ecclesiastes," 1093.

their hate and their envy have already perished, and forever they have no more share in all that is done under the sun.

The principle. Solomon's point is that the living can reckon with the reality of death and in so doing embrace the joy a God-centered life has to offer.[114] If all a person has lived for is this life, "under the sun," even if they lived like a majestic lion, they have truly lost everything and led a meaningless existence. They already have enjoyed their reward, and there is nothing else good for them after death (*cf* Lk 6:24).

The proverb. In this way the proverb rings true. The *lion,* "mightiest of the beasts" (Pro 30:30), was admired in the ancient world. The *dog,* on the other hand, was a despised scavenger (Exo 22:31; 1 Kgs 14:11), notorious for its uncleanness (Pro 26:11).[115] The poor dog of a person who prepares for death by fearing the Lord is far better off than the dead lion of a person who never thought of death, and now is in misery forever. It reminds us of the rich man and the beggar (Lk 16:19-31). The faithless rich man after death lived "in anguish" in the flame so that he couldn't cool his tongue there in Hades. But the poor man who was rich in faith was brought to Abraham's side in God's paradise. What good were the rich man's riches without faith in the Lord?

God's mercy and love extend in this life, but then comes judgment day (Heb 9:27). For the Christian, life and death are both important, and we want to honor God in both. With Paul we have a Christ-centered philosophy of life and death.

Philippians 1:20-21 | Christ will be honored in my body, whether by life or by death. [21] For to me to live is Christ, and to die is gain.

The past. When the dead die, they "know nothing" (9:5a). This is not an argument for annihilationism, but a radical wakeup call that when your life is over, most of what you done is unrecognized, and "the memory of them is forgotten" (9:5b). If all you have is this life, you are eventually forgotten forever.

The perishing. If all you have is this life, it will all perish with you when you die. Solomon's making a very clear distinction between two ways of living. He's saying, "If all you have is what is 'under the sun,' you're done. You have no more influence under the sun. Your love dies,

---

[114] Garrett, *Ecclesiastes,* 331.
[115] Eaton, *Ecclesiastes,* 143.

your hate dies, your envy dies with you. All that you lived for dies. You leave everything here when you die."

Only the living have a hope because they're still alive (9:4a). Jesus asked this question in Mark 8:36, "For what does it profit a man to gain the whole world and forfeit his life?" While we are alive, we can choose to know the Lord, to seek his reward, to make a difference that will last long after we die. Those who die living for what is merely "under the sun" in this life will die having lost everything. Truly, "forever they have no more share in all that is done under the sun." How sad to live for what is so temporal, finite, and fleeting.

THE PRACTICE OF MEANINGFUL LIVING (9:7-10)

Knowing that God is providentially guiding the godly to a higher purpose, we can navigate the difficulties and understand the practice of meaningful living. Let's look at the practice and disciplines of a meaningful, Christ-centered life.

Ecclesiastes 9:7-10 | Go, eat your bread with joy, and drink your wine with a merry heart, for God has already approved what you do. [8] Let your garments be always white. Let not oil be lacking on your head. [9] Enjoy life with the wife whom you love, all the days of your vain life that he has given you under the sun, because that is your portion in life and in your toil at which you toil under the sun. [10] Whatever your hand finds to do, do it with your might, for there is no work or thought or knowledge or wisdom in Sheol, to which you are going.

Solomon tells us we should dive into all that life offers. We are to be all there, giving all that we have to the situation in front of us. Work hard. Play hard. Be all there with your family. And do it all for the glory of God. That's the life God wants us to live on this painful planet.

The Discipline of Enjoying Friends

A meaningful life engages with friends. We see how friendship is connected to food, to laughter, and to worship.

Ecclesiastes 9:7 | Go, eat your bread with joy, and drink your wine with a merry heart, for God has already approved what you do.

Friendship and food. Godly friendships are vital for a growing, meaningful life. Friendships are best enjoyed over food! Eating in

Scripture is almost never alone. It is a picture of friendship and com-
munion. Solomon says, eat dinner! Eat your bread and drink your wine.
He's not saying that we should be hedonists. He's already explained in
the first half of the book that food and pleasure will never satisfy. But if
God has first place in your life, you ought to enjoy the blessings of God
and form God-honoring relationships with people.

Friendship and laughter. Laughing with friends is also prescribed
by Solomon. We are to have "a merry heart." Good food is to be enjoyed
with good friends who have good senses of humor. This is how you
practice for heaven. Encourage people all around you by eating with
them! Jesus certainly enjoyed time with his friends, so much so that
they called him a drunkard and a glutton.

> *Luke 7:34* | The Son of Man has come eating and drinking, and you
> say, 'Look at him! A glutton and a drunkard, a friend of tax collectors
> and sinners!'"

We are commanded to enjoy the gifts God gives us. We have this
same sentiment in the Psalms.

> *Psalm 104:14-15* | You cause the grass to grow for the livestock
> and plants for man to cultivate, that he may bring forth food from the
> earth [15] and wine to gladden the heart of man, oil to make his face
> shine and bread to strengthen man's heart.

Do you want to live deep? Do you want to find significance?
McDonald's in your car is not dinner. Hot pockets in the office are not
dinner. Go home. Spend time with your family. Know your spouse and
your kids. We say life is so busy today. Life was busy then as well. Use
mealtimes to build relationships—and be encouraging to people. Be
"merry." It's a command.

Friendship and worship. Sometimes we try to separate the secular
and the sacred. We think of laughter with friends as separate from singing hymns and listening to preaching. But notice Solomon brings God
into the midst of friendship and laughter. He says you should laugh
with friends "for God has already approved what you do" (9:7b). The
idea is very clear that Solomon is not speaking of hedonism, but of a
godly enjoyment of the gifts of God for the glory of Christ. Remember
the words of Paul.

> *1 Corinthians 10:31* | Whether you eat or drink, or whatever you do, do
> all to the glory of God.

From the small things (like eating and drinking and laughing) to the big things (like prayer and Bible study), everything you do is sacred and should be done for the glory of God. You are accepted by God. You are approved—you are walking in faith—your motive is not mere pleasure but pleasing God. So go ahead and enjoy all things for the Lord.

The Discipline of Enjoying Life

Those who live a meaningful life are a blessing to people, filled with joy, lifting people up.

Ecclesiastes 9:8a | Let your garments be always white.

White garments are a comfort in the unforgiving heat of the middle east. They signify someone enjoying life. White garments were the "dress-up clothes" of the ancient Near East.[116] In both the Old Testament and the New Testament, white garments are symbolic of joy and are worn on joyous, festive occasions.[117] They were worn by war heroes in a victory parade, by slaves on the day they gained their freedom, and by priests on the high holy days of Israel (e.g., 2 Chr 5:12). To put this into a contemporary context, the Preacher is telling us to put on tuxedos and evening gowns so we can dance the night away.[118] Be an encouragement to people. He's saying, "Do dinner, laugh, enjoy friends. Let conversation be deep and rich, smile and enjoy, and then do not stand at the center of your universe." One of the best ways for us to keep the good things of life in their proper perspective is to praise the Giver for all of his gifts.[119]

1 Timothy 4:4 | Everything created by God is good, and nothing is to be rejected *if* it is received with thanksgiving.

You have been blessed to be a blessing. You've been blessed by God. Give thanks, do dinner, and be a blessing to others.

The Discipline of Enjoying God

Ecclesiastes 9:8b | Let not oil be lacking on your head.

---

[116] Ryken, *Ecclesiastes*, 214.

[117] Jay E. Adams, *Life under the Son: Counsel from The Book of Ecclesiastes* (Woodruff, SC: Timeless Texts, 1999), 95.

[118] Ryken, *Ecclesiastes*, 214

[119] Ibid., 218.

Oil, in both the Old Testament and New Testament, is a reference to the anointing presence of God in the Holy Spirit (1 Sam 16:13). It is a symbol of gladness in the Holy Spirit (Psa 45:7). Without a right walk with God, we cannot have an enjoyable, meaningful life. The ancient saints put this upon their head on the way to the tabernacle and temple. Since we are the temple of the Holy Spirit, we should always carry the sweet aroma of Christ in us (*cf* 1 Cor 6:19; 2 Cor 2:15).

Solomon tells us to wear the sweet perfume of worship. We are to do this "day and night," always meditating on the word of the Lord (Psa 1:2). To anoint someone's head with oil (*cf* Psa 23:5) was to pour out something richly scented, like cologne—what the Bible terms "the oil of gladness" (Psa 45:7) in a celebratory worship of Yahweh. This is an important part of getting ready for a celebration—not just looking good but also smelling good, especially in a hot climate. He's saying, get ready for the worship gathering and festival. We are going to worship the Lord![120] Put your worship on—the sweet fragrance of Christ!

The Discipline of Enjoying Family

Ecclesiastes 9:9 | Enjoy life with the wife whom you love, all the days of your vain life that he has given you under the sun, because that is your portion in life and in your toil at which you toil under the sun.

God alone is the source of all the gifts of earthly life. We are to enjoy the bread and wine, the festivity and work, our marriage and love.[121] Enjoy God by enjoying his gifts. Here he specifically compels men to love their wives.

Solomon says, "Enjoy your wife, but remember, it's going to be some work." Keep your gaze on Christ, and you will learn to enjoy your wife and invest in her. You need to enjoy dinner. Talk with your family. Talk with friends. Don't forget the dishes. There are dishes to wash. Beds to make. Diapers to change. Walls to paint. Vehicles to fix. There's going to be some serious work if you want to enjoy your wife. You'll not be able to enjoy your wife if you are not first enjoying God.

I have found through my own marriage, closeness and companionship must be worked at, and it does not come easily. If you really want

---

[120] Ibid.
[121] Kidner, *The Message of Ecclesiastes*, 83.

to want to get really deep down to the core of who your wife is, married men, you are going to need to spend some time with her. You need to learn to communicate.

> 1 Peter 3:7 | Likewise, husbands, live with your wives in an understanding way, showing honor to the woman as the weaker vessel, since they are heirs with you of the grace of life, so that your prayers may not be hindered.

It matters that you talk with her. It matters how you talk with her! We are to listen, "showing honor to the woman as a weaker vessel."

Let's be honest. You cannot enjoy the wife God has given you if you are wishing you were married to someone else. Solomon is basically saying: "The grass is not greener on the other side." And if it is, it's because *you* have stopped watering the grass.

You say, "But you don't understand my husband" or "You don't understand my wife." Listen, if your spouse was at one time lush, green pasture—what happened to the grass? *You* did! Men, water your marriage with deep humility. Honor and cherish your wife. Have compassion toward her weaknesses. Lift her up when she's discouraged. If you want to enjoy life with your spouse, you cannot seek to change them; you need to change you! What is your goal? You will enjoy your spouse once you "toil" and work hard on your own attitudes and reactions.

If you are not right with your spouse, it is very likely that you are not right with God. You are not doing what he's called you to do. In fact, Peter says in the verse we just read, that if you're not right with your spouse, then your prayers are hindered. Enjoy and engage in married life if you are married. Put God at the center of your marriage, and you will find your marriage enjoyable.

The Discipline of Enjoying Work

A meaningful life engages in hard work.

> Ecclesiastes 9:10 | Whatever your hand finds to do, do it with your might, for there is no work or thought or knowledge or wisdom in Sheol, to which you are going.

The Scriptures here are pleading with you to be a good worker. God blessed us with work before the Fall. There is a joy and satisfaction in working hard. Previous generations called this the work ethic. There is something that happens when we've done a good job and get to step back and look at it. There is a feeling that we did a good job, that we accomplished something. You know vacation is going to be difficult for me if there is nothing to do. I can't just go and sit—so we have various activities planned. You know it's true. You come home from vacation sometimes exhausted because it takes more energy than work!!

Let me say something to the younger people. Turn off mine sweep or pac man or wii, or Atari, or whatever it is. Turn off the computer or the video games and do something productive. Parents, I want you to know it drives me crazy to see our young people glued to a portable video game or computer. I allowed it once recently, and it convinced me that it's not a good idea. Parents you need to limit screen time. If your kids are in front of videos, video games, computer, TV for more than a short amount of time a day—you are teaching them to waste time.

Conclusion

Let me paraphrase what Solomon is saying: "Go to dinner and invest in relationships with people. Don't horde everything you've been given. Follow the still small voice of God. Pour into deep relationships, specifically your spouse. Work hard. And in the end, find what God has asked and be obedient to it." So many people are looking for meaning in all the wrong places. On his first assignment for a Chicago newspaper, a rookie reporter drove a company car to a car-crushing plant, parked in the wrong spot, and returned from interviewing the manager just in time to see the vehicle being compacted into scrap metal.[122]

I think so many people are like that reporter, except it's not their car being crushed, it's their life. They invest themselves in something big, but temporal. All temporal things can be taken away. Invest your life in the eternal—that's what counts. People search for the "good life" here on this earth, and they are always severely disappointed. The one who trusts in the Lord will never be disappointed.

---

[122] De Witt Wallace, Lila Acheson Wallace, *The Reader's Digest*, vol 117 (Pleasantville, NY: Reader's Digest Association, July 1980), 128.

16 | ECCLESIASTES 9:11-18

ADMONITIONS FOR MEANINGFUL LIVING

*The words of the wise heard in quiet are better than the shout-
ing of a ruler among fools.*
ECCLESIASTES 9:17

We've all heard of rags to riches Cinderella stories, but have you heard of riches to rags? I read an article recently of Charles Prestwood of Conroe, Texas. Prestwood retired in October 2000 after 33 years at Enron—most of them as a pipeline operator. He applied himself, used his intelligence and hard work for his job and life, and in the end, he had $1.3 million in Enron stock in his 401(k). But after the company collapsed several years ago, he lost every penny. He learned the hard way that you cannot put your trust in anything or anyone on this earth. True happiness and meaning comes from the Lord alone. So many people put their hopes in this life and end up bitterly disappointed.

We know that true joy is not found in attaining the American dream, but in attaining salvation in Christ. Solomon knows that we need to be warned regularly not to put our trust in this world, but to keep our eyes and our gaze fixed on Jesus. Are your eyes fixed on Jesus for happiness and contentment? How can we avoid the heart break that occurs from trusting in man and in riches. How can we live a wise, Christ-centered, fulfilling, and meaningful life?

Ecclesiastes 9:11-18 | Again I saw that under the sun the race is not to the swift, nor the battle to the strong, nor bread to the wise, nor riches to the intelligent, nor favor to those with knowledge, but time and chance happen to them all. [12] For man does not know his time. Like fish that are taken in an evil net, and like birds that are caught in a snare, so the children of man are snared at an evil time, when it suddenly falls upon them. [13] I have also seen this example of wisdom under the sun, and it seemed great to me. [14] There was a little city with few men in it, and a great king came against it and besieged it, building great siegeworks against it. [15] But there was found in it a poor, wise man, and he by his wisdom delivered the city. Yet no one remembered that poor man. [16] But I say that wisdom is better than might, though the poor man's wisdom is despised and his words are not heard. [17] The words of the wise heard in quiet are better than the shouting of a ruler among fools. [18] Wisdom is better than weapons of war, but one sinner destroys much good.

Jeremiah said something similar. "Cursed is the man who trusts in man... blessed is the man who trusts in the LORD" (Jer 17:5-7). Solomon gives us another admonition: "Some trust in chariots and some in horses, but we trust in the name of the LORD our God" (Pro 20:7).

Key thought: The best intelligence and hard work are not enough to have a happy, contented life. We need to look beyond what this world can provide and look to another world, another kingdom for our joy. Trusting in Christ brings meaning and joy to life.

DON'T TRUST IN HUMAN POWER (9:11)

Don't put your trust in your natural abilities. Most people when they get into trouble, they feel like they can "figure it out". They are smart enough to get out of trouble. The wise know that the greatest strengths of the human being are at best limited. We need a larger purpose and firmer foundation than mere human strength, abilities, and giftings.

Human Power Disappoints

Natural abilities can attain only temporary success. Here Solomon describes the "rat race" that no one can win. Exerting every human advantage is like turning your car wheels on ice. All you're going to do is spin the wheels and go nowhere. The best you can hope for from a secular point of view is chance. Solomon speaks from this worldview for a moment to make a point. Without Christ, life is unsatisfying and unpredictable. Five accomplishments are listed, none of which guarantees success or prosperity.[123]

Ecclesiastes 9:11 | Again I saw that under the sun the race is not to the swift, nor the battle to the strong, nor bread to the wise, nor riches to the intelligent, nor favor to those with knowledge, but time and chance happen to them all.

Fast runners do not always win the races. The bravest men do not always win the battles. The wisest do not always earn a living—sometimes they live in poverty. Intelligent people do not always get rich. And the capable people do not always rise to high positions. Life at its core is completely unpredictable.

Life is bigger than success or prosperity. There is a grand purpose beyond the rat race. "Fear God" and follow his commands and his way of living (12:13). This is the life of knowing and growing in God. We call it discipleship. It's the way God designed life to be lived. Amidst the pressures of difficulties, trials, tragedies and sins, the believer is pressed into the mold of Christ.

Don't get sucked into this life of busyness. The rat race is out there, and you can utilize all your natural abilities to win the race, to win the battle, to be very successful, and even to attain high position. But what are you really living for?

Solomon is warning against leaning on our natural abilities. What I've learned is that there are men and women who excel at business from the day they were born. They didn't have to go to business college, they just excel at it. There are guys who excel at being an athlete. They didn't do anything, they were just born, but they were given the right combination of speed and size.

---

[123] Eaton, *Ecclesiastes*, 148.

Think about Shaquille O'Neil, an NBA basketball player. He's 7'3", weighing over 300lbs. But he didn't do anything to get that. He didn't knock on the womb and go, "Alright, I need height and size." God gave it to him. It was a natural gifting. The word of warning here is no matter how successful you are in business, athletics, education, whatever field you're in, natural gifting will never bring about contentment or true meaning and success. True meaning in life is found in fearing God.

The joy of meaningful living is not attained through your natural abilities, but through faith in the Lord. Everything you can attain with your natural abilities can be broken, stolen, tarnished, and eaten by moths and rust. No one has the gift of natural contentment. We must seek supernatural contentment in Christ, living under his love and guidance.

God's Providence Directs

It is not stated, but it is implied that we need something more than natural human power. We need to trust in more than mere human ability or human strength, or human wisdom or human intelligence and knowledge. We need to trust in the Lord's providence and direction.

Ecclesiastes 9:11b | But time and chance happen to them all.

Despite the general pattern of biblical teaching that speaks of long life and blessing to the wise and godly, it is not always the case that those with the greatest physical, intellectual, or spiritual powers will succeed and prevail. Everyone should be prepared to encounter many such anomalies in the course of one's life.[124]

Two things limit all human activity: time and chance. We are all given only so much time. We are all given very limited time on this earth. Some live very short lives, but even the longest of lives is "vapor that appears for a little time and then vanishes away" (Jas 4:14). Chance means that from the human perspective, sudden and unexplainable events take place. Solomon is not abandoning the truth of God's sovereignty over all; he is merely looking at the arbitrary nature of life from a human rather than theological perspective.[125]

Since we are limited beings at best, we must trust in the one who is unlimited, the one who "works all things according to the counsel of his

---

[124] Rogland, "Ecclesiastes," 1094–1095.
[125] Garrett, *Ecclesiastes*, 332.

will" (Eph 1:11). If your goal is to get you what your natural abilities can get you, you are going to get robbed of your contentment and meaning. If your identity is to succeed in the rat race, what happens when sickness or tragedy take your natural ability away? Don't put your identity in the rat race! Don't base your happiness on the rat race! Seek to put God at the center of your life and let him direct your path.

Matthew 6:33 | Seek first the kingdom of God and his righteousness, and all these things will be added to you.

Proverbs 3:5-6, NKJV | Trust in the Lord with all your heart, and do not lean on your own understanding. ⁶ In all your ways acknowledge him, and he will direct your paths.

A brand-new driving student is instructed not to look at the road directly in front of the car's hood. Focusing on what is immediately ahead will result in a beginning driver's swerving from side to side. Instead, new drivers are told to focus their eyes farther down the road. Not only does this help them to see and anticipate potential obstacles or dangers that are approaching, but it helps them to steer more steadily as well. In a similar way Solomon is continually urging his hearers to maintain part of their focus on their ultimate destinies in order to be able to navigate their lives successfully. [126]

DON'T TRUST IN HUMAN PLANS (9:12)

Don't put your trust in your plans if you want to live a wise, meaningful Christ-centered life.

Ecclesiastes 9:12 | For man does not know his time. Like fish that are taken in an evil net, and like birds that are caught in a snare, so the children of man are snared at an evil time, when it suddenly falls upon them.

All your well laid plans can be destroyed with one event. You don't get a meaningful life by mere human planning alone. You can plan for the college education, the family, the house, the car, the kids, the whatever, and it can all be destroyed in a moment. You must trust in the Lord. God might test you with severe illness. You may be a righteous man like Job, but your wife threatens to leave you in your darkest hour.

---

[126] Rogland, *Ecclesiastes,* 1095.

Is your life not meaningful if tragedy occurs? Of course it is, because a meaningful life is not about the swift or the strong or the knowledge and riches you have. Meaningful living is not about your bank account or health care plan. All that could be taken away in a second. That's what Solomon says here.

Things happen that you never can see coming. So, it's better to put your faith in something beyond the sun rather than under it, where in an instant, you can get snared up in it like a bird or get hung up in a fish in a net. Solomon elsewhere gives us good advice.

Proverbs 3:5-6 | Trust in the Lord with all your heart, and do not lean on your own understanding. [6] In all your ways acknowledge him, and he will make straight your paths.

DON'T TRUST IN HUMAN POSITION (9:13-18A)

Don't put your trust in human position if you want to live a wise, meaningful Christ-centered life. All people are placed where they are by the sovereign of God.

Wisdom is Better than Human Politics

Human position is very disappointing. Look at politics from ancient to modern and you will be gravely disappointed. The majority of politicians are not going to appreciate godly wisdom. Solomon tells a story to illustrate this. He basically says, "I saw this thing happen one time, and I think there's a lot of wisdom in it, so pay attention to the story." This story is going to illustrate that true, godly wisdom is often despised on this earth.

Ecclesiastes 9:13-16 | I have also seen this example of wisdom under the sun, and it seemed great to me. [14] There was a little city with few men in it, and a great king came against it and besieged it, building great siegeworks against it. [15] But there was found in it a poor, wise man, and he by his wisdom delivered the city. Yet no one remembered that poor man. [16] But I say that wisdom is better than might, though the poor man's wisdom is despised and his words are not heard.

Whether the poor man delivered the city by diplomacy or military strategy is not the issue. The point is that the city owed its survival to him, but he received no reward or lasting respect. Wisdom is usually sought out only in desperate times; otherwise, the majority of humanity live for themselves with ungrateful, self-centered attitudes.[127]

This means that if you live a wise, godly life, you may not be appreciated by the citizens of earth. People may not listen to your godly wisdom. Are you ok with that? People may profit from your wisdom and then forget you. Are you ok with that? You may not be appreciated in your family or in your marriage for living for God. Are you ok with that? Your workplace may think ill of you for being a Christian. Are you ok with that? Wisdom is often not appreciated.

Yet, in the end, wisdom is always vindicated. This is a test to see if you are truly wise. A truly wise person will walk in wisdom because it is right, not because it is merely helpful or profitable or advantageous. Often wisdom is advantageous, but the truly wise still do the right thing even if they are despised or forgotten.

The point is wisdom is better than human power. Solomon observed it. We can think of prominent examples. How about Isaiah and Hezekiah, with no army against the Assyrian military of 185,000 soldiers. We read about it in 2 Kings.

> *2 Kings 19:35-36* | That night the angel of the Lord went out and struck down 185,000 in the camp of the Assyrians. And when people arose early in the morning, behold, these were all dead bodies. [36] Then Sennacherib king of Assyria departed and went home and lived at Nineveh.

Seeking the author of all power, the one who "removes kings and sets up kings" (Dan 2:21)—is much greater than having massive human power yourself. Human power is so limited compared to true wisdom.

Wisdom is Better than Haughty Rulers

Some will value quiet godly counsel and see the superiority of God-centered wisdom.

> **Ecclesiastes 9:17** | The words of the wise heard in quiet are better than the shouting of a ruler among fools.

A wise man does not feel the need to do a lot of shouting. He knows it is not the loud word that moves people's hearts and changes the world for good, but the wise word.[128]

---

[127] Garrett, *Ecclesiastes*, 334.
[128] Ryken, *Ecclesiastes*, 226.

Right words carry more weight than the politically powerful! What is spoken wisely should be spoken calmly, and then it will be heard with the weight it deserves and calmly considered. The loud spouting of passion lessens the force of reason, instead of adding any force to it.[129]

Set aside the loud and spectacular and quietly consider what would please God. Set aside the mere pragmatic and consider what would honor God. The fear of the Lord is the beginning of wisdom. Stop trying to get the next big idea, politically posturing and using people. Instead, choose to please God with the quiet wisdom of the Spirit from his word.

Do you find the quiet instruction of the word of God in the peace of your private meeting place as a vital part of your life? Are you in the word, reading it over and over and over again? Can you tell me about wisdom from the books of Moses or the prophets or the New Testament? Can you tell me what each book of the Bible is about because you read it so much? That's where you are going to find a meaningful life.

Better than political posturing is the blessing and richness of the Lord through his wisdom.

Wisdom is Better than Human Weapons

Ecclesiastes 9:18a | Wisdom is better than weapons of war.

Godly wisdom is more profitable for peace keeping than the greatest human weapons of war. Wisdom comes from fearing God. That's where the real power in this world can be found.

Think about the Philistines. They had weapons. They had their champion. But David had wisdom, a sling, and a rock (1 Sam 17:1-54). If you have the fear of the Lord, it doesn't matter how small you are!

Think about the apostles. They were unlearned men, and they turned the most powerful, cruel, war mongering empire in the history of the world (Rome) upside down through Christ, the wisdom of God.

This nation (the United States) was founded on the wisdom of the Lord. Our forefathers wanted to put the Lord first. We do have great weapons, but our nation's defense is first and foremost founded on the true wisdom and fear of God. Without the trust that comes from godly wisdom, we would be no different than so many third world countries that have weapons and no wisdom and turn on each other.

---

[129] Henry, *Commentary on the Whole Bible*, 1050.

DO TRUST IN GODLY WISDOM (9:18B)

Will you trust man's power and position or even their armies and weapons. If you trust man, you are cursed, for one sinner can do so much damage.

Don't Trust Man

Ecclesiastes 9:18b | But one sinner destroys much good.

In the end, godly, Christ-centered wisdom is what really makes the difference. We do not trust in perfect people, or perfect political change. Even though wisdom is much more important than weapons of war, yet a perfect outcome is not possible on this earth since, "one sinner destroys much good." Don't trust in the power of wisdom of itself.

Your life must not turn on the hinge of other people's decisions. All it takes is one woman to go, "I will not forgive. I will not forgive him." All it takes is for person to say concerning missions, "I don't care what it says. My money is mine. I'll do what I want with my money." And that attitude can spread. It takes one spouse to say "the marriage is over", and destroy their lives, the children's lives, and many others as well. All it takes is one to say, "Forget the wisdom of God. I'll follow my own wisdom." The warning to all of us is: "Don't be reckless!" Don't play with sin—it will destroy you! If you play with snakes, you might get bit. I know of many children who played with matches and are disfigured today. Sin will do much worse to us. We cannot play with sin.

Genesis 4:7 | Sin is crouching at the door. Its desire is contrary to you, but you must rule over it.

If you trust in yourself, sin will overtake you.

Do Trust the Lord

Ecclesiastes 9:18a | Wisdom is better than weapons of war, but one sinner destroys much good.

Trust in the Giver of wisdom. Why? It's better than weapons of war. Wisdom comes from fearing the Lord. If you don't fear him, you are depending on sinners, and even "one sinner destroys much good" (9:18b). Look how fragile life is. You can make all the right choices, but that's not enough. One sinner can undue it all. The implied point,

218

begging us from the verse is that we should submit to God's guidance and trust him for wisdom. We must trust the Lord implicitly.

The meaningful life is described here over 3000 years ago, and it is still the wisest life you can live.

Philippians 1:21 | For me to live is Christ and to die is gain.

Matthew 6:33 | Seek first the kingdom of God.

Ecclesiastes 12:13 | Fear God and keep his commandments, for this is the whole duty of man.

It's not always popular or very sensational. It doesn't always go along with our plans. It's certainly not attained by natural ability. But it is the most meaningful life a human being can live!

Conclusion

Don't lean on your natural ability. Trust in something bigger than you. And in the end, find what God has asked and be obedient to it. Shine the light of Jesus to others. Be selfless. Trust in God even when you are not appreciated. Trust God when it is not popular. Live a predictable, dependable life of prayer and reading the Scriptures and quietly living them out every day in the smallest areas of life.

As a young man in college, I had various jobs. One interesting one was being a security guard for the largest collection of religious art in the western hemisphere. Several of the artifacts there are now in the Museum of the Bible in Washington, D.C. One of the paintings I guarded was Rembrandt's depiction of Christ. It's considered a masterpiece. Yet compared to how God sees you, that Rembrandt is worthless.

We are called God's "masterpiece" (Eph 2:10). If you want to live a meaningful life, let God do his work in his way through is wisdom. We must not trust in human power and plans. We must trust in the Lord. He's working on his masterpiece. What he has begun, he will complete (Phil 1:6).

17 | ECCLESIASTES 10:1-11

A WARNING AGAINST FOOLISH LIVING

*Dead flies make the perfumer's ointment give off a stench; so a
little folly outweighs wisdom and honor.*
ECCLESIASTES 10:1

People are infamous for not heeding warnings, especially when there are tornadoes or hurricanes. But no one is more infamous at not heeding a warning than the man who lived right near Mount St Helens. The final eruption of Mount St. Helens in May of 1980 was not a sudden event. For two months prior to the massive blast—the most deadly and destructive in American history—earthquakes and volcanic activity signaled a major event was underway. Authorities had plenty of time to sound the alarm and warn those living nearby of the looming danger. Yet despite the seriousness of the threat, some people chose to disregard the warnings.

The best known of those who refused to evacuate was Harry Randall Truman. The eighty-three-year-old man was the owner and caretaker at the Mount St. Helens Lodge at Spirit Lake. He had survived the sinking of his troop ship by a German submarine off the coast of Ireland during World War I, and he was not about to leave just because scientists thought there was danger. Truman told reporters, "I don't have any idea whether it will blow. But I don't believe it to the point that I'm going to pack up." On May 18, 1980, Truman and his lodge were buried beneath 150 feet of mud and debris from the volcanic eruption. His body was never found.[130]

It is foolish to recognize the danger of meaningless living and think that we will somehow be exempt from the consequences if we linger. If we believe Scripture's warnings, we will surely flee from foolish living. A fool is one who forgets God, so to heed the warning, we need to live with Christ at the center of everything.

Ecclesiastes 10:1-11 | Dead flies make the perfumer's ointment give off a stench; so a little folly outweighs wisdom and honor. [2] A wise man's heart inclines him to the right, but a fool's heart to the left. [3] Even when the fool walks on the road, he lacks sense, and he says to everyone that he is a fool. [4] If the anger of the ruler rises against you, do not leave your place, for calmness will lay great offenses to rest. [5] There is an evil that I have seen under the sun, as it were an error proceeding from the ruler: [6] folly is set in many high places, and the rich sit in a low place. [7] I have seen slaves on horses, and princes walking on the ground like slaves. [8] He who digs a pit will fall into it, and a serpent will bite him who breaks through a wall. [9] He who quarries stones is hurt by them, and he who splits logs is endangered by them. [10] If the iron is blunt, and one does not sharpen the edge, he must use more strength, but wisdom helps one to succeed. [11] If the serpent bites before it is charmed, there is no advantage to the charmer.

Let us heed Solomon's warnings to us. He's warning us about the danger of foolish living. Your life is precious. Don't play around with foolishness and sin. It will destroy you in more ways than you can imagine.

Key thought: We need to avoid living like fools who take no thought of God. Truly meaningful living happens when we put God at the center of our thoughts and life.

---

[130] Shirley Rosen, "The Old Man and the Mountain," *The Columbian*, April 1, 2010, https://www.columbian.com/news/2010/apr/01/the-old-man-and-the-mountain/.

IDENTIFYING FOOLS (10:1-3)

Solomon tells us to flee from foolish living, and he ought to know. He has launched into an experiment of sorts, demonstrating that life without the Lord at the center is vain and foolish. Solomon gives us several identifying marks of a fool.

Identity marks can be important. Do you know the difference between a black bear and a brown bear? Knowing the difference could save your life. By the way, it's not just the color. Brown bears can be black and black bears can be brown. One type of brown bear is a grizzly. You've got to play dead with them and hope they walk away. With a black bear, you've got to make yourself look big, waving your arms and making loud noises. If you can't identify the bear, it could be the end of your life.

Our DNA has identity markers. I found out that though my family is from Scotland, my ancestors are mostly Vikings. They invaded Scotland, but the Christians there tamed the Vikings within one generation. DNA can also give us identity markers for diseases within the family. Identity markers can be vital.

Solomon here gives us a warning to avoid foolish living by identifying the essence of a fool. The first identity marker is that they are careless with their lives. They work so hard only to throw it all away.

Fools are Careless

Here's Solomon's first warning: fools are careless and can ruin a lot of good with a little bit of folly. They can have everything in their lives together, but they make excuses in one or two areas of their life, and it sinks them.

Ecclesiastes 10:1 | Dead flies make the perfumer's ointment give off a stench; so a little folly outweighs wisdom and honor.

Carelessness can destroy a lot of good in your life. It doesn't take much to ruin what has the potential for much blessing. A little fly in the perfume gives off a disgusting stench. In the same way a little sinful activity cancels out a great deal of wisdom.[131]

Though miniscule, they flies can ruin a lovely fragrance and not only make it a stench, but actually turn it into an instrument for

---

[131] Garrett, *Ecclesiastes*, 334.

destruction. The phrase "dead flies" renders the Hebrew "flies of death," which could be speaking of flies that bring death by spreading deadly diseases. [132] In the same way, we are reminded of the Old Testament's "Baal-zebub," or "lord of the flies" (2 Kgs 1:2–3, 6, 16) who makes his appearance in the New Testament as "Beelzebul," that is, the "prince of demons" (Mt 12:24).[133] Satan loves sending killer flies our way.

It's like a story I'm told that occurred before I was born but will never be forgotten. My cousin, Tom Black, saved up all his money and bought a brand new 1967 Shelby Cobra. Had he kept it until today it would be worth around five million dollars. Sadly, as he was driving it home from the dealer, with no insurance, he got distracted and totaled his brand-new car. The pristine automobile was now a pile of scrap. A little folly destroys the very best of things. One small moment of indiscretion has power to ruin not just a car, but a life.

Of course, we are not concerned about cars here, but the lives of people. Remember all sin is influenced by the "lord of flies," the "prince of the power of the air" (Eph 2:2). Giving into sin is inviting the enemy's demonic stench into your life. With a little sin in your life, he can destroy a lot of good. And he's got a lot of killer flies to send your way.

You could have built a reputation in your life for many years, over a period of twenty or thirty years. You could be known for being a wise and honorable citizen. And then, in a moment of foolishness, you can mar that reputation. A tiny amount of folly may destroy a family, ruin a reputation, bring heartache into a marriage.[134]

Think of the pastor who faithfully serves, and then ends in a moral crash. Sad, but it happens every day. The tempter stops at nothing and no one and we are all prone to have a great fall. I can tell you that I have clean hands and a pure heart. I am blameless by the grace of God. But there is no one, including pastors and teachers of the word, that are above temptation. I often pray to the Lord: If I am going to compromise my testimony, please kill me before it would ever happen. Jill and I have prayed since we were teenagers. "Lord, do not allow us to enter

---

[132] Rogland, "Ecclesiastes," 1098.

[133] Ibid.

[134] Alistair Begg, "Dead Flies and Little Birds," *Truth For Life* (A Study in Ecclesiastes, December 8, 2002), https://www.truthforlife.org/resources/sermon/dead-flies-and-little-birds/.

into ministry if we are going to bring shame and dishonor to your name."

These killer flies come in many shapes and sizes. There may be some young ladies and young men that have kept themselves pure, but in a night of heated passion will lose their purity and give away that which is priceless, and dirty what God intends to be precious and reserved for a man who has pledged his life to that girl for life. You have that perfume spoiled by the nasty fly of fornication.

You may have a good reputation, but your habit of gossip is tarnishing your testimony. You love the Lord and have served him for many years, but you are hooked on a substance or drugs or on alcohol. You think you can have a few and be ok, but if you're honest, you know you are hooked. You are an honorable man or woman, but you have a life dominating sin of pornography that no one knows about. You have the reputation of being godly, but behind closed doors, you are often flaming with anger and pride. Perhaps you love the word of God and have much of it hidden in your heart, but when things go wrong your mouth is filled with curse words and bitterness. There could be a husband or wife who, in a moment of despair throws away ten, twenty, or thirty years of marriage for some relief in the arms of a forbidden lover. Don't allow you're the pain in your life to blind you. Don't allow those killer flies into your life.

Solomon is telling all of us to not be careless but wise. Your life is precious. Handle it with care. Get rid of these deadly flies. Don't allow Satan, the lord of the flies, to ruin your testimony. Walk in the light. Bring it out in the open and clean up that perfume so that you can be an aroma for Christ.

If you have some killer flies in the ointment of your life, the Lord of grace and mercy can heal that ointment and cleanse you from the stench of sin and Satan. Look to the cross for forgiveness and restoration. Be wise and flee the flies of foolishness and sin.

Fools Can Be Brilliant

Foolish people are not necessarily stupid people. Some of the most brilliant people in the world are fools that live a meaningless life. Folly stinks up the lives of some of the most brilliant and wise and honorable people! It comes to characterize a person. A little folly stinks so much that it far outweighs all the wisdom and honor of a man's life.

Ecclesiastes 10:1 | Dead flies make the perfumer's ointment give off a stench; so a little folly outweighs wisdom and honor.

Think of Einstein. We know him as the most brilliant scientist ever to live. God is not impressed with Einstein's knowledge. God gave Einstein that knowledge. If Einstein's brilliance were cologne, it would be the best kind. But Einstein was also a notorious fornicator. He lived a very scandalous life, especially at the time, rejecting marriage, and instead shacking up with his girlfriend. In understanding so much, he denied the existence of a personal God. The man was so brilliant, but so foolish.

Another modern example is Elon Musk. Here is a man with a genius level IQ of 155, the founder of PayPal, Tesla, and SpaceX, yet when asked about God, considers himself agnostic.[135] How can someone who is so brilliant miss the biggest and most important thing? Because a person can be brilliant and be a fool at the same time.

The fool trusts in himself and in his own brilliance. He counsels himself that with all his or her brilliance, a little folly is permissible. We as God's people are called to abandon foolishness and walk in true wisdom. What is true wisdom? It's abandoning all hope in yourself and in your own wisdom, and it's taking refuge in Christ and his word by faith.

Fools Are Controlled by the Flesh

Ecclesiastes 10:2 | A wise man's heart inclines him to the right, but a fool's heart to the left.

With apologies to left-handers, the Bible generally treats the right side as the good side: "The right hand was associated with a strength which saves, supports and protects."[136] One paraphrase I think gets the gist of it: "A wise man's heart leads him aright, but a fool's heart leads him astray" (Jerusalem Bible). The wise person is led by the Spirit of God, and a fool is led by his own fallen thinking. At a basic minimum

---

[135] Terry Mattingly, "On Religion: Elon Musk, the Babylon Bee and the Teachings of Jesus," *Herald/Review Media* (Sierra Vista, AZ: Herald/Review Media, February 20, 2022), https://www.myheraldreview.com/news/faith/on-religion-elon-musk-the-babylon-bee-and-the-teachings-of-jesus/article_da8e400e-749a-11ec-9b9d-bf1c09ce6f83.html.

[136] Eaton, *Ecclesiastes*, 133.

THE PROCLAIM COMMENTARY: ECCLESIASTES

this proverb is teaching that the wise and fools are headed in opposite directions.[137]

The Heart of the Wise

Ecclesiastes 10:2a | A wise man's heart inclines him to the right.

The wise or regenerate person has a new nature that inclines him to do what is right. He trusts in the Lord and has no confidence in himself.

Philippians 3:3 | We are the circumcision, who worship by the Spirit of God and glory in Christ Jesus and put no confidence in the flesh

The Spirit of God leads the child of God into holiness (*cf* Eze 36:25-27; Eph 4:22-24). The wise do not trust their own heart. We crucify our own finite understanding (Pro 3:5-6). The wise person will choose to please God in the depth of his heart. There is a struggle, but God's child yields to the Spirit.

Galatians 5:16-17 | I say, walk by the Spirit, and you will not gratify the desires of the flesh. [17] For the desires of the flesh are against the Spirit, and the desires of the Spirit are against the flesh, for these are opposed to each other, to keep you from doing the things you want to do.

It's not that God's people are rid of the old nature, but we are dead to it and alive to God (Rom 6:11). While the sinful nature wars against us, we already have the victory over it, but it requires crucifixion to the flesh to gain that victory (Rom 7:21-25; Gal 5:24). We crucify the flesh by walking in the Spirit (Gal 5:16, 25). We now have eyes to see our flesh and fallen thinking for what it is: dangerous and destructive. The wise person does not have confidence in his own fallen and finite perception of reality. We are very, very prone to making wrong judgments with our heart. As the old hymn says, "Prone to wander, Lord, I feel it—prone to leave the God I love."[138] We don't lean on our own understanding, but we instruct our heart with the word of God. Only then can God's word be a lamp to our feet and a light to our path (Psa 119:105). A

---

[137] Roland E. Murphy and Elizabeth Huwiler, *Proverbs, Ecclesiastes, Song of Songs* (Grand Rapids, MI: BakerBooks, 1999), 101.

[138] Robert Robinson, "Come Thou Fount of Every Blessing," *Wyeth's Repository of Sacred Music, Part Second* (1758, repub., State College, PA: Pennsylvania State University Press, 1964).

swimmer in the ocean of life is quite vulnerable, but when we have the radar and submarine of God's word, our ability to see clearly is infinitely enhanced.

The Heart of the Fool

Ecclesiastes 10:2b | But a fool's heart to the left.

The fool's own heart leads him astray. He is "dead in trespasses and sins," enslaved to the world, the flesh, and the devil (Eph 2:1-3). Solomon tells us that the fool leads by his "gut"—how he feels in the moment. He's led by animal instinct instead of God-centered wisdom. There is a selfish nature in all of us—what the Bible calls "the flesh," and it always leads to foolishness. The fool trusts in himself. He doesn't think in the moment of temptation about the future, about what might happen, only the here and now. What feels good right now is what guides the fool into recklessness. The fool has an unchanged heart, and he hopes in himself and in his own corrupted way of thinking. He thinks he's right.

Proverbs 14:12 | There is a way that seems right to a man, but its end is the way to death.

The human heart can lead us terribly astray. The fool's heart leads him to the world. He's intoxicated by it. Most of the world's population is controlled by their emotions, by their lust, by their pleasures. People let their heart lead, and they end up as addicts, or they end up divorced and alone. They end up losing so much. They don't see it coming because they are self-deceived.

Jeremiah 17:9 | The heart is deceitful above all things, and desperately sick; who can understand it?

We cannot hope to be led in the right way without help from above. Truly we rejoice with the Psalmist, "the testimony of the LORD is sure, making wise the simple" (Psa 19:7). Which way does your heart incline—toward God or away from him? Do you have a growing appetite for the word of God, or does the Bible taste stale? Are you moving toward or away from God in prayer? Are you getting more serious about sin, or have you stopped pursuing personal sanctification? Understand that the inclination of the heart determines the direction of the life.

Fools Lack Sense

Fourth, the fool demonstrates his foolishness, yet he himself is unaware. He lacks godly character or good sense. Everyone but him seems to know it!

Ecclesiastes 10:3 | Even when the fool walks on the road, he lacks sense, and he says to everyone that he is a fool.

Sin is so blinding that it will deceive the sinner. The fool is self-deceived. He believes his own foolishness and is unaware of his own folly. It does not take much to see the evidence of foolishness because it is on display in a fool in the normal conduct of life.[139] Even a Christian for a time can become foolish. Peter says that if a Christian is not growing in the faith, he can become "so nearsighted that he is blind, having forgotten that he was cleansed from his former sins" (2 Pet 1:9).

The idea is when the fool is walking down the street in public, the way he acts and the way he talks expresses to everyone that he is a fool. The fool thinks he's the center of the universe. He revels and celebrates his own folly. A fool is not teachable but thinks he already knows it all.

Proverbs 18:2 | A fool takes no pleasure in understanding, but only in expressing his opinion.

Proverbs 12:15 | The way of a fool is right in his own eyes, but a wise man listens to advice.

Don't ever think you can't learn something from someone. Be teachable. Be humble. Listen and consider what you hear. How do you get sense and wisdom? Before you walk down the street—before you go out in public, get alone with God! He is the way, the truth, and the life. You want to walk the way with sense, get to know Christ and his word.

You may ask, how do you deal with such people? Solomon tells us in the rest of the chapter how to avoid foolish living.

AVOIDING FOOLISH LIVING (10:4-11)

How are we to deal with those whose lives are meaningless and full of folly? Folly is simply life without God. Unbelief is the root of all sin.

Psalm 14:1 | The fool has said in his heart, no God.

---

[139] Belcher, *Ecclesiastes*, 346.

How do you deal with those who live meaningless lives? You put God at the very center of your life, walking in the light of his presence and wisdom. Solomon now begins to contrast the fool with a person of wisdom and the fear of the Lord. The first mark of a wise person is calmness and self-control.

Be Calm

Calmness in the midst of chaos is a wonderful mark of one who fears the Lord. We can be calm with the most foolish of people. Solomon gives a specific example of calmness with an unhinged ruler. When dealing with a fool, even if he's a high official, don't be controlled by your emotions.

Ecclesiastes 10:4 | If the anger of the ruler rises against you, do not leave your place, for calmness will lay great offenses to rest.

How do the wise deal with someone who blows their top? Solomon tells us, "Don't leave the room. Don't storm out. Be calm." The God fearer is always more concerned about the presence of the Lord than the presence of man, even if the man is a great ruler. Often the deference that is seen will "lay great offenses to rest" and bring the powerful ruler back to his senses.

When we get angry, most of us are tempted to either clam up or blow up. A growing Christian is going to do neither. We grow in nine-fold aspects of the fruit of the Spirit, one of which is "self-control" (*cf* Gal 5:22-23). Solomon goes further in another proverb.

Proverbs 25:28 | A man without self-control is like a city broken into and left without walls.

Some men can control and guide companies, but they cannot control their own heart or their words. The fool is often controlled by emotions, and that includes fools in high places. God's people are called to walk in the calming presence of God. Fearing God brings a calmness to the soul even in the most chaotic situations.

Be Alert

Be alert. Solomon tells us that folly is found in every place. And wisdom can be found in the most unlikely places. The wise person stays alert to the fact that when fools are in charge, there is a reversal of the right order of society.[140] Fools are exalted and the wise are set aside as slaves.

Ecclesiastes 10:5-7 | There is an evil that I have seen under the sun, as it were an error proceeding from the ruler: [6] folly is set in many high places, and the rich sit in a low place. [7] I have seen slaves on horses, and princes walking on the ground like slaves

In the Old Testament horses were associated with royalty and with the wise and rich.[141] Solomon is saying that we live in a maddening world where the wicked are in power and the righteous are left behind. In this inversion of society, stupidity, folly, immorality, and wickedness is exalted and put up like a crown achievement to be pursued. And sadly, those who are competent and have integrity are treated like slaves who walk on the side of the road. "Truth is trampled in the streets" (Isa 59:14). Woe to us when those in power are "those who call evil good and good evil" (Isa 5:20).

You can tell where a society is at by looking at who it honors. A hundred years ago, the famous people were doctors and scientists and astronauts. Now, you can't turn on the TV without learning about the "idiot of the day." Today we don't have news, we have something called "infotainment." It's basically the "freak of the week", and people get famous for being stupid. And if you are really, really stupid, you might even get your own reality TV show! People who ought to be penniless because they are fools, are actually making money off their own stupidity.

That which should be exalted is thrown to the side like a slave. And that which should be despised is celebrated. Wickedness and folly are celebrated, and righteousness and godliness are despised.

Be Harmless

Solomon then warns us to understand folly's destructive nature. The wise person is not conniving and manipulative. He gives a proverb how a manipulative person will usually pay a high price. The wise know that those who serve themselves will eventually hurt themselves.

---

[140] Belcher, *Ecclesiastes*, 348.
[141] Schultz, "Ecclesiastes," 447.

Ecclesiastes 10:8 | He who digs a pit will fall into it, and a serpent will bite him who breaks through a wall.

Dig a pit to trap someone, and you are likely to fall in it! Break through a wall to steal something, and you might find a snake lurking for you! While the consequences of sin are not always this immediate, anyone who does evil is taking an unnecessary and dangerous risk. We always reap what we sow, though it's not always immediately recognizable.

The wise flee from manipulative practices and are harmless. Jesus said his people were to be "shrewd as snakes and as innocent as doves" (Mt 10:16, NIV). God's child is innocent as a dove, not seeking malice against anyone. But he is wise, not easily fooled or taken advantage of. Jesus said his followers are to "turn the other cheek" and "resist not evil" (Mt 5:39) recognizing sometimes the godly will have to suffer harm, but that we need not be self-seeking or looking for vengeance. We trust God is working out his perfect plan, so manipulation and vengeance are worthless to us.

Be Ready

The godly are responsible and think through their actions. They don't just drift through life. They are ready and sharp in their character. They avoid the destructive nature of a fool. A fool takes no advice and very little precaution as we see from Solomon's proverbs.

Ecclesiastes 10:9-10 | He who quarries stones is hurt by them, and he who splits logs is endangered by them. **10** If the iron is blunt, and one does not sharpen the edge, he must use more strength, but wisdom helps one to succeed.

In quarrying large stones, there is great danger to be injured or maimed. In cutting logs, my wife's family will tell you that it's great money, but you might die if a tree falls on you. If you don't sharpen your knife, you'll have to use more muscle.

Some of these things seem so elementary, yet most of us are like proud people who don't want to read instructions! If you take such care in your secular work of logging or quarrying, how much more should you seek the wisdom of God, since "wisdom helps one to succeed." According to 2 Peter 1:3, the word of God has everything we need for life and godliness. When we refuse to look into it and take heed to it, we are going to get hurt! Be responsible to apply God's wisdom to your life in every area (*cf* Psa 1:1-3).

Be Courageous

Finally, Solomon tells us in a proverb that there is danger in not applying the wisdom and understanding we already have.

Ecclesiastes 10:11 | If the serpent bites before it is charmed, there is no advantage to the charmer.

In ancient times, before there was animal control, there were those who knew how to deal with snakes. They were called "charmers." You see them in the cartoons caricatured, but it was something that was necessary, as Solomon alludes to. If the charmer waits to use his skill and as a result gets bit, his charming skill is of no use to him. The charmer has to be courageous and waste no time in charming the snake, otherwise, it could be the end of the charmer.

What is Solomon saying? If you have wisdom stored up in your mind but don't live it out and walk in it in your life, it will be of no use to you. If you know the word and don't apply the word, it does you no good. You're going to get bitten by the world! If you know you need to cut off a temptation and you leave it there, you shouldn't be so surprised when you fall. You may miss the bite here and there, but eventually you are going to get bitten!

Conclusion

So how should we approach the foolishness of sin? How should we approach those whose lives are so prone to foolishness and sin? The most merciful thing we can do is to warn people of the frailty and uncertainty of life and the imminence of their ultimate meeting with God. Our message hasn't changed. Turn from this world of sin. It's folly. Turn in faith to Jesus. He will save you. Life can end suddenly. Sin is destructive. Without Christ's mercy, you will pay for your own sin in hell forever. Repent and turn to Christ. Live for him.

Walking in this world without Christ is like driving in a blizzard. When I was only nineteen years old, I took a trip to Harrisburg, Pennsylvania in the middle of a blizzard. At one time it started snowing sideways! We saw semitrucks jackknifed on both sides of the road, and visibility was limited. We turned on the radio and heard the warnings: "Blizzard advisory: visibility limited. Shelter in place." We took the next exit and found a motel just before they sold their last vacancy. The next morning, we couldn't even find our van in the parking lot. It was buried, so we were stuck there for an entire day before we could make our way back on the highway. We heard of those who stayed on the road and the pile up of cars. We could have been one of them.

You hear about these fifty car pile ups in the fog or snow or rain. That's how it is in the world living without Christ. There are blizzards of foolishness, and you will skid out and destroy your life. Stay sheltered and safe in Christ with great wisdom and fear of the Lord. Be careful! Be wise! Walk with Christ. Avoid meaningless living!

18 | ECCLESIASTES 10:12-20

THE WASTE OF A MEANINGLESS LIFE

The lips of a fool consume him.
ECCLESIASTES 10:12

John Piper shares a story from the February 1998 edition of Reader's Digest, which tells about a couple who "took early retirement from their jobs in the Northeast five years ago when he was 59 and she was 51. Now they live in Punta Gorda, Florida, where they cruise on their 30-foot trawler, play softball, and collect shells."

This is what a lot of people are banking on! That they can get to the end of their life and do nothing! What a waste! This is the dream: Come to the end of your life—your one and only precious, God-given life—and let the last great work of your life, before you give an account to your Creator, be this: playing softball and collecting shells. Picture them before Christ at the great day of judgment: "Look, Lord. See my shells." That is a tragedy.[142] Most people waste their life and live for trinkets. They live for that which is passing away!

---

[142] John Piper, *Don't Waste Your Life* (Wheaton, IL: Crossway Books, 2018), 46.

Key thought: Everything in a life without Christ is wasted. Our words, our work, our purpose, our potential, and even our peace are all thrown to the side as meaningless things that last only for this life.

Three thousand years ago, the wisest man ever to live (outside of the Lord) wrote a book telling us not to waste our life. Let's listen to what he had to say.

Ecclesiastes 10:12-20 | The words of a wise man's mouth win him favor, but the lips of a fool consume him. **13** The beginning of the words of his mouth is foolishness, and the end of his talk is evil madness. **14** A fool multiplies words, though no man knows what is to be, and who can tell him what will be after him? **15** The toil of a fool wearies him, for he does not know the way to the city. **16** Woe to you, O land, when your king is a child, and your princes feast in the morning! **17** Happy are you, O land, when your king is the son of the nobility, and your princes feast at the proper time, for strength, and not for drunkenness! **18** Through sloth the roof sinks in, and through indolence the house leaks. **19** Bread is made for laughter, and wine gladdens life, and money answers everything. **20** Even in your thoughts, do not curse the king, nor in your bedroom curse the rich, for a bird of the air will carry your voice, or some winged creature tell the matter.

Living this life without Christ is a total waste. Jesus asked an important question in Matthew 16.

Matthew 16:26 | What will it profit a man if he gains the whole world and forfeits his life? Or what shall a man give in return for his life?

This wasted life begins with the words of a fool. Those who do not know Christ spend a lot of their words on selfishness and sin. This leads to complete madness and to a person ending up in eternity without Christ.

FOOLS WASTE THEIR WORDS (10:12-14)

Ecclesiastes 10:12-13 | The words of a wise man's mouth win him favor, but the lips of a fool consume him. **13** The beginning of the words of his mouth is foolishness, and the end of his talk is evil madness.

Words are indicators of the state of our heart. When Solomon speaks on how to spot a fool or a wise person, the first marker is to take note of their words. Jesus taught us to understand a person's heart, examine their words.

Matthew 12:34 | How can you speak good, when you are evil? For out of the abundance of the heart the mouth speaks.

The Wise Person's Words Edify

The heart of a wise person is evident by his words.

Ecclesiastes 10:12a | The words of a wise man's mouth win him favor.

What is really said is that his words are literally "grace." Certainly, wise words include charm as well as kindness; but the wise person at their best is disinterested in any self-interest. Words identify what is in the heart. True wisdom springs from the basic humility which is the beginning of a heart of wisdom.[143] The wise person is gracious and is empathetic to the good of others. Paul likely had this verse in mind when he instructed the believers at Colossae and Ephesus about their speech.

Colossians 4:6 | Let your speech always be gracious, seasoned with salt, so that you may know how you ought to answer each person.

Ephesians 4:29 | Let no corrupting talk come out of your mouths, but only such as is good for building up, as fits the occasion, that it may give grace to those who hear.

The wise man is not self-centered or self-serving but is generous and gracious to others with his words. The wise person's words win him favor because they are rational, reasonable, respectful, easy to listen to, pure and sincere, and bring the advantage of genuine wisdom to the person who hears them. James speaks of this gracious wisdom.

James 3:17 | The wisdom from above is first pure, then peaceable, gentle, open to reason, full of mercy and good fruits, impartial and sincere.

These words are obviously kind, appropriate, helpful and attractive.[144] Very simply, his words will edify and help others around him to grow. To see the stark contrast between the wise man and the fool, you simply need to examine their words. The fool's words are self-destructive.

---

[143] Kidner, *The Message of Ecclesiastes*, 92.
[144] Eaton, "Ecclesiastes," 617.

The Fool's Words are Self-Destructive

A fool according to Psalm 14 is very simply someone who denies or forgets God. Solomon tells us how the greatest danger of the fool's words are towards his own self.

Ecclesiastes 10:12b | But the lips of a fool consume him.

In contrast to the wise person's words, the fool's words are destructive. Literally, the words of a fool "eat him up." Because the fool is morally opposed to God, he becomes mentally unstable. He cannot control his inner being. His words are like piranhas, they swim out of his mouth only to devour him. His words consume him by damaging his reputation (10:3), setting a trap for his own life, leaving him in ruin (Pro 14:3; 18:7). The fool blurts out whatever is on his mind and doesn't stop to consider who might be hurt by it, and in the end, he destroys himself, alone, with no one to help him.[145] There he is on judgment day, alone before God, condemned by his own words that demonstrate his unbelief. Because of his words, he is consigned to eternal torment in the lake of fire (Mt 12:36ff; *cf* Rev 20:11-15)[146] Only with God's help through a change of heart can we learn to control our tongue.

Matthew 15:18-20 | What comes out of the mouth proceeds from the heart, and this defiles a person. [19] For out of the heart come evil thoughts, murder, adultery, sexual immorality, theft, false witness, slander. [20] These are what defile a person.

We cry out with David:

Psalm 141:3 | Set a guard, O LORD, over my mouth; keep watch over the door of my lips!

The words that come out of our mouth reveal our spiritual state. This is why Solomon told his young son Rehoboam to guard his heart.

Proverbs 4:23 | Keep your heart with all vigilance, for from it flow the springs of life.

The only way to control the tongue is to transform the heart. In the end, the lost will be brought before Christ on the day of judgment, and

---

[145] Wiersbe, *Be Satisfied*, 119.
[146] Eaton, *Ecclesiastes*, 154.

their words will "eat them up" and "consume" them. Words are fitting evidences as to who we love and what we live for.

The Fool's Words are Depraved

Ecclesiastes 10:13 | The beginning of the words of his mouth is foolishness, and the end of his talk is evil madness.

The source of the foolish talk is traced to the inner character (*cf* Mt 12:34).[147] The beginning of all his words is foolishness, because he has a foolish, God-forgetting heart. While this is sad, an unbeliever leads himself to irrationality and madness, because sin is irrational at it's core. The end of his talk is evil madness or "delusion."[148] Sin can never be satisfied, so depraved madness most certainly ensues. The heart of a fool produces a mouth that is a cesspool. What kinds of words do fools utter? They utter depraved words that are evil madness.

Abusive words are depraved. Paul says that we are to "put away" all sinful speech, including "obscene talk from your mouth" (Col 3:8). The word obscene means "filthy, abusive, and vulgar."[149] The lost person talks this way. Anyone who continues in abusive talk and won't acknowledge their sin will not inherit the kingdom of heaven. This is the teaching of the New Testament.

1 Corinthians 6:9-10 | Or do you not know that the unrighteous will not inherit the kingdom of God? Do not be deceived: neither the sexually immoral... nor revilers [*verbal abusers*] ... will inherit the kingdom of God.

Do depraved words flow from your mouth on a regular occasion? Cursing at your spouse or another person is abuse. Someone who swims in verbal abuse will not inherit heaven. God delivers his children from abusive talk.

Sexually explicit words are depraved. Sex talk outside of marriage is filthy talk. If you have sexually suggestive speech, you are a fool. Do you watch and listen to filthy things? Moral depravity flows from the heart. If you watch the filth of porn, or you look at it, even so-called

---

[147] Eaton, *Ecclesiastes*, 154.
[148] Belcher, *Ecclesiastes*, 353.
[149] Johannes P. Louw and Eugene Albert Nida, *Greek-English Lexicon of the New Testament: Based on Semantic Domains* (New York: United Bible Societies, 1996), 392.

"soft porn," it's because your heart longs for filth. You are a rebel, and you need to repent.

1 Corinthians 6:9-10, NLT | Don't fool yourselves. Those who indulge in sexual sin...—none of these will inherit the Kingdom of God.

Deceptive, sneaky words are depraved. The lost, unbelieving fool lies regularly. He or she doesn't want accountability, so they are willing to lie even about even non-important things. They lie to themselves first and foremost. Self-deception is the greatest poison because it means you believe your own lies. If you are a fool, then you are hiding from God, hiding from accountability. You are comfortable living with lies. If you will not walk in the light with other believers with accountability, then you may have a lying heart. A lying heart will exclude a person from heaven.

Revelation 21:8 | All liars shall have their part in the lake which burns with fire and brimstone, which is the second death.

Unfortunately, much of the mass media is dominated by those who pull down moral standards with their words rather than build them up.[150] They use their words and shows to normalize sin, so that their "evil madness" of depravity seems ordinary and even right.

The Fool's Words Lack Self-Control

Jesus said, "Out of the abundance of the heart the mouth speaks" (Mt 12:34). And the fool's words flow and multiply. They just slip out of his or her mouth without self-control.

Ecclesiastes 10:14 | A fool multiplies words, though no man knows what is to be, and who can tell him what will be after him?

The fool also spews out far too many words. This verbosity arises from too high a regard for his own opinions.[151] Not only is the fool given to endless talk, but he even boldly boasts about his plans and purposes. He has no trust in God, so he feels he can create his own future. He's the "master of his own destiny."[152] A wise person on the other hand speaks very few words.

---

[150] Wright, *Ecclesiastes*, 1187.
[151] Garrett, *Ecclesiastes*, 336.
[152] Leale, *Ecclesiastes*, 147.

Proverbs 17:27-28 | Whoever restrains his words has knowledge, and he who has a cool spirit is a man of understanding. [28] Even a fool who keeps silent is considered wise; when he closes his lips, he is deemed intelligent.

An amazing thing happens to us when we get saved. We begin a battle. We start wrestling against our flesh and putting to death our sinful nature. That battle shows up in our words. If your words haven't changed then you cannot claim a true born-again experience. For the true believer, we can testify that we don't talk like we used to. That means sometimes things go through our mind that we have to reject. But someone who doesn't know Christ or a believer who is losing this battle, will often say whatever comes to mind.

2 Corinthians 10:5, KJV | Casting down imaginations, and every high thing that exalts itself against the knowledge of God, and bringing into captivity every thought to the obedience of Christ.

If you are growing in Christ, you will learn not to speak before you think. A true believer speaks intentionally to edify, not mindlessly for pride and self-indulgence. Whether we eat or drink or, I might add, speak, we do all to the glory of God (1 Cor 10:31), knowing that "every careless word" will be taken into account at the day of Christ (Mt 12:36). The one who does not have his eyes on Christ just says whatever comes to mind.

FOOLS WASTE THEIR PURPOSE (10:15)

Fools waste their purpose for living. We often ask, "Where did we come from and where are we going?" The fool works hard but he easily loses his way to his goal.

Ecclesiastes 10:15 | The toil of a fool wearies him, for he does not know the way to the city.

A fool is truly lost. He has no purpose. He can't find his way to his destination. He doesn't know what his purpose in life. Life wearies him.

A Christian has the end goal in mind. He is ultimately toiling for a city "not made with [human] hands" that is not located on this earth (Heb 9:11). It's a place that Paul describes as "eternal in the heavens" (2 Cor 5:1). Our ultimate purpose is to be "conformed to the image" of Jesus Christ (Rom 8:29). When your days are filled with headaches and frustration, sadness, disappointment and even serious tragedy and ill-ness, your purpose of knowing Christ gives you strength to carry on (Neh 8:10).

The person without Christ who doesn't know where he's going, what he's trying to be, what he's trying to accomplish, they tend to get exhausted by life because they're walking, but they're not going any-where. They exemplify the treadmill that is so apparent through Eccle-siastes, running their guts out but not going anywhere.

Solomon is saying that a person who has no idea where he's going, no idea who he's trying to become, no idea what life holds for him, no goals, not going anywhere, tend to get overwhelmed and wearied by life and lose their way.

FOOLS WASTE THEIR POTENTIAL (10:16-17)

Fools waste their potential. The following verses are applied to the national leadership but give principles to us all. Whole nations choose fools who act like self-indulgent children to be their rulers. They may be gifted, but they are so self-indulgent they waste their potential.

Ecclesiastes 10:16-17 | Woe to you, O land, when your king is a child, and your princes feast in the morning! **17** Happy are you, O land, when your king is the son of the nobility, and your princes feast at the proper time, for strength, and not for drunkenness!

Solomon says that the nation is cursed who have foolish rulers who live self-indulgent lives and often neglect the needs of their subjects. And oh, how happy is the land whose rulers exercise proper self-re-straint for they can greatly benefit their nations (1 Kgs 3:9–14, 28).[153] The picture of the 'child', petulant, is contrasted with 'the son of nobles', someone who may well be as young, but who has grown into his posi-tion and has been prepared for it.[154]

We live in such a situation today in the United States. The strong, well-educated, balanced men of our day do not want to enter into poli-tics. Politics today are filled with self-indulgent narcissists. Today we are seeing what foolishness looks like on a national level.

What Solomon is saying is there is trouble when people don't grow up right. They don't learn maturity. They don't learn to wait until the

---

[153] Barry, *Faithlife Study Bible*, Eccl 10:16.
[154] Winter, *Opening up Ecclesiastes*, 134.

right time to do something. They are given a leadership position before they are ready for it. They are children. Now they may not be physically children but may simply be immature.

They end up eating not for health and sustenance, but simply to party! They end up wasting their potential and their credibility. We've all met people who were super intelligent but had no self-control and never wanted to grow up. What a waste!

God wants us as Christians to grow up. He wants us not to be like the boy-king who can't finish anything but his next meal. He doesn't know what commitment is. God wants us to be faithful and finish the tasks that we start and to do what we do well. Sometimes we want to give up and indulge in life and just forget about the hard stuff. You'll never grow that way. Those who can't wait end up throwing their life away as self-centered, self-indulgent people. They are the whiners and complainers that never reach their potential and never get anything done!

FOOLS WASTE THEIR MONEY (10:18-19)

Fools waste their money.

Ecclesiastes 10:18-19 | Through sloth the roof sinks in, and through indolence the house leaks. [19] Bread is made for laughter, and wine gladdens life, and money answers everything.

God gives us many precious gifts. There are some who live life to eat all they can, enjoy all they can, and get all they can. People live for vacation, and not for what is important.Do you get the picture? While the roof is sinking in, the house is leaking, but the person ignores it and goes on living for himself. Now it is true that bread is made for laughter and wine does gladden life, and money does have its place. But do you see the misplaced priorities?

God has given us many good gifts. Every good thing is from heaven. Every good gift is from the Father who never changes (Jas 1:17). But the fool abuses God's gifts and uses life for himself. Listen, what ever God has prospered you with, use it wisely. Put God first. Don't be lazy. Don't procrastinate. All laziness and procrastination point to is selfishness.

FOOLS WASTE THEIR MIND (10:20)

Fools waste their mind. Self-centered people who walk in the flesh are not careful with their thoughts and what passes through their mind. The wise though are careful what they think in private because it comes out in the life.

Ecclesiastes 10:20 | Even in your thoughts, do not curse the king, nor in your bedroom curse the rich, for a bird of the air will carry your voice, or some winged creature tell the matter.

You know what this is all about? Gossip and bitterness and unforgiveness. Do any of struggle with that? We shouldn't even curse the king—an easy target that will probably never hear, much less those we are closest to. God may allow them to hear what we say.

Application: Have you ever run your mouth and get busted? I mean, have you ever walked into a room and there's like nine other people dogging somebody and you say one line but it's that one line that gets back to the person?

Here's an important truth. If you talk bad about others, you will not be trusted. People will wonder what you say about them behind their backs!!

The wise man understands that he lives in a sinful broken world, of which he is a part. We have to realize there's plenty in our own lives for people to talk bad about.

But here's the part that got me. I think I do a decent job of not bad-mouthing people out loud with my mouth, but he even says that the wise man, he won't even do it as he lays in bed at night.

You know you've had an argument with someone and you are laying in bed at night going, "Oh, why didn't I say that to him? That's so good." And you are just tearing them down in your mind. Solomon says—a wise man won't do that! That's a waste!

You know what the wise person does when they lay in bed at night? He says, "You know what, I don't battle flesh and blood, but I wrestle with spirits and principalities. I pray for my enemy. I will pray for his heart. I pray for my heart. Maybe I'm seeing wrong." That's the wise man. Otherwise you are wasting your time with all that bitter poison in your heart. It doesn't hurt them. It hurts you! Don't speak bad even in your thoughts. It will come back to haunt you!

Conclusion

It's easy to waste your life. Live with yourself as the focus. Don't worry about self-denial for Christ or others. A wise person is careful to please Christ in every area of their life.

"In April 2000, Ruby Eliason and Laura Edwards were killed in Cameroon, West Africa. Ruby was over eighty. Single all her life, she poured it out for one great thing: to make Jesus Christ known among the unreached, the poor, and the sick. Laura was a widow, a medical doctor, pushing eighty years old, and serving at Ruby's side in Cameroon. The brakes failed, the car went over a cliff, and they were both killed instantly. I asked my congregation: Was that a tragedy? Two lives, driven by one great passion, namely, to be spent in unheralded service to the perishing poor for the glory of Jesus Christ." [155]

The wise life is one of a single focus. "Seek first the kingdom of God and his righteousness". "For me to live is Christ". Put Christ as your overall focus of life, live for His kingdom and crucify yourself, and you will be wise and not waste your life!

---

[155] John Piper, *Don't Waste Your Life*, 45.

19 | ECCLESIASTES 11:1-12:8

MEANINGFUL LIVING FOR YOUNG AND OLD

Remember also your Creator in the days of your youth, before the evil days come and the years draw near of which you will say, "I have no pleasure in them."

ECCLESIASTES 12:1

In In September 1942, Viktor Frankl, a prominent Jewish psychiatrist and neurologist in Vienna, was arrested and transported to a Nazi concentration camp with his wife and parents. Three years later, when his camp was liberated, most of his family, including his pregnant wife, had perished – but he, prisoner number 119104, had lived. In his bestselling 1946 book, Man's Search for Meaning, which he wrote in nine days about his experiences in the camps, Frankl concluded that the difference between those who had lived and those who had died came down to one thing: Meaning, an insight he came to early in life. When he was a high school student, one of his science teachers declared to the class, "Life is nothing more than a combustion process, a process of oxidation." Frankl jumped out of his chair and responded, "Sir, if this is so, then what can be the meaning of life?" How can one be happy regardless of the unhappy circumstances of life?

As he saw in the German concentration camps, those who found meaning even in the most horrendous circumstances were far more resilient to suffering than those who did not. "Everything can be taken from a man but one thing," Frankl wrote in Man's Search for Meaning, "the last of the human freedoms – to choose one's attitude in any given set of circumstances, to choose one's own way."

Frankl worked as a therapist in the camps, and in his book, he gives the example of two suicidal inmates he encountered there. Like many others in the camps, these two men were hopeless and thought that there was nothing more to expect from life, nothing to live for. "In both cases," Frankl writes, "it was a question of getting them to realize that life was still expecting something from them; something in the future was expected of them." For one man, it was his young child, who was then living in a foreign country. For the other, a scientist, it was a series of books that he needed to finish.[156]

For the Christian, our purpose is to reflect Jesus Christ in all we do. We want to be conformed in our heart and character to his likeness. We know that it is dangerous to put one's hope in anything that is not guaranteed. Our purpose and joy is to finish the race Jesus put us in, becoming more and more like Christ. Paul said it well.

> 2 Timothy 4:7 | I have fought the good fight, I have finished the race, I have kept the faith.

How do we get to that place of pure happiness in Christ? In chapters 8-10, Solomon has been admonishing us to live a meaningful life. Solomon is now ready for his conclusion and personal application. What he does is present numerous pictures for living life to its fullest. Three thousand years ago, the wisest man ever to live (outside of the Lord) wrote a book telling us how to live a meaningful life in a very meaningless world. Is money all there is? Is my job all there is? Is the answer pleasure? It falls short. Family? The pursuit of pleasure? They fail. What's the answer? Live life for God. Solomon paints the portrait of a meaningful life in chapters 11-12. Let's listen to what he had to say.

> **Ecclesiastes 11:1-10** | Cast your bread upon the waters, for you will find it after many days. ² Give a portion to seven, or even to eight, for you know not what disaster may happen on earth. ³ If the clouds are full of rain, they empty themselves on the earth, and if a tree falls to the south or to the north, in the place where the tree falls,

---

[156] Viktor E. Frankl, *Man's Search for Meaning an Introduction to Logotherapy* (Boston: Beacon Press, 1963).

there it will lie. [4] He who observes the wind will not sow, and he who regards the clouds will not reap. [5] As you do not know the way the spirit comes to the bones in the womb of a woman with child, so you do not know the work of God who makes everything. [6] In the morning sow your seed, and at evening withhold not your hand, for you do not know which will prosper, this or that, or whether both alike will be good. [7] Light is sweet, and it is pleasant for the eyes to see the sun. [8] So if a person lives many years, let him rejoice in them all; but let him remember that the days of darkness will be many. All that comes is vanity. [9] Rejoice, O young man, in your youth, and let your heart cheer you in the days of your youth. Walk in the ways of your heart and the sight of your eyes. But know that for all these things God will bring you into judgment. [10] Remove vexation from your heart, and put away pain from your body, for youth and the dawn of life are vanity.

Ecclesiastes 12:1-8 | Remember also your Creator in the days of your youth, before the evil days come and the years draw near of which you will say, "I have no pleasure in them"; [2] before the sun and the light and the moon and the stars are darkened and the clouds return after the rain, [3] in the day when the keepers of the house tremble, and the strong men are bent, and the grinders cease because they are few, and those who look through the windows are dimmed, [4] and the doors on the street are shut— when the sound of the grinding is low, and one rises up at the sound of a bird, and all the daughters of song are brought low— [5] they are afraid also of what is high, and terrors are in the way; the almond tree blossoms, the grasshopper drags itself along, and desire fails, because man is going to his eternal home, and the mourners go about the streets— [6] before the silver cord is snapped, or the golden bowl is broken, or the pitcher is shattered at the fountain, or the wheel broken at the cistern, [7] and the dust returns to the earth as it was, and the spirit returns to God who gave it. [8] Vanity of vanities, says the Preacher; all is vanity.

The Bible pictures the life of the Christian prospering. Think of Psalm 1, how the blessed man's delight is in the law of the Lord, day and night, and how he "shall be like a tree, planted by the rivers of water, bringing forth its fruit in its season, and whatever he does shall prosper" (Psa 1:3). I want that prosperity that depends on God and God alone. God has a plan for you, and it is prosperity in Christ. Just make sure it's real prosperity that you get. There's nothing in the Bible that says we will millionaires. It doesn't promise us a life of luxury. What is this prosperity? So many times, we look at a man who has gone through several marriages, whose kids are rebellious, who has an ulcer, addicted to some alcohol or something like that, and he's got a big bank account. We say he's prosperous. He's not prosperous. He's a miserable failure. We are talking about biblical prosperity—the kind that God wants you to have, which is only available through Christ.

I recently read of an old prospector who had been out mining for gold out in Nevada somewhere—out in the West somewhere—and he had found what he thought was the mother lode. But what he found was what they call "fool's gold." It was mica; it wasn't gold at all. He had loaded down his old burro with it, and started out across the desert, ran out of water, and he and the old burro died. They found him there— the old burro lying down, the saddlebags full of nothing but fool's gold. But the old prospector wrote before he died, "Died rich." He had nothing but fool's gold in the saddlebags. Now a lot of people have even real gold, but they are very much like that old prospector: they don't understand what real riches are.[157]

LIFE IS AN ADVENTURE (11:1–6)

Be courageous! You must trust God. Ruthlessly follow God's adventure for you. Let the Spirit lead you by his word. When I was a child, I lived in Louisiana. In the summertime we would find the biggest Cypress tree and jump into a 30ft deep creek. Sometimes we would fall distances of 70ft! I would travel to see my father in the summer times. Life to me was an adventure. Of course, at that time, the only one I was trusting was myself, and many times, my adventures ended in disaster. When I was a boy of fifteen, I came to know Jesus Christ, and the greatest adventure of my life began. I used to use adventure simply for my own entertainment. Now I journey the adventure of faith so that I might see lives changed, and people conformed to the image of Christ!

Here in the first six verses, Solomon uses two illustrations to show how we must trust God: a merchant who sends out ships (11:1-2) and a

[157] Adrian Rogers, "The Principles of Prosperity," in *Adrian Rogers Sermon Archive* (Signal Hill, CA: Rogers Family Trust, 2017), Eccl 11:1–10.

farmer who plants seed everywhere (11:3-6). For both, you must have faith. Ultimately the outcome is up to God.

Live Like a Merchant

Consider the courage of a merchant. Invest!

A Merchant Invests Willingly

Ecclesiastes 11:1 | Cast your bread upon the waters, for you will find it after many days.

Solomon himself was involved in various kinds of trade and investment, so it was natural for him to use this illustration. It would be months before the ships would return with their precious cargo; but when they did, the merchant's faith and patience would be rewarded.

Solomon was a trader; he was an investor. He would invest money in ships, and he would set them to sail out across the sea. He was casting his bread upon the water. And they would go out and stay out for as long as three years. For when they came back, they came back with incredible riches. I think probably this is where we get the statement, "when your ship comes in."

You reap what you sow. You will be repaid with heavenly treasure for your investment, so have the courage to follow Christ and put him first, just like the merchant takes the chance by sending his grain out in many directions. Not all will be successful, but some will. So it is with following Christ.

When God calls you to "cast your bread upon the waters," he's asking you to invest in the kingdom. Don't die with a house and a heart full of junk! Give courageously of yourself, of your time, of your resources! Rather than hoarding, we need to give of ourselves and invest in expanding the kingdom. That's how we can "lay up treasure in heaven" (Mt 6:19-21). If we hoard here, it will be eaten by moths, and it will rust and could be stolen.

A Merchant Invests Broadly

Ecclesiastes 11:2 | Give a portion to seven, or even to eight, for you know not what disaster may happen on earth.

To "give a portion to seven, or even to eight" is a way of saying, "do not put all your eggs in one basket." In business this would be called "diversifying investments." Rather than focusing narrowly on a single product or service, many companies try to widen their interests.[158]

Join the adventure of God's kingdom. What Solomon is saying is that the wise man will invest everything he has in the life of faith.[159] Put on the mind of a investor. This goes for your gifts in ministry. Serve in a variety of ways. Diversify. Every man should be willing to teach in some way. Read and explain the word to your family. Every woman should be willing to work in the children's ministry. We should all help with meals for the sick. That's all of our responsibility. Diversify your investment. Don't say, "Well, I teach Sunday School, so I don't need to attend prayer meeting." Cast all of your bread upon the water. Give it all. And do it in a diversified way. Cast your net broadly for a diverse hall.

Live Like a Farmer

Consider the courage of a farmer (vs. 3-6).

The Christian life is like a farm. You can't tell if or when bad weather is coming way in advance. The Christian, like the farmer, farms in the midst of dangerous conditions.

Don't Focus on Fear but Faithfulness

Ecclesiastes 11:3 | If the clouds are full of rain, they empty themselves on the earth, and if a tree falls to the south or to the north, in the place where the tree falls, there it will lie.

What is he saying? He's saying, "Get ready. Sooner or later, there's a storm that's going to come. Sooner or later, there's going to come a rainy day, and it's going to blow over some trees. And when it blows over those trees, the way the tree falls, that's where it's going to lie." Life is filled with unexpected disasters. Expect them, but don't let it detour you from serving God. Learn from the farmer. Storms come and destroy. Trees fall and rot. You can't stop them. We all have storms that destroy and healthy trees that suddenly fall to the ground. Tragedies happen. Is your life predictable? Are you faithful in the little things? Do you follow through?

[158] Ryken, *Ecclesiastes*, 256.
[159] Eaton, *Ecclesiastes*, 140.

Don't Depend on Luck but on God's Promises

Ecclesiastes 11:4-5 | He who observes the wind will not sow, and he who regards the clouds will not reap. ⁵ As you do not know the way the spirit comes to the bones in the womb of a woman with child, so you do not know the work of God who makes everything.

If you are waiting for ideal circumstances, you will never plant or harvest. You've got to have a steadiness in life—a predictability. The winds blow. The trees fall. But you can expect the farmer to sow in the spring and harvest in the autumn. "Knee high by the fourth of July" means that the farmer planted on time in the springtime. Are you trusting in God's promises for the future?

The one who "regards the clouds" looking for a sign "will not reap." Superstition should never be a part of the believer's life or decision-making process. Solomon is saying that a person claiming to wait for a sign from heaven to tell him when to start working his fields would, in fact, be a lazy fool seeking to avoid hard work. Hence these verses provide another practical exhortation to diligence.[160]

Just as we do not understand the mystery of life in the womb, we also do not understand the mystery of growth and plenty in the field. What makes the wind blow the way it does? Why do we have times of drought and plenty? It's all in the mysterious providence of God. Our trust must not be in making wishes, gambling, or superstition. Some people clap their hands twice to make their car start. Some athletes have a ritual before a game so they can win, or their lucky shoes or lucky laces. All of that is worthless bologna. It is nothing. We don't regard clouds or lucky shoes or a lucky pendant. We live by faith in the promises of God.

Like the farmer, we must trust God for what each day brings. Just as nobody knows how the fetus is formed in the womb (Psa 139:14–15), so nobody knows the works of God in his creation. God has a time and a purpose for everything (3:1–11), and we must live by faith in his word.

Don't be Apathetic but Walk in Faith

Ecclesiastes 11:6 | In the morning sow your seed, and at evening withhold not your hand, for you do not know which will prosper, this or that, or whether both alike will be good.

---

[160] Rogland, "Ecclesiastes," 1104.

A farmer can't make his crops grow by sheer will power or by superstitious rituals. He has to trust in God. Our trust and hope is not in the weather but in the God who controls the weather. Therefore, use each day wisely (11:6). The farmer works hard, even though he cannot be perfectly assured of the outcome! He "redeems the time" (Eph 5:15–17).

In the same way, we need to work hard, trusting God to bless at least some of the tasks we have accomplished. If, as finite humans, we can never be sure which endeavors will prove fruitful, then the right approach to life is to give ourselves to the responsibilities at hand and trust the Lord for the outcome.[161]

The merchant and the farmer work hard. Just as the merchant sends out more than one ship, so the farmer works more than one crop. The Christian should be diligent as well, going through open doors. Talking to everyone God places in your path about Christ. Who knows what the Lord will do? Are you living by faith? Are you giving of yourself—investing yourself in people? As Paul said, "Some plant, some water, but God gives the increase" (1 Cor 3:6).

LIFE IS A GIFT (11:7-10)

Now Solomon begins to rejoice and celebrate the gifts of God. The believer is always humble, grateful, and generous knowing that everything is a gift from above (Jas 1:17).

Life is a gift—enjoy it (11:7–12:8). Live it to the fullest. Be committed! Rejoice in the gift of life (11:7–9). What a joy it is to anticipate each new day and accept it as an amazing gift from God! I was born two and a half months premature, so I was always taught to appreciate life. If you know me, I live about every moment as if it is my last. I'm almost hyper-focused on life. What a joy to savor each moment.

Enjoy Each Moment

Enjoy each moment since every second we have is an undeserved gift from God. Some feel guilty for enjoying God's good gifts, but Solomon's theology is quite different. Joy should be one of the central attributes of a growing Christian.

---

[161] Eaton, *Ecclesiastes*, 162–163.

Ecclesiastes 11:7 | Light is sweet, and it is pleasant for the eyes to see the sun.

Solomon is saying—appreciate waking up! Enjoy life from the moment you open your eyes. Take God's sweet sunlight in. Take time to smell the roses! Solomon's explaining that life can be very, very, very beautiful. He's referencing those days where you wake up and everything works. Like you wake up happy. Your bum back's not hurting, your legs aren't hurting, your relationships are just working. In fact, it feels like you've fallen into rhythm in terms of where you stand in God's universe. I think we've all had that day where the music just sounded better. Take all the light and the color of life that God has given you and enjoy it.

I'm a firm believer in Deuteronomy 33:25, "As are your days, so shall your strength be." God gives sufficient grace and strength for each moment (2 Cor 12:8-10). Now when I awake early each morning, I thank God for the new day; and I ask him to help me use it wisely for his glory and to enjoy it as his gift.[162]

I love to cut the lawn, and then just look at it. I know I've seen it a thousand times, but I love to walk around the house and just see the beauty of the trees. I love cleaning something up and looking at it. Taking in the joy of life. Just looking at my children sleeping. Savoring that first cry of the baby in the morning, because I know I can comfort my sweet child. Enjoy life. Take time to smell the roses!

Enjoy Each Stage of Life

Enjoy each stage of life. Enjoyment of life is to be life-long, the characteristic of *many years*. Two notes of warning are sounded. First, death makes a response to the life of joy an urgent matter, for earthly life cannot be enjoyed in retrospect.[163]

Remember to Live So You Can Enjoy Old Age

We will not always be young. Time is ticking away. So, enjoy life since old age is threatening when darkness and pain will be here in greater quantity.

---

[162] Wiersbe, *Be Satisfied*, 129.
[163] Eaton, *Ecclesiastes*, 164.

Ecclesiastes 11:8 | So if a person lives many years, let him rejoice in them all; but let him remember that the days of darkness will be many. All that comes is vanity.

Enjoy all of life. Life is truly a vapor, so savor each moment. It quickly slips away when "the days of darkness will be many." Eyes dim. Limbs hurt. The mind slows. They say, "you don't know what you've got until it's gone." Take time now before the difficult days of old age come. So while you and I have breath, while you and I have this opportunity for sweet life and the feel of the sun, let us pursue life because it will get difficult.

Rejoice in Your Youth

Ecclesiastes 11:9a | Rejoice, O young man, in your youth, and let your heart cheer you in the days of your youth.

Especially be diligent to enjoy your youth. He's not saying, "Party while you are young." No that would be wasted living. He's saying, "Prepare yourself in your youth. Get wisdom in your youth. Enjoy the immense advantages of youth. Chase life—chase Jesus—chase it to the fullest." The truth is most of the time, you're going to blink, and old age will be here. Your back's going to hurt, if not now, eventually. And your knees are going to creak, if not now, eventually. But as much as you can help it, enjoy life deeply."

Enjoy Life with Inner Virtue

Enjoy life but be careful that you enjoy it in a way that pleases God.

Ecclesiastes 11:9b | Walk in the ways of your heart and the sight of your eyes. But know that for all these things God will bring you into judgment.

The walk. All our doings are to be dedicated to God, from the most menial to the most vital. "Whether therefore you eat or drink, or whatever you do, do all to the glory of God" (1 Cor 10:31). We are called in everything to be conformed and transformed into the image of Christ (Rom 8:29; Rom 12:1-2). God gives us "all things richly to enjoy" (1 Tim 6:17), but it is always wrong to enjoy the pleasures of sin. Our walk (meaning our thoughts, desires, and actions) must be honorable to God. Since we belong to Christ, we are to "walk worthy of the calling" with which we are called (Eph 4:1). We are not to put pleasures in the place of God but use them for the glory of God.

The heart. For a young person or an older person to truly be joyous, there must be a carefulness in "the ways of your heart." That means the Bible is to be meditated on as a means to know the Lord personally. All else is rubbish compared to this (Phil 3:8; Psa 34:8).

The eyes. Solomon also mentions the "sight of your eyes." What and who we look at will shape us. Having a close relationship with our spouse if we are married is vital. Having faithful eyes for your marriage partner is vital since God made man and woman to be one in marriage. It is our marriage that reflects our relationship with God. Single people have an even greater joy as they are not burdened by all the cares of marriage but can serve the Lord without distraction. All service to God must be done in purity and chastity with heart and eyes and body devoted to him who is worthy of everything we are and do.

The judgment. All people will be brought into judgment for their works. This in no way means we merit our salvation since it is a "free gift" (Eph 2:8-9; Rom 6:23). Rather, "by their fruit you shall know them" (Mt 7:16). No one who has the practice of sinning is a true child of God (1 Jn 3:6). The adulterer, fornicator (including the perpetual pornographer), homosexual, thief, greedy person, abuser, drunkard and drug user, and all liars will be tormented in the lake of fire (Rev 21:8; 1 Cor 6:9-11). The good works of a Christian are predestined by God (Eph 2:10) and are the fruit of the Spirit who moves in all who by faith enter the new covenant and causes them to obey his statutes and keep his judgments (Eze 36:25-27). Some indeed will be "saved by fire" (1 Cor 3:15), that is, there will be true fruit of regeneration with faith and repentance, but the works may be wood, hay, and straw, mixed with man-pleasing perhaps (1 Cor 3:10-15). All believers will stand before the tribunal of Christ "so that each one may receive what is due for what he has done in the body, whether good or evil" (2 Cor 5:10). Yet, it is at this judgment seat where God will "wipe away every tear" from our eyes (Rev 21:4) since there is "no condemnation" for all who are in Christ (Rom 8:1). Indeed, because we are justified by the blood of Christ (Rom 5:9), with our sins place upon Christ, and his robes of righteousness placed upon us (2 Cor 5:21), he can say to us, "Well done, good and faithful servant, enter into your rest" (Mt 25:23).

Enjoy Life with Inner Peace

The incredible insight into the vexation of worry or bitterness and its effects on the body is breathtaking. Solomon literally says, "Banish anxiety," enjoying inner peace, and you will also "cast off the troubles of your body."[164]

Ecclesiastes 11:10 | Remove vexation from your heart, and put away pain from your body, for youth and the dawn of life are vanity.

Quiet your vexed and anxious soul. We need to know how to quiet our noisy soul. There's a lot of noise in our hearts at times. Frustration, anxiety, fear, depression, jealousy, bitterness. Those are not the fruit of the Spirit! Remove this vexation from your heart. This state of your heart will bring pain to your body. Noisy souls lead to physical problems, so deal with your heart issues, and at the same time you'll renewing your body. A lot of body pain comes from the heart. Sin and idolatry make us miserable. Anytime there is noise in the soul, there is an idol in the heart. By renewing our mind, recommitting ourselves to Christ, we are literally renewing neuropathways in our brain, making new and healthy connections that will refresh the body.

Learn to live with inner peace in your youth if possible. The robust physical health of youth is a gift to be embraced in its time, since it will eventually pass as "vanity." These are precious years and should not be squandered by spending too much time with the "vexations" of one's heart nor by engaging in practices that prove harmful to one's body.[165] Yet this kind of inner peace is fairly rare among young people. My father always referred to youth as being "young and dumb." Someone once said, "Youth is wasted on the stupid." Solomon is saying, "Don't waste your youth. Deal with your issues while you are young, and you'll be able to enjoy life more as you grow older.

Let's learn from the painful lessons of life while we are young. Deal with your junk and your issues now. Don't fake it. Deal with your sinful habits now. The thing about deep roots is that they never come up on the first pull. I'm not even a farmer—I just know that. Take a stab at the painful lessons of life when you are young and learn them.

---

[164] Schultz, "Ecclesiastes," 450.
[165] Rogland, "Ecclesiastes," 1108.

LIFE IS FLEETING (12:1-8)

Youth are called to "remember" the Lord from their earliest days. To "remember" our Creator is more than simply bringing him to mind. It is a call to reverence and surrender in all of life that finds its fulfillment in verse 13, "Fear God."[166] Worship God and grow in your relationship with him because your life passes by so fast!

The Rapidity of Youth

Ecclesiastes 12:1 | Remember also your Creator in the days of your youth, before the evil days come and the years draw near of which you will say, "I have no pleasure in them."

Your decisions in your youth affect your whole life. I find Solomon's wisdom striking. Solomon is perhaps an old man at this point, and he is pleading with young men and women to not forget about Jesus in this small window of your life that will affect the next decades of your years. Remember God now, while you still have a whole lifetime to live for his glory. As Charles Bridges once said, "Many have remembered too late—none too soon."[167]

He says, "Not now. Don't forget about your Creator now. Not now. Now when you're choosing husband and wife, not when you're choosing a job and a calling, not when you're choosing future, not when you're choosing college. Don't forget about Jesus now, because how you handle the now is going to play out in the rest of your life. Often in our youth we choose the pathway for our legacy." There's coming this day when we'll be ready for heaven—where we'll have very little pleasure for living on earth. We'll just want to be with the Lord, and it won't seem to be coming quick enough for us. So, make good and godly choices now. Your youth is fleeting, so lay a godly foundation for your life well. Build the house of your life on the rock, Jesus Christ, not on the shifting sands of this world's philosophy and fads.

The Loss of Mental Vitality

Remember God now, because old age is coming! You'll lose mental vitality. Solomon is now moving into metaphors for old age. When

---

[166] Winter, *Opening up Ecclesiastes*, 147.
[167] Charles Bridges, *A Commentary on Ecclesiastes* (1860; repr. Edinburgh: Banner of Truth, 1961), 294.

258

people get old most eventually lose their mental sharpness. The atrophy of old age and death was never the plan of God. Sin brought old age and death into the world.

Ecclesiastes 12:2 | Before the sun and the light and the moon and the stars are darkened and the clouds return after the rain.

Solomon says, "While you still have your mind you should chase after Jesus. When it comes to your mind, the sun and moon and stars are darkening, and the storm clouds are coming."

Solomon is talking about mental vitality and mental illumination. Young people have creativity, good memory, and wit. We still have a sharp mind. There's coming a day when all of a sudden, we can't find our car keys ever, and we're taking about this herb that's supposed to increase our memory, but we don't really remember what it was called. So chase after Christ with your whole heart and mind while you still have vitality

Be encouraged by this as well: your Creator remembers you, even if you do not always remember him. The security of our salvation does not depend on our remembrance of God but on his promise to remember us. [168] So the psalmist prayed that God would guide him even into old age.

Psalm 71:17-18 | O God, from my youth you have taught me, and I still proclaim your wondrous deeds. So even to old age and gray hairs, O God, do not forsake me.

The Loss of Physical Mobility

Growing old and facing death are some of the hardest experiences in life. The Bible is honest about this, but not bitter. In fact, this passage contains some of the most beautiful words ever breathed. The Holy Spirit took special pains to treat aging and dying with dignity.[169] From dust we came, and to dust we will return, with weakness, but the power of Christ rests even more upon us as we grow older. Solomon uses very poetic language to describe our decline.

[168] Ryken, *Ecclesiastes*, 271–272.
[169] Ibid., 271.

Ecclesiastes 12:3 | In the day when the keepers of the house tremble, and the strong men are bent, and the grinders cease because they are few, and those who look through the windows are dimmed.

As we grow old, we lose our stability with trembling hands ("the keepers of the house"). Our posture declines since "the strong men are bent" – that's the muscles in our back and legs! The stairs you used to hop up and down are now too difficult on your once strong knees.

To make matters worse, when we grow older, sometimes our "grinders cease because they are few," that is, you won't have many teeth so a soft food diet is an advantage. To top it off, Solomon says that while we once used to see perfectly fine, now our "windows are dimmed." In old age we don't see well.

The Loss of Hearing

Ecclesiastes 1:4 | And the doors on the street are shut—when the sound of the grinding is low, and one rises up at the sound of a bird, and all the daughters of song are brought low.

The shutting of doors refers to the ears, as people shut doors when they want to exclude outside noise. Solomon is talking about losing hearing, even to the point of deafness, as indicated by the sounds of grinding and singing fading out.[170]

One rises up at the sound of a bird —reference to how difficult it becomes to sleep through the night, the older you get. All the daughters of song are brought low—you can't hear people when they sing. There are certain tones you can't hear.

The Loss of Youth

Ecclesiastes 12:5 | They are afraid also of what is high, and terrors are in the way; the almond tree blossoms, the grasshopper drags itself along, and desire fails, because man is going to his eternal home, and the mourners go about the streets.

Gone are youthful adventures. "They are afraid also of what is high, and terrors are in the way." Natural fear is more common due to physical decline. What used to be fun and exciting is now terrifying. You used to think heights and fast cars, etc. were great. Now you just want to stay alive. Some take it as referring specifically to the shortness

---

[170] Garrett, *Ecclesiastes*, 342.

of breath that makes it difficult to walk up a hill and the stiffness of limbs that makes movement hard for older people.[171]

Gone are youthful looks. Solomon compares old age to the white blossoms of an almond tree. "The almond tree blossoms." The thing about an almond tree is it will go white, and the wind will carry away the blossoms. This is a reference to white hair or the lack of hair, either one. There was a time when our hair, our muscle tone, and even our skin was a lot younger.

Gone is youthful mobility. "The grasshopper drags itself along." As we get older, we move slower with increased difficulty of walking. As the years go on, the muscles get stiffer. Getting out of bed, or walking up the stairs actually looks like to a *wounded grasshopper* dragging itself along.

Gone is youthful zeal. "Desire fails, because man is going to his eternal home, and the mourners go about the streets." In old age, we can even lose our zest for life. This may include our natural libido (*cf* 1 Kgs 1:1–4), but we also lose the desire for living, longing to go to our eternal home, when the mourners go about the streets on their way to our funeral.[172]

The Loss of Life Itself

The final act of dying is pictured in four expressions.[173] The pictures in this verse have met with a variety of interpretations, but they certainly describe total collapse.

Ecclesiastes 12:6 | Before the silver cord is snapped, or the golden bowl is broken, or the pitcher is shattered at the fountain, or the wheel broken at the cistern.

The silver chain of life snaps. This likely simply to the silver chain from which the lamp hangs, representing our soul. When the silver chain is snapped, the light suddenly hits the ground, and the light goes out. Could this perhaps also refer to our body's chain of DNA? When we die our DNA chain snaps and goes back to the dust with our body, but our soul goes to the Lord. In both cases, the chain will one day

---

[171] George A. Barton, *A Critical and Exegetical Commentary on The Book of Ecclesiastes* (Whitefish, MT: Kessinger, 2006), 189.

[172] Rogland, "Ecclesiastes," 1109.

[173] Eaton, *Ecclesiastes*, 170.

atrophy and snap. Our soul goes back to be with Jesus. "To be absent from the body" is "to be present with the Lord" (2 Cor 5:8). The silver corded soul is snapped out of the body and is now with the Lord.

The golden bowl of oil is crushed. The *'golden bowl'* is used as a receptacle for oil which feeds the lampstand in the tabernacle and temple (Zech 4:2).[174] The menorah's lamp as a result, goes out. The feast is over. It's time to go home to be with the Lord. The light of the mind goes out. The brain's mental capacity, as the golden bowl, is crushed.

The clay pitcher is broken to pieces so that no water can be brought from the fountain back home. This could be referring to the heart, described as a cistern or fountain out of which life itself flows.[175] The heart, which used to distribute life to the body is now broken.

The wooden wheel that lowers the bucket into the well has itself been broken. The wheel of the lungs and throat shut down, and the breath of life is extinguished.[176] James says it well.

> James 4:14, NKJV | For what is your life? It is even a vapor that appears for a little time and then vanishes away.

At death, life as we know it is over. The immaterial part of us (the silver cord) returns to God in fellowship. The golden bowl of our brain and mind is done. The clay water pitcher of the heart stops. The wheel for the water well, representing our lungs, stop. We leave this earth, and we are forever with the Lord. Glory and Hallelujah.

The Solemnity of Death

Death is the most solemn of occasions. Solomon earlier told us for this reason it's better to go to the "house of mourning" rather than the "house of feasting" so that the living will lay the solemnity of death to heart (7:2). We go back to God. While death is no longer our enemy, we need to take it seriously and live our life in the most meaningful way.

> Ecclesiastes 12:7-8 | And the dust returns to the earth as it was, and the spirit returns to God who gave it. [8] Vanity of vanities, says the Preacher; all is vanity.

---

[174] Belcher, *Ecclesiastes*, 398.
[175] Garrett, *Ecclesiastes*, 342.
[176] Wright, *Ecclesiastes*, 1194.

Dust returns to dust (*cf* Gen 2:7; 3:19)! Life is frail! Solomon could have said with James how life is fleeting like a vapor (Jas 4:14). The return of the spirit to God refers to death. All life comes from God, and we will all return to him.[177] We should all consider what happens one second after you die? Death is sobering not mainly because it is the end of life but the beginning of eternity.

But of course, he describes it for us in living color. Truly, if this life is all there is, it is vanity! Life without Christ is tasteless and tedious, and vain. All is vanity without Jesus at the center. That's not the case though. Christ is our all in all. For me to live is Christ (Phil 1:21). So live life to its fullest. It's so short. God wants us to serve him from the cradle to the grave and enjoy the good gifts he's given.

Conclusion

Live life for the Lord with all your might now while you can. Live a meaningful life. How do you do that? You give our life to Christ and live life for his glory.

To illustrate what I mean let me tell you about two men buried in Cairo Egypt, one named William Borden, a Christian missionary, and the other named Tutankhamun, who we know better as the famous Egyptian monarch, King Tut.

The streets of Cairo are hot and dusty. If you go down a trash filled alley, you'll go past Arabic signs to an overgrown graveyard for American missionaries. In a forgotten alley in Cairo, with trash blowing back and forth, you'll notice a sun-scorched tombstone that reads: "William Borden 1887–1913." William Borden was a Yale graduate and heir to great wealth, but he rejected a life of ease in order to bring the gospel to the Muslim world and point them to the only Savior: Jesus Christ.

Borden would have been on the "Forbes Riches Persons" list were he alive today. Refusing even to buy himself a car, Borden gave away hundreds of thousands of dollars to missions. After only four months of zealous ministry in Egypt, he contracted spinal meningitis and died at age twenty-five. If you dust off the epitaph on Borden's grave, you'll read about his love for God and sacrifices so that the Muslim people would know Christ. The final sentence of the epitaph is unforgettable.

Apart from faith in Christ, there is no explanation for such a life.

---

[177] Garrett, *Ecclesiastes*, 343.

Not far from Borden's grave is the Egyptian Museum. The King Tut exhibit is mind-boggling. Tutankhamun died at age seventeen. He was buried with solid gold chariots and thousands of golden artifacts. His gold coffin was found buried within a gold tomb which was buried inside another gold tomb. The ancient Egyptians believed in an afterlife—one where they could take earthly treasures. But all the treasures intended for King Tut's eternal enjoyment stayed right where they were for more than three thousand years, until Howard Carter discovered the burial chamber in 1922.[178]

We should be struck by the contrast between these two graves. Borden's was obscure, dusty, and hidden off a back street littered with garbage. Tutankhamun's tomb glittered with unimaginable wealth. Yet where are these two men now? One, who lived in opulence and called himself king, is in the misery of a Christless eternity. The other, who lived a modest life in service of the one true King, is enjoying everlasting reward in his Lord's presence. Eternity will demonstrate who and who did not to live a meaningful, Christ-centered life.

Choose to remember your Creator while you are young. Build a legacy on Christ, not on the fleeting world. Before we know it, we will see Christ. The only legacy that lasts is one that gives all glory and honor to him.

---

[178] Richard Emmons, "A Missionary First, Last, and All the Time," *Israel My Glory*, Richard Emmons September/October 2010.

20 | ECCLESIASTES 12:9-14

THE LAST WORD ON MEANINGFUL LIVING

Besides being wise, the Preacher also taught the people knowledge, weighing and studying and arranging many proverbs with great care.

ECCLESIASTES 12:9

For many people, life is perplexing and problematic, and many people are living life cynically. Some try to check out using alcohol, drugs, immorality, or entertainment. Many people, even young people are so hurt by life that they are jaded. Once there was a survey of college students on the meaning of life. Some of the answers were quite cynical. One quoted Socrates who said, "Life is a disease for which the only cure is death." Another said, "Life is a jail sentence that we get for the crime of being born." Another said, "Life is a joke that isn't even funny." We're all familiar with Erma Bombeck, who said, "If life is a bowl of cherries, why do I always get the pits?" People are trying to figure out what life is really all about.[179]

For the Christian, our philosophy of life can be summed up with Paul's words who said, "For to me, to live is Christ, and to die is gain"

---

[179] Adrian Rogers, "A Perspective on Life," in *Adrian Rogers Sermon Archive* (Signal Hill, CA: Rogers Family Trust, 2017), Ec 12:10–14.

266

(Phil 1:21). David said, "Your unfailing love is better than life itself; how I praise you" (Psa 63:3). Paul defined the purpose of life as being "conformed to the image of God's Son," so that everything in life can be called good since it is molding us into the imprint and likeness of Christ (Rom 8:28-29). Paul may have said it best when he proclaimed Christ as the center of life to the Philippians.

> *Philippians 3:8, NLT* | Yes, everything else is worthless when compared with the infinite value of knowing Christ Jesus my Lord. For his sake I have discarded everything else, counting it all as garbage, so that I could gain Christ.

Solomon's last word on the meaningful life is very simple: fear God. Magnify him as big as he is. Glorify him. Life becomes worth living when we see everything in its proper perspective. We are called to magnify and fear God by Solomon. Only then can we really enjoy life. John Piper illustrates this beautifully.

> Magnify has two distinct meanings. In relation to God, one is worship, and one is wickedness. You can magnify like a telescope or like a microscope. When you magnify like a microscope, you make something tiny look bigger than it is. A dust mite can look like a monster. Pretending to magnify God like that is wickedness. But when you magnify like a telescope, you make something unimaginably great look like what it really is. With the Hubble Space Telescope, pinprick galaxies in the sky are revealed for the billion-star giants that they are. Magnifying God like that is worship.[180]

Life under the sun is tasteless and vain unless life is lived under the Son of God. Solomon tells us this no less than 39 times. Nothing matters without Christ. But if Jesus is at the blazing center of your life, everything matters.

Ecclesiastes 12:9-14 | Besides being wise, the Preacher also taught the people knowledge, weighing and studying and arranging many proverbs with great care. [10] The Preacher sought to find words of delight, and uprightly he wrote words of truth. [11] The words of the wise are like goads, and like nails firmly fixed are the collected sayings; they are given by one Shepherd. [12] My son, beware of anything beyond these. Of making many books there is no end, and much study is a weariness of the flesh. [13] The end of the

---

[180] John Piper, *Don't Waste Your Life*, 32.

matter; all has been heard. Fear God and keep his command-ments, for this is the whole duty of man. **14** For God will bring every deed into judgment, with every secret thing, whether good or evil.

Solomon gives us the final word on meaningful living. He tells us to live by example and live with the fear of God always before you. In other words, live so that God is big, and everything else will be in its proper perspective.

A natural reading of the epilogue gives the impression that it is in-tended to be a straightforward commendation of the Preacher's words (12:9–12) and a summary of their primary message (12:13–14).[181]

LEAD BY EXAMPLE (12:9-12)

Like Solomon, we ought to have a passion for teaching and influ-encing others for Christ. Christians are not invested in money or things primarily but in people. In King Solomon's conclusion, we get a fantas-tic insight into the wise king as a teacher. The book after all is called "Ecclesiastes" which is Latin for "preacher" or "teacher." Solomon is one who proclaims the true wisdom of God, and if we put on our New Testament glasses on, we can see Jesus, who Paul describes as "the wis-dom of God" incarnate (1 Cor 1:24).

Teach Diligently

Wisdom is certainly a gift. Solomon was given the gift of wisdom directly from God. All Christians are given a foundational wisdom at regeneration. Yet, in order to teach others, there must be a diligence exercised. Though Solomon is described as "the Preacher" who is a wise teacher, he describes his diligent efforts in preparing to teach.

Ecclesiastes 12:9 | Besides being wise, the Preacher also taught the people knowledge, weighing and studying and arranging many proverbs with great care.

Who are we to teach? Solomon was called to "teach the people." We are to seek to teach everyone. We are to make disciples of our chil-dren, friends, family—every creature (Mt 28:18-20). Though Solomon

[181] Rogland, "Ecclesiastes," 1111.

268

was king, he was humble, knowing that he was a sinner, not above anyone else.

What are we to teach? Solomon taught "knowledge" and "many proverbs" or wise sayings from the word of God. This "knowledge" is a summary word for the entire book of Ecclesiastes. It is only God-breathed scripture that will transform people in any meaningful way. The central theme of Ecclesiastes and all of God's word is that we must "seek first the kingdom" or "Fear God" as Solomon says. Therefore, Christ should be enjoyed first and then everything else can be enjoyed. Without surrender to Christ, we surrender to lesser things that keep us miserable and vexed in our spirit with confusion, anger, and anxiety, longing for a satisfaction in idols that can only be found in Christ.

How we are to teach? We read: "Besides being wise, the Preacher also taught the people knowledge, weighing and studying..." *Teach with great preparation.* Before the king would teach, he prepared "...weighing and studying and arranging many proverbs with great care." The word "weighing" means to "ponder, to sift, to search out: with "careful evaluation, indicating honesty, thoroughness and diligence."[182] The activities of studying, writing, arranging, and so on are to be understood as the Preacher's typical work and do not refer exclusively to the book of Ecclesiastes itself.[183]

We too are to study and meditate and pray over God's word diligently, day and night (Psa 1:2). We are to renew our minds each day through the word (Eph 4:23). *Teach with great care and compassion.* Put yourself in the shoes of the people you are teaching. They are all hurting. Their only hope is the plain word of God. Peter asks, "Do you have the gift of speaking? Then speak as though God himself were speaking through you" (1 Pet 4:11, NLT).

Teach Practically

It's not enough to simply give data dumps of information. Knowing the word is not enough. God's people need to walk in the word. Teaching should be applied with great practicality.

Ecclesiastes 12:10a | The Preacher sought to find words of delight.

---

[182] Eaton, *Ecclesiastes*, 174.
[183] Rogland, "Ecclesiastes," 1112.

The word "delight" means "winsome, easy to grasp, readily applied" like the "gracious words" of our Lord (Lk 4:22).[184] It's delightful and easy to be received and applied to our lives. True wisdom is filled with love for the person we are communicating to, otherwise we come off as a noisy, clanging cymbal (1 Cor 13:1). James is clear that the word should not just be considered and then forgotten (Jas 1:22-25), but the one who puts the word into practice "will be blessed" in the doing of it (cf Psa 1:1-3). Christians should not be about mere theory but doing. Yet it should not be communicated in a way that is pushy or legalistic. The word should be spoken with an irresistible graciousness demonstrating the beauty of glory of God.

> James 3:17-18 | The wisdom from above is first pure, then peaceable, gentle, open to reason, full of mercy and good fruits, impartial and sincere. [18] And a harvest of righteousness is sown in peace by those who make peace.

This kind of teaching brings delight even to the most calloused of hearers. I think of the great Ben Franklin, who was never accused of being a Christian, yet could not resist the logic of George Whitefield's preaching. Not only did Franklin befriend the great evangelist, but the Philadelphia printer admired Whitefield, printed his sermons and his life's story, supported his philanthropic endeavors, and even dreamed of founding with him a colony in the Ohio country. Indeed, Franklin did not hold to the beliefs of Whitefield, but he was so impressed at how sincerely Whitefield believed, preached, and delighted in Christ and his word.[185]

Teach with Conviction

When teaching is presented with sincerity and truth it can bring great penetration and conviction to the heart.

Ecclesiastes 12:10b-11a | And uprightly he wrote words of truth. [11] The words of the wise are like goads, and like nails firmly fixed are the collected sayings.

Solomon was sincere and "upright" as "he wrote words of truth." He sincerely grasped the word of God for himself first before he taught

---

[184] Leale, *Ecclesiastes*, 172.
[185] David T. Morgan "A Most Unlikely Friendship — Benjamin Franklin and George Whitefield." *The Historian* 47, no. 2 (1985): 208–18.

his hearers. These were not merely motivational concepts but sincerely held beliefs that the king lived by.

When the sincere word is taught, the Spirit uses it as a *goad*—a pointy stick that would poke an animal to move him forward. So God's word is like the goads for cattle, or we might say spurs for a horse – God's word pushes us, spurs us on toward the goal of Christ-likeness.

The word of God, Solomon says, is like a nail we can firmly hang our life upon. We need to fasten our lives upon God's word because it is "firmly fixed."

Teach with Authority

Solomon reveals the true author of the book of Ecclesiastes: the words are given by one Shepherd. The God-breathed Scripture is authoritative because of who it comes from: the Almighty who lowers himself to forgive and shepherd wandering sheep.

Ecclesiastes 12:11b | They are given by one Shepherd.

A shepherd leads his sheep. And though there were many wise and holy men who "spoke from God as they were carried along by the Holy Spirit" (2 Pet 1:21), we can rest assured that "they are given by one Shepherd." The words of Scripture are inspired words of authority from "one Shepherd," from the Lord himself.

Teach Exclusively

To be able to see lives change, don't teach beyond the word of God. Our foundation is the Bible. The sixteenth century reformers cry of sola scriptura remains our cry today. Salvation is found in the Bible alone, by grace alone through faith alone, to the glory of God alone. Don't go beyond the gospel found in the Bible.

Ecclesiastes 12:12 | My son, beware of anything beyond these. Of making many books there is no end, and much study is a weariness of the flesh.

It is a waste of time to look for something to change us outside of God's word. There are many books written, and many methods taught that people say are the answer. There is no other answer outside of God's sufficient word, of which Peter speaks of.

The apostle Peter is clear that the Scriptures are all we need for life and godliness (2 Pet 1:3). God's word is profitable and applicable for "teaching, for reproof, for correction, for training in righteousness" that the Christian might have every tool for a godly life (2 Tim 3:16-17).

LIVE BY FEARING GOD (12:13-14)

A meaningful life is a practical living out of God's word with a reverent awareness of his presence (12:13-14). Everywhere angels appear the first words are normally: "Fear not!" How much more should we fear the one who created the angels and who worship him day and night. Listen to the words of Solomon. He sums up the entire book in two verses.

> **Ecclesiastes 12:13-14** | The end of the matter; all has been heard. Fear God and keep his commandments, for this is the whole duty of man. ¹⁴ For God will bring every deed into judgment, with every secret thing, whether good or evil.

We are told that in the Hebrew there is a "stylistic crudeness" in the way Solomon says, "The end of the matter." It's abrupt. He's saying, "Let me give you the main point: Fear God." What a tremendous summary these two verses are. They summarize our entire salvation—past, present, and future.

The past. "The end of the matter; all has been heard." Meaning in life comes from knowing the Lord. Nothing makes sense without a Christ-centered worldview. The preacher-king has demonstrated how knowledge without Yahweh is meaningless (1:1-18). Indeed, nothing in life can be enjoyed without him, be it pleasure (2:1-11), work (2:11-26), or time itself (3:1-15). Injustice has no satisfying answer without the Judge of the earth at the center (3:16-22). All is empty and passing without a heart devotion to the Lord, including our relationships on all levels (4:1-16), our worship (5:1-7), our wealth (5:8-9), and all our possessions (6:1-12). Without faith and hope in Christ, the ugly enemy of death will win (7:1-6). Knowing Christ transforms your character (7:7-10) and the radiance of your countenance (8:1-8). Fearing God brings contentment (8:9-11), purpose (9:1-10), and discernment (9:11-18). Knowing the Lord warns us against foolish living (10:1-11) or wasting our life (10:12-20). The most adventurous life is a Christ honoring life (11:1-10). Life is fleeting, so lay the foundation of fearing God in your youth (12:1-14).

The present. Fear God. This is the entire duty and purpose of man. Be conformed to Christ in your heart, your affections, your thoughts, actions. Be sanctified in obedience. Keep his commandments. The Spirit will cause you to walk in his statues and keep his judgments. Be faithful to your vows to God. Grow in sanctification and your relationship with Christ. He will be your God, and you will be people. You are to forsake all others and have no idols in place of him.

The future. There's a day coming when all of our works will be revealed. At first when we consider that "God will bring every deed into judgment, with every secret thing, whether good or evil," it may bring great dread and terror. This is a proper response to the transcendent God judging us. Yet for the believer, "there is no condemnation" (Rom 8:1). Christ has paid it all and taken away all sin, but there will be a judgment of our works and rewards given or loss suffered. All Christians will be brought before Christ's tribunal, not for condemnation but for commendation.

> *1 Corinthians 3:13-15* | Each one's work will become manifest, for the Day will disclose it, because it will be revealed by fire, and the fire will test what sort of work each one has done. [14] If the work that anyone has built on the foundation survives, he will receive a reward. [15] If anyone's work is burned up, he will suffer loss, though he himself will be saved, but only as through fire.

For the lost, all who live magnifying the things of this life, putting themselves at the center, they have a judgment of condemnation. "These will go away into eternal punishment, but the righteous into eternal life" (Mt 25:46).

The Meaning of Fearing God

> **Ecclesiastes 12:13a** | The end of the matter; all has been heard. Fear God.

If fearing God is the key to our entire salvation and meaning for life, we have to ask, what exactly does it mean to fear God? Clearly, fearing God is the entire point of the book. Solomon declares by the Holy Spirit that it is indeed the "whole duty" and purpose of man.

> Simply put, fearing God means seeing him in his greatness, and allowing that greatness to dwarf every other pleasure or misery, so that our joy comes from God alone.

Relationally, fearing God means to live in right relationship with God, trembling before him and yet also resting in his love, as a child fears their father. You grow in the fear of the Lord by gazing upon the beauty of his attributes and by seeking an ever-deepening relationship with him.[186] Our standing does not come from us meeting legal requirements or earning God's favor. Fearing God's judgment leads to a dread that leads to misery. The fear that God brings his child leads to an awe that leads to wonder and joy for his forgiveness (Rom 8:1). God blesses us and lavishes us with love, forgiveness, compassion, provision, protection, guidance, grace, mercy, and countless other things even though we are the least deserving. Many mistakenly assume that God's good gifts are given in response to things we do that please him, but we need to remember that God's blessings are gifted to us, not earned by us. They are based completely on the work of Christ's atoning sacrifice on our behalf and his imputed righteousness to us as a result. We should therefore relate to God not merely on a functional level, but on a relational level of Father to child.

Practically in our daily life, fearing God means to magnify him as the transcendent being who rules above all your finite and constantly shifting circumstances. Very hard things happen to God's people. What about all the promises he has made to care for and reward those who fear him (Heb 11:6)? Does going through adversity mean that he hasn't kept those promises? By no means! Some of those promises will not be realized this side of eternity. This doesn't mean that God has somehow gone back on his word — that's impossible. It just means that our hope is not in this temporary life but in our life to come. As we become convinced of his greatness, we will fear him—stand in awe of him—and also trust him. We cannot separate trust in God from the fear of God. We will trust him only to the extent that we genuinely stand in awe of him.[187] His fear will keep us from allowing lesser things—idols—take control of our lives and infest us with misery. Oswald Chambers said, "The remarkable thing about fearing God is that, when you fear God,

---

[186] Jerry Bridges, *The Joy of Fearing God* (Colorado, Springs, Colorado: WaterBrook Press, 2016), 236.

[187] Ibid.

you fear nothing else; whereas, if you do not fear God, you fear everything else."[188]

Affectionately, it means to recognize and revere the beauty of God's holiness. In order to render heartfelt worship to God, we must be gripped in the depth of our being by his majesty, holiness, and love; otherwise, our praise and adoration may be no more than empty words.[189] As we appreciate and delight in who God is, we will love him more, proclaiming with David, "Because your steadfast love is better than life, my lips will praise you" (Psa 63:3). Affectionately we are blown away by the beauty and cost of God's love.

Theologically, fearing God is the exercise of faith in the transcendent God, producing reverence, love, awe, curiosity, surrender, obedience, and faithful devotion. The concept of fearing God is akin to biblical faith or trust. The greatness of God teaches us that God is able to save us, and the goodness of God tells us he delights in saving and loving us. This moves us to trust in him with exclusive devotion and worship.

The Demonstration of Fearing God

We can speak of fearing God theoretically, but what does it look like when it is adopted into our life? How does one practically fear the Lord? Very simply: we "keep his commandments."

Ecclesiastes 12:13b | Fear God and keep his commandments.

If we fear God, our lives will be characterized by submission and joyful obedience to God. Someone said, "The only part of the Bible you truly believe is the part you obey."[190] If we fear God, we will keep his commandments (Jn 14:15). Obedience for the Christian is not merely legal but devotional. Obedience is Spirit-birthed submission, causing the child of God to see God's way as irresistible in beauty and glory.

We must go beyond simple submission when it comes to God. We must desire to obey him, not merely because it's the right thing to do but because we love and revere him. If we are truly submissive to the

---

[188] Timothy George, *J.I. Packer and the Evangelical Future: The Impact of His Life and Thought* (Grand Rapids, MI: Baker Academic, 2009), 52.

[189] Bridges, *Joy of Fearing God*, 48.

[190] Ajith Fernando, *Deuteronomy: Loving Obedience to a Loving God* (Wheaton, IL: Crossway, 2012), 116.

authority of Scripture, then we will obey the commands therein out of our fear of the Lord.

The Joy of Fearing God

Ecclesiastes 12:13c | Fear God and keep his commandments, for this is the whole duty of man.

A meaningful life is a satisfying life. Man's highest calling, purpose, and destiny is to fear our transcendent God. Why are people miserable chasing after temporary dreams? Why is one Super Bowl never enough? Why do people go from marriage after marriage and relationship to relationship? Because we were made for something bigger!

Fearing God means being consciously aware that God is omnipresent and omniscient. He is everywhere at all times, which means that he sees all and knows all. This includes our innermost thoughts that we would never consider saying out loud and our inner motives that we may not even be aware we have. This realization should cause us to:

1. *Enjoy the presence of God.* Remember that the Lord is always with us. He will never leave us nor forsake us. It should remind us not to be afraid during trials. No matter how egregious our sins may be, our Father loves us and forgives us of those sins. That is where joy in fearing the Lord is to be found. [191] In the Old Testament, the presence of God was manifested in the garden to Adam, to Moses in the burning bush, to Israel in the glory cloud, and to us by the indwelling Spirit. God's presence in the glory cloud protected the people of Israel from the burning sun during the day and was a warming and comforting light and protection during the night. When Moses approached God's glorious presence, his face glowed, and so the one who fears the Lord today has a countenance that is changed (8:1). As we gaze upon him in fearful reverence and love, we behold "the glory of the Lord, are being transformed into the same image from one degree of glory to another" (2 Cor 3:18).

2. *Enjoy the righteousness of God.* The day will soon be here when we meet God face to face. Be very aware of our thoughts, words, and actions knowing that even if no one else knows, God knows and will call us to account for those things on Judgment Day. Because of the cleansing blood of Christ, we are not terrorized by Judgment Day since only

---

[191] Bridges, *Joy of Fearing God*, 183.

unbelievers will be condemned. Believers will never suffer condemnation for their sins (Rom 8:1), but commendation for their works (1 Cor 3:13-15), though they merit nothing. We will cast all our crowns before the Lord.

3. *Enjoy the person of God.* God's greatness leaves us marveling and wanting more of him. We cherish and worship the Lord as we magnify his glory. We read in his word what he has revealed to us about himself, and we are left in utter amazement at who he is and what he has done for us. His holiness, wisdom, sovereignty, love, power, and beauty are incomprehensible and beyond compare. His altogether otherness is something our fallible human minds cannot even fathom. God wants us to see and understand that he is inconceivably great, that nothing or no one can possibly compare with him.[192]

The Outcome of Fearing God

A meaningful life is a far-sighted life. What is man's ultimate concern? Our works matter because they accurately display a person's heart.

Ecclesiastes 12:14 | For God will bring every deed into judgment, with every secret thing, whether good or evil.

Solomon says in the Proverbs: "Keep your heart with all vigilance, for from it flow the springs of life" (Pro 4:23). Judgment is coming. As I said before, all Christians will be brought before Christ's tribunal, not for condemnation but for commendation. "It is appointed for man to die once, and after that comes judgment" (Heb 9:27).

Vanity of vanities! Everything is vain without Christ. It's not that nothing matters. In fact, everything matters. Do you know the transforming love of Christ? He alone makes life meaningful and worth living. He is life itself.

1 John 5:12 | He who has the Son has life; he who does not have the Son of God does not have life.

Conclusion

Fearing God is seeing him as he is, and it takes your breath away. There is an epiphany that is like the fireworks of the heart and mind.

---

[192] Ibid., 57.

Living without the fear of God is like being blind to all beauty. C.S. Lewis captured it so well.

> We are half-hearted creatures, fooling about with drink and sex and ambition when infinite joy is offered us, like an ignorant child who wants to go on making mud pies in a slum because he cannot imagine what is meant by the offer of a holiday at the sea. We are far too easily pleased.[193]

Aurelius Augustine, North African bishop says, "You arouse us to delight in praising you; for you have made us for yourself, O Lord, and our heart is restless, until it finds rest in you."[194] Solomon in all his wisdom, tells us to dive into all pleasure and beauty and wealth and joy and all good things by diving into God himself.

---

[193] C. S. Lewis, *The Weight of Glory and Other Addresses* (New York: HarperOne, 2001), 26.

[194] Aurelius Augustine, *Confessions of St. Augustine, Book 3*, Bishop of Hippo (London: Griffith Farran Browne & Company Limited, 1886), 1.

SELECTED BIBLIOGRAPHY

In order of appearance in the commentary

COMMENTARIES

Warren W. Wiersbe, *Be Satisfied*, "Be" Commentary Series (Wheaton, IL: Victor Books, 1996).

Philip Graham Ryken, *Ecclesiastes: Why Everything Matters*, Preaching the Word (Wheaton, IL: Crossway Books, 2010).

R. N. Whybray, *Ecclesiastes, The New Century Bible Commentary* (Grand Rapids, MI: Eerdmans, 1989).

Duane A. Garrett, *Proverbs, Ecclesiastes, Song of Songs*, vol. 14, The New American Commentary (Nashville: Broadman & Holman Publishers, 1993).

Michael A. Eaton, *Ecclesiastes: An Introduction and Commentary*, vol. 18, Tyndale Old Testament Commentaries (Downers Grove, IL: InterVarsity Press, 1983).

Jim Winter, *Opening up Ecclesiastes*, Opening Up Commentary (Leominster: Day One Publications, 2005).

Donald R. Glenn, "Ecclesiastes," in *The Bible Knowledge Commentary: An Exposition of the Scriptures*, ed. J. F. Walvoord and R. B. Zuck, vol. 1 (Wheaton, IL: Victor Books, 1985).

Robert B. Hughes and J. Carl Laney, *Tyndale Concise Bible Commentary*, The Tyndale Reference Library (Wheaton, IL: Tyndale House Publishers, 2001).

J. Stafford Wright, "Ecclesiastes," in *The Expositor's Bible Commentary: Psalms, Proverbs, Ecclesiastes, Song of Songs*, ed. Frank E. Gaebelein, vol. 5 (Grand Rapids, MI: Zondervan Publishing House, 1991).

John D. Barry et al., *Faithlife Study Bible* (Bellingham, WA: Lexham Press, 2012, 2016).

T. M. Moore, *Ecclesiastes: Ancient Wisdom When All Else Fails: A New Translation and Interpretive Paraphrase* (Downers Grove, IL: InterVarsity, 2001).

Carl Friedrich Keil and Franz Delitzsch, *Commentary on the Old Testament*, vol. 6 (Peabody, MA: Hendrickson, 1996).

Thomas H. Leale, *Ecclesiastes*, The Preacher's Complete Homiletic Commentary (New York; London; Toronto: Funk & Wagnalls, 1892).

Max Rogland, "Ecclesiastes," in *Psalms–Song of Solomon*, ed. Iain M. Duguid, James M. Hamilton Jr., and Jay Sklar, vol. V, ESV Expository Commentary (Wheaton, IL: Crossway, 2022).

Derek Kidner, *The Message of Ecclesiastes: A Time to Mourn, and a Time to Dance*, ed. J. Alec Motyer and Derek Tidball, The Bible Speaks Today (England: Inter-Varsity Press, 1984).

Richard P. Belcher Jr., *Ecclesiastes: A Mentor Commentary*, Mentor Commentaries (Ross-shire, Great Britain: Mentor, 2017).

Carl Schultz, "Ecclesiastes," in *Evangelical Commentary on the Bible*, vol. 3, Baker Reference Library (Grand Rapids, MI: Baker Book House, 1995).

Jay E. Adams, *Life under the Son: Counsel from The Book of Ecclesiastes* (Woodruff, SC: Timeless Texts, 1999).

Roland E. Murphy and Elizabeth Huwiler, *Proverbs, Ecclesiastes, Song of Songs* (Grand Rapids, MI: BakerBooks, 1999).

Charles Bridges, *A Commentary on Ecclesiastes* (1860; repr. Edinburgh: Banner of Truth, 1961).

Ajith Fernando, *Deuteronomy: Loving Obedience to a Loving God* (Wheaton, IL: Crossway, 2012).

SERMONS

Adrian Rogers, "The Principles of Prosperity," in *Adrian Rogers Sermon Archive* (Signal Hill, CA: Rogers Family Trust, 2017).

Adrian Rogers, "A Perspective on Life," in *Adrian Rogers Sermon Archive* (Signal Hill, CA: Rogers Family Trust, 2017).

Alistair Begg, "Dead Flies and Little Birds," *Truth For Life* (A Study in Ecclesiastes, December 8, 2002), https://www.truthforlife.org/resources/sermon/dead-flies-and-little-birds/.

ANCIENT SOURCES

Aurelius Augustine, *Confessions of St. Augustine, Book 3*, Bishop of
    Hippo (London: Griffith Farran Browne & Company Limited,
    1886).

Origen Adamantius, "Origen against Celsus," in *Fathers of the Third
    Century: Tertullian, Part Fourth; Minucius Felix; Com-
    modian; Origen, Parts First and Second*, ed. Alexander Rob-
    erts, James Donaldson, and A. Cleveland Coxe, trans. Frederick
    Crombie, vol. 4, The Ante-Nicene Fathers (Buffalo, NY: Chris-
    tian Literature Company, 1885).

John Bunyan, *The Fear of God* ((London: The Religious Tract Society,
    1839).

Martin Luther, "Notes on Ecclesiastes," in *Luther's Works*, trans. and
    ed. Jaroslav Pelikan, 56 vols. (St. Louis: Concordia, 1972).

John Wesley, *Selections from the Writings of Rev. John Wesley* (New
    York: Methodist Book Concern, 1929).

John Wesley, *Sermons on Occasions*, volume 1, (1829; repr. Nashville,
    TN: Abington Press, 1984).

Flavius Josephus. *Antiquities of the Jews*.

John Calvin, *Institutes of the Christian Religion*.

Charles Bridges, *A Commentary on Ecclesiastes* (1860; repr. Edin-
    burgh: Banner of Truth, 1961).

Matthew Henry, *Matthew Henry's Commentary on the Whole Bible:
    Complete and Unabridged in One Volume* (Peabody: Hendrick-
    son, 1994).

HISTORICAL AND BIOGRAPHICAL

Timothy George, *J.I. Packer and the Evangelical Future: The Impact
    of His Life and Thought* (Grand Rapids, MI: Baker Academic,
    2009).

David T. Morgan "A Most Unlikely Friendship — Benjamin Franklin
    and George Whitefield." *The Historian* 47, no. 2 (1985).

Walter A. Hazen, *American Black History* (St. Louis, MO: Milliken,
    2004).

Jim Elliott, *The Journals of Jim Elliot: Missionary, Martyr, Man of
    God*, ed Elisabeth Elliot (Grand Rapids, MI: Revell, 2002), 265.

DICTIONARIES AND LEXICONS

Johannes P. Louw and Eugene Albert Nida, *Greek-English Lexicon of the New Testament: Based on Semantic Domains* (New York: United Bible Societies, 1996).

COUNSELING & DISCIPLESHIP

C. S. Lewis, *Mere Christianity*, C.S. Lewis Signature Classics (San Francisco: HarperOne, 1980).

Jerry Bridges, *The Joy of Fearing God* (Colorado, Springs, Colorado: WaterBrook Press, 2016).

John Piper, *Don't Waste Your Life* (Wheaton, IL: Crossway Books, 2018).

Randy Alcorn. *Money, Possessions, and Eternity: A Comprehensive Guide to What the Bible Says about Financial Stewardship, Generosity, Materialism, Retirement, Financial Planning, Gambling, Debt, and More* (Carol Stream, IL: Tyndale House Publishers, 2003).

C.S. Lewis. *The Weight of Glory* (New York: HarperCollins, 1949).

Edoardo S. Miciano, *The Faith Factor: Living Out What We Believe* (Eugene, OR: Wipf & Stock Publishers, 2016).

Greg Beale, *We Become What We Worship: A Biblical Theology of Idolatry* (Downers Grove: Intervarsity Press, 2008).

Tony Reinke, "We Become What We Worship," Desiring God, August 22, 2012, https://www.desiringgod.org/articles/we-become-what-we-worship.

David Powlison. *Breaking Pornography Addiction.* http://ccef.org/breaking-pornography-addiction-part-1

JOURNALS

Andrew T. Jebb, Louis Tay, Ed Diener, and Shigehiro Oishi. "Happiness, Income Satiation and Turning Points around the World." *Nature Human Behaviour* 2, no. 1 (2018): 33–38. https://doi.org/10.1038/s41562-017-0277-0.

BACKGROUNDS

Wisdom in Israel and in the Ancient Near East edited by M. Noth and D. W. Thomas, (Leiden, Netherlands: Brill Publishers, 1955).

Cole Newton, "Background on Ecclesiastes," *B. C. Newton: Rooted Theology for the Unwithered Church*, Blog. December 15, 2020.

TOPICAL
Viktor E. Frankl, *Man's Search for Meaning an Introduction to Logotherapy* (Boston: Beacon Press, 1963).
Dr. Hugh Moorhead, *The Meaning of Life* (Chicago Review Press, December 1988).
Robert Robinson, "Come Thou Fount of Every Blessing," *Wyeth's Repository of Sacred Music, Part Second* (1758, repub., State College, PA: Pennsylvania State University Press, 1964).
Hope Jahren, *Lab Girl* (New York: Knopf Doubleday Publishing Group, 2016).
Edward L. Bernays. *Propaganda* (New York: Horace Liveright Publisher, 1928).
Jesse Jackson in Daniel K. Williams, *Defenders of the Unborn: The Pro-Life Movement Before Roe v. Wade* (New York: Oxford University Press, 2019).
Tony Evans in Daniel York, *I Keep Asking* (Warrenton, OR: Norseman Ventures, 2001).
Star Parker, ed., "Policy Report: The Effects of Abortion on the Black Community," *Library of Congress* (Center for Urban Renewal and Education, June 2015).
T.S. Eliot. *The Rock*. Directed by E Martin Browne and R. Webb-Odell, 28 May 1934, Sadler's Well's Theatre, London, England.

NEWS ARTICLES
Shirley Rosen, "The Old Man and the Mountain," *The Columbian*, April 1, 2010.
Terry Mattingly, "On Religion: Elon Musk, the Babylon Bee and the Teachings of Jesus," *Herald/Review Media* (Sierra Vista, AZ: Herald/Review Media, February 20, 2022).
De Witt Wallace, Lila Acheson Wallace, *The Reader's Digest*, vol 117 (Pleasantville, NY: Reader's Digest Association, July 1980).
Mark Shanahan, "Despite Living Quiet Life, Madonna Has a Lot to Say," Boston.com (The Boston Globe, June 9, 2005), http://archive.boston.com/ae/celebrity/articles/2005/06/09/despite_living_quiet_life_madonna_has_a_lot_to_say/.

Eleanor Blau, "Declaration of Independence Sells for $2.4 Million." *The New York Times*. 14 June 1991.

Richard Emmons, "A Missionary First, Last, and All the Time," *Israel My Glory*, Richard Emmons September/October 2010.

PROCLAIM PUBLISHERS

WENATCHEE, WASHINGTON

You may obtain this, and many other fine resources made available by Proclaim Publishers by contacting us:

Web:
proclaimpublishers.com

Email:
contact@proclaimpublishers.com

Postal Mail:
Proclaim Publishers
PO Box 2082
Wenatchee, WA 98807

SOLI DEO GLORIA

www.ingramcontent.com/pod-product-compliance
Lightning Source LLC
Chambersburg PA
CBHW030715110426
42739CB00030B/420